"A searing indictment of the way public policy was pursued, and the cost to children's lives and professionals' futures, that shows us how to change child protection for the future."
Baroness Armstrong of Hill Top, House of Lords

"A coruscating critique of a society's response to child sexual abuse which sees prime ministers, princes and popes protecting the establishment and turning their backs on violated children, prioritising their purse strings and the powerful above those deemed not worthy of as much as a backward glance."
Karen Ingala Smith, nia, The Femicide Census

"A significant milestone in national and global narratives on child sexual abuse ... offers much-needed insight following the Independent Inquiry into Child Sexual Abuse ... a game changer."
Natasha Phillips, child rights journalist

"With forensic clarity, Beatrix Campbell reveals the staggering extent of failures to protect children from sexual abuse. This book marks a turning point in child protection history."
Michael Salter, University of New South Wales

"Beatrix Campbell shines a spotlight on the sacrifice of honourable paediatricians, social workers and the sexually abused children they correctly identified, on the altar of systemic denial and subsequent cover up."
Arnon Bentovim, The Child and Family Practice

"A shocking indictment of state neglect and complicity in child sexual abuse. Essential reading for anyone who cares about truth, accountability and justice."
Harriet Wistrich, lawyer and Director of the Centre for Women's Justice

SECRETS AND SILENCE

Uncovering the Legacy of
the Cleveland Child Sexual Abuse Case

Beatrix Campbell

First published in Great Britain in 2023 by

Policy Press, an imprint of
Bristol University Press
University of Bristol
1-9 Old Park Hill
Bristol
BS2 8BB
UK
t: +44 (0)117 374 6645
e: bup-info@bristol.ac.uk

Details of international sales and distribution partners are available at
policy.bristoluniversitypress.co.uk

British Library Cataloguing in Publication Data
A catalogue record for this book is available from the British Library

ISBN 978-1-4473-4114-7 paperback
ISBN 978-1-4473-4116-1 ePub
ISBN 978-1-4473-4115-4 ePdf

Cover design: blu inc
Front cover image: iStock/Picsfive

CONTENT WARNING

This book contains graphic descriptions of child sexual abuse.

Dedicated to
Mrs T, heroine of her own life.

And in memory of Sinéad O'Connor, who sang
beauty into the horror of child abuse and misogyny
bequeathed by the Catholic Church; whose eloquence
and discipline made the worst bearable; whose hurt
and heroism synchronised precisely with the era of
rediscovery – when we played her music at our child
abuse conferences – and denial described in this book.

Contents

About the author

Beatrix Campbell is an award-winning writer, broadcaster and political activist. Her book *Wigan Pier Revisited* – one of Virago's bestsellers – won the Cheltenham Literature Festival Prize.

She has written about politics, crime, community, gender, child abuse and sexual politics for a range of publications from *The Guardian*, *The Independent*, the *New Statesman*, *Marxism Today* to OpenDemocracy and *Byline Times*. She has participated in many TV and radio programmes, including *Any Questions* and *Question Time*. She has also written acclaimed plays with co-author Judith Jones.

Described as a charismatic speaker and campaigner, she has received many awards, including the Nancy Astor Media Awards Campaigning Journalist of the Year, six honorary doctorates and an OBE for services to equality.

Acknowledgements

Despite expecting that this book would be critical of her report, Baroness Elizabeth Butler-Sloss graciously and candidly shared her thoughts about the events in Cleveland in 1987 and the subsequent Inquiry.

Sir Liam Donaldson declined to be interviewed. David Mellor declined to respond to questions. Sir John Major and Lord Robin Butler explained to me that they had no recollection of the events.

Thanks to: Richard Barker, Sue Barker, Danya Glaser, Deborah Cameron, Richard Scorer, Michael Salter, Pauline Conroy, Fiona Montgomery, Tim Tate and Chris Hobbs for critically reading and re-reading all or some of the text, and especially to Liz Kelly, with whom I have conferred and to whom I've been saying for years, 'Help me think about this …'

Thanks to the many lawyers, practitioners and survivors who have shared their experiences and who, for professional and personal reasons, cannot be named.

I'm grateful to Marietta Higgs, Geoff Wyatt, Sue Richardson, Marjorie Dunn, Heather Bacon, Peter Morrell, Celia McKeown, Deborah Glassbrook, Charles Pragnall, Stuart Hill, Hilary Armstrong, Wendy Shepherd, Tink Palmer, Joy Trotter, Nigel Speight, Joyce Sturdy and Sir David Behan for sharing their experiences of Cleveland.

Thanks to Marjorie Orr, Betsy Stanko, David Finkelhor, Roland Summit, Richard Krugman, Joe and Laurie Braga, Ross Cheit, Hollida Wakefield, Sarah Nelson, Nigel O'Mara, Sir William Utting, Edwina Currie, Angela Hegarty, David Conn, Oonagh Gay, Maurice Frankel, Lucy Delap, Jennifer Crane, Jonathan Foster, Jacqui Saradjian, Rocco Pagnello, Sandra Lawn, Elizabeth Sheehy, Peter Garsden, David Greenwood, Clare Hyde, Arne Mhyre, Joyce Adams, Astrid Heger, John McCann, Geoff Debelle, Alison Steele, Joanne McCarthy, Nicola Gavey, Chris Atmore, Helen Buckley, Niall Meehan, Zlakha Ahmed,

Amina Lone, Adele Gladman, Lorraine Radford, Nick Davies, Dean Nelson, Alison Taylor, Liz Davies, Tom Watson, Caroline Lucas, Marcia Willis-Stuart, Alison Grief, Peggy Ray, Wendy Wheeler, Graham Davies, Nigel Parton, Bernard Gallagher, Bonnie Fisher, Arnon Bentovim, Margaret McCurtain, Chris Moore, Jan Welbury, Elaine Arnold, Ietje Jonker-Bakker, David Southall, Jenny Pearce, Simon Court, Eileen Fairweather, Peter McKelvie, Susan McKay, Liz McNulty, Bernice Andrews, Joyce Plotnikoff, Simon Bailey, Elizabeth Mansfield, Steve Trafford, Martin Calder, Elizabeth Letourneau, John Carr, David Greenwood, Gavin Millar and Andrew Arden. Gratitude and fond memories of the late Louis Blom-Cooper, Frank Docherty, Ouaine Bain, Fiona Reay and Jane Wynne. Particular thanks to Sharon Meir, Danielle Billotti and Gorana Arnaud, to Andrea Dawson, Adam Dawson for help with production, and finally thanks to Policy Press.

I am especially blessed by Judith Jones: she has been sharing her wisdom, wit, humanity and stamina while living with these events and with me for three decades.

During the writing of this lamentable tale, a new generation, Joe, Beth, Amelie, Acer and Ringo, have been inspiring joy-bringers.

This work received no funding from any organisation.

Prologue

'Are there a few of us, like me?'

A message flew onto my computer screen: 'I am one of the Cleveland children. I have recently been trying to piece my childhood together.' But she could not access any documents, 'And my mother won't give me answers.' It was a never-to-be forgotten moment, a sight I never expected to see.

It was written by a 40-year-old woman, a cake maker and school cook, who made contact in 2017 after learning that I was writing another book about the 1987 Cleveland child abuse crisis in the North of England that defined child protection politics for the next three decades.

The woman is Minnie,[1] and she belongs to a modern myth: that 121 children living in the industrial city of Middlesbrough in the county of Cleveland were seized from their parents because of 'unfounded suspicions' and dodgy diagnoses of sexual abuse by two consultant paediatricians, Dr Marietta Higgs and Dr Geoff Wyatt.[2]

Remarkably, she is the first and only Cleveland child to share her odyssey and to tell her story *before* and *after* delving into her records. We meet a few days later and she asks: 'Are there a few of us, like me...?' The answer is that after a public inquiry and millions of words written about the UK's biggest child abuse controversy, the world is no wiser. Shamefully, the Cleveland children were not followed up, and nothing was learned about them or from them. What did it mean to be a 'Cleveland child'?

When Minnie reached her 40th birthday in 2017, she decided to become a detective in her own life and to seek the truth about the Cleveland case.

She had always remembered the day in early June 1987 when she was ten years old and she met Dr Higgs at Middlesbrough General Hospital for a medical examination:

'I remember the feeling I had when I first saw her, because she was *a woman*, and I associate her with that day when I was admitted to hospital. Oh, my word, I remember being happy then, and clean. I had a nice bed, clean sheets, it was snuggly and people were nice to me.'

Her recollection of life on Children's Ward 9 was that 'it was as if somebody had opened the curtains and opened the windows and let in the fresh air. I felt like I was on holiday.'

Minnie had always known that what had been going on at home was a nightmare. And she had always known that she was a Cleveland child because the saga was played out on the news, Dr Higgs was on television and the adults around her were always complaining about her. 'Everybody was demonising her, everybody was saying she is a bad person, a bad person. But to me, she was my saviour.'

Her questions, challenges and quandaries are an accusation; they are the consequences of the inquiry's determined 'not-knowing' – or not telling – what had happened to the children. What was she to think? Was Dr Higgs the 'baddie'? Had she harmed – abused – Minnie?

'I'd love to bake her a cake, I'd love to meet her and say to her: "You saved me. If it wasn't for you..."' Even the medical examination was untroubling – those parts of her body had not belonged to her anyway: 'I remember seeing her in hospital, showing her my bits, and my life got better.'

She had also known that it was her older brother who had blown open the family secret in 1986. At that time her brother was attending a special school for 'maladjusted' children because of 'failure to thrive'.[3] In 1986 he told his school and his aunt about the gross things his stepfather was doing. A *guardian ad litem* – a specialist appointed by the court to look after the rights and best interests of children – aware of potential risk to the other siblings, referred Minnie to a paediatrician, Dr Myint Oo, one of the consultants who saw many of the Cleveland children and offered several second opinions. Dr Oo kept an open mind about the possibility of sexual abuse. Both children were taken into care.

Minnie thinks her school was already alive to problems at home with her stepfather: 'One day a teacher stayed behind with me because he'd come to the school looking for me; the teacher got hold of me and hid me under the work top.' She recalls her stepfather's 'horrible cider breath', his naked body, thrusting his genitals in her face, his sadism and elaborate cruelty towards her brother, his roars at her mother: 'Get up them fucking stairs, you know what your job is…' And she remembers the day when their mother burst into the bedroom, saw the stepfather with the children, caught in the act, and then fled, shouting, leaving him to it.

In all this, Minnie had tried to become invisible: 'My brother complained, and he was beaten quite severely. I grasped the situation, I made myself a recluse, I said very little. I knew when something was going to kick off, I'd make myself absent.' One day in 1986 she noticed a sign somewhere about Childline, a pioneering confidential telephone helpline for children, and she told her mother she might make a call. 'She said to me "what do you want to do that for?!" I shut up. I never talked.'

In June 1987, nine months after her brother's explosive revelations and medical examinations that indicated rape and anal abuse, the children were not expected to return home. Minnie was referred to Dr Higgs, who confirmed medical signs of abuse.[4] That's when she became a Cleveland child.

There was a room in Middlesbrough General Hospital where:

> 'people were talking and someone was saying, "There's nowhere else to put her, this is a Place of Safety." In hospital I felt so liked, and so loved. They'd take me to brush my teeth. A lady, blonde, she was on the ward a lot, she would hold me by the hand. She was always smiling.'

The medical examination was nothing compared with the horrors of home: 'I remember playing with a doll in hospital and I pointed out where I was touched. This wasn't unusual to me, the sexual bit. I remember things *going on* at home…' While in hospital, according to a confidential analysis given to the inquiry, when a nurse gave Minnie a dish of semolina, 'she volunteered that it looked "like what comes out of daddy"'. The summary recorded that her mother admitted seeing an abusive scene involving the stepfather and the children. The police response, according to a confidential legal schedule given for the inquiry, is one line long: 'No further action'.[5]

By then the system was in crisis: some parents were protesting; the police were refusing to investigate; and politicians were going to the press. Minnie's mother joined Middlesbrough MP Stuart Bell's crusade against Dr Higgs. For Minnie, hospital had been a respite, but not for long. On 9 July Minister of Health Tony Newton had announced a public inquiry, and suddenly Dr Higgs was gone, relieved of her duties to focus on the inquiry, and the girl lost the woman she had regarded as her 'saviour'.

Thereafter, her memories of Dr Higgs and the hospital became fogged in a public legend that transmogrified her own experience into a grotesque fairy tale, populated by innocent children snatched by a megalomaniac freak – 'that woman'.

Minnie was sent to foster care. Towards the end of 1987, at her mother's insistence, she was picked up by a social worker and taken to a party hosted by advocates for accused adults – Parents Against Injustice and Stuart Bell – to celebrate the triumphant campaign to restore children to their homes.

Her mother told me when I interviewed her for this book that she had been encouraged to fight the paediatricians by a local lawyer and by Parents Against Injustice: 'I wanted Stuart Bell to turn round and get someone different than Geoff Wyatt and Marietta Higgs to check my kids.' Why? She said she didn't really believe that her daughter had been abused.[6] 'But here is the irony,' comments Minnie about that party, 'it was all smiles, as if it was all OK. I felt like screaming!'

She has screamed over the years, and screamed again after she read her social services records in 2017.

Much worse

A few weeks after our first conversation, my mobile phone rings. It is Sunday night, around 10 o'clock. I answer, and a man's voice says, 'Hello, I'm sorry … it's…' It is Minnie's husband. He is calling because she can't, because her sense of herself, who she was and who she is, has been 'bombed'.

While he talks, Minnie's voice clatters in and out of the soundscape. It seems that she can't talk, but she can't stop talking. So he talks to this stranger on the phone: 'We've not met, I'm sorry to bother you at this time of night … but … she's very upset … we don't know what to do…' The 'bomb', he explains, is three social services files, collected from a solicitor a few days earlier. This archive of official interventions in her childhood has just detonated the story she had believed for three decades: Minnie discovers that life in her family was worse, much worse than she had remembered.

Three thick ring binders, hundreds of pages of social services records, sitting on her worktable, seemingly inert, pristine, unopened. Yet they were full of danger. Then she and her husband opened the files and delved into the maze of procedures, an inventory that tells her life story – except that it doesn't; it is only a record of what institutions heard, decided and did. They contain filleted episodes, punctuated by black marker pen redactions, erasing the bits she is not allowed to read because they are about someone else – her brother. The files, from her birth to the end of her childhood, disclose years of havoc, risk and hapless neglect exploding into criminal sexual sadism.

She had expected that. But they also describe cruelty that began at the very beginning of her life, and went on and on. During and after her years in care, she tried to support her mother: 'there's nothing tenacious about my mother, she's weak. I felt for her'. The files changed all that: 'Reading those files changed my life', Minnie says, horrified by her mother's part in making her life horrible, and ashamed that she had tried to make this family work, that she had allowed her mother anywhere near her own children. That threw her into 'throbbing pain, eyes running, nose running. You think about it that much that it actually hurts.'

According to the files, when she was only a few months old, she was committed to care because her 'proper development is being avoidably prevented'. When she was a year old, social services received a 'distressed' call from her mother to report that the child's bottom was 'full of bruises'. Her back and thighs were bruised too. The babysitter was blamed.

At two years old, she suffered burns on her wrist, arm and shoulder. Her mother said she had fallen in the fire. There was a drug overdose – she had taken pills. She was taken to hospital following a cut; when she received stitches she had shown 'no emotion at all … made very little sound whatsoever'. Her mother was worried that people would think she was 'a battered baby'.

There were several visits to hospital. At three years old, after many injuries, her mother's friends warned that they would make an official complaint if they had proof that she was harming her daughter. One day she arrived at nursery with a black eye and an injury to the back of her head. That summer the nursery called social services about another assault.

In the autumn the mother asked that the child be placed in care because she couldn't cope. Then her mother wanted her back home; she said she missed the child's company: 'she finds it difficult to complete her housework in an empty house'. There were more case conferences, more reported non-accidental injuries, many illnesses, including dysentery, more absences from nursery. The mother admitted kicking her daughter – she said she had 'booted' her because the child couldn't find her shoe. 'A piece of plastic was embedded' in the back of her head. Between 1977 and 1980 she was in and out of local authority care: 'the family seems to have drifted from one crisis to another'.

This was Minnie's life, unsafe and unprotected. A year later, her mother married a violent drunk. The family tumbled along hopelessly until 1986: this was the year that her brother told people that they were being beaten and sexually assaulted by their stepfather.

Now Cleveland's children's services were focused, and for the first time professionals were galvanised to get the children out of harm's way. In October 1986, the local authority acquired interim care orders.[7] In November there was a contested hearing, and a woman police officer gave evidence that there was sexually abusive activity in the household, witnessed by the mother. But according to the records, the juvenile court did not 'accept expert witnesses', and technicalities 'prevented a full airing of concerns for these children'. Between November and February social services tried to get the case transferred to a wardship court 'as a matter of urgency'. The county's child abuse consultant,

Sue Richardson, specialist health visitor Marjorie Dunn, social workers and the police officer all put up a fight for Minnie. The stepfather was informed of the allegations against him, and in May Minnie's school reported that he turned up 'demanding his daughter, very angry, shouting'.

In June social services finally succeeded. The process had taken nine months and Minnie did indeed see Dr Higgs. Dr Oo confirmed grave medical signs. All the while Minnie remained in hospital or in care, and she thrived. She was admitted to the specialist Nuffield Unit in Newcastle between June and September for an assessment by the eminent child psychiatrist Prof Israel Kolvin. During this time Prof Kolvin had been appointed chairperson of an independent panel of experts to provide second opinions on the Cleveland cases. He was distinguished, somewhat cautious, one of the grandees who gave evidence to the inquiry, at which he articulated a conservative, passive approach to interviewing children that was endorsed by the inquiry. Minnie has been unable to access Kolvin's report, and the social services records merely report that Kolvin had noted a 'lack of disturbance' in her and his unit felt unable to make any recommendations for her future. (See Prof Kolvin, Chapter 2, evidence to the inquiry.)

What was to be done? There was a long history of abuse and neglect, there had been witnesses, her brother had described serious sexual violence against himself and his sister, and there were medical findings of rape and buggery. But by the autumn, strategic energy around Minnie evaporated: the inquiry was having a chill effect, focus had faded and there was a U-turn, a new mission – to get her back home.

And so, between the end of December 1987 and the end of January 1988, when the inquiry came to an end, there were six weekend stay-overs back at the family home, all part of a rehabilitation assessment. Her foster carers warned social services that in fact things were deteriorating. Staff restructuring in Cleveland led to the withdrawal of Minnie's key social worker. She had lost Dr Higgs and now another advocate. According to the files, the child's 'perspective on the situation was not known'. The entire safeguarding strategy – insofar as there was one – was collapsing.

There had to be a decision: a case conference was concerned that if rehabilitation was rejected, Professor Kolvin's report might be weaponised and 'there will be a fight in court'. It was now clear: there would be no prosecution of the alleged rapist, and no coherent protection plan. But there could be no rehabilitation either. In April 1988 it was mooted in social services that Minnie might benefit from the Safe and Strong group organised by the Child Resource Centre – set up in June 1987 to support the Cleveland children. The group was designed to educate and empower children. But apparently Minnie didn't qualify, because, it was said, she had 'never indicated that she'd been sexually abused'.

'What!' gasped the Centre's director Deborah Glassbrook, when I reported this to her nearly 30 years later. 'That was the whole point. The Centre was a safe space, the concept was that there weren't any secrets that the child mustn't tell. The fact that she had not said anything – and lots of children hadn't – didn't matter. I'm so sorry she didn't come.'

Here was a girl whose survival strategy had been to shut up. But her brother had talked and talked, and Minnie acknowledges that by speaking up he had contributed to her survival: 'he was half of my story', she told me.

Throughout her childhood she never spoke about what had happened to her at home: 'For me to say something would mean there would be uproar.' Glassbrook expected uproar and anger: 'I'm always surprised that children aren't angry and aggressive and in a state when this stuff happens to them.' The Centre anticipated it and accommodated it, but the Centre was not available to Minnie.

In October 1991 the court granted a full care order: parental responsibility was shared with the local authority. She remained with her foster parents. They loved Minnie – her foster father 'gave her away' when she married – but it had been tough. They had not been told that she was a Cleveland child. She was still in regular contact with 'home' when she was 14 years old and inevitably the foster care placement broke down. When she was 15 she moved to a children's home.

Glued lips

By then Minnie's life was in peril. If Prof Kolvin had noticed 'no signs of disturbance' in 1987, there were many a few years later. According to the files, she made several suicide attempts by tying a cord or laces tightly round her neck. Ambulances were called, she fought, she roared. She was panicking about her brother and her mother. She kept running away. According to her social services files, after returning from visits to her mother Minnie 'glued her lips together'.

Amid all this, somehow, she managed to study. She wanted to be a firefighter, took and passed examinations and got a place at college. She had stamina and willpower. But treatment plans tangled her in her family, and the enmeshment intensified – amazingly, she was sent to family therapy with them. She kept trying to strangle herself.

By 1993 her brother's situation threw the authorities' entire approach into chaos. He was sent to prison. But Minnie's entrapment intensified – she was back with her mother and visiting her brother in prison twice a week. Her social services records note that she 'continues to bear the scars of her traumatic and abusive family life'. They provide insight into a classic prehistory of danger and drift, suddenly marshalled by Cleveland's health and social services in 1986, then derailed during the inquiry, and drift resumed. Professional intelligence haemorrhaged, and Minnie choked and struggled to survive.

For a few months, between October 1986 and June 1987, her woes and injuries had attracted serious and strategic attention: this was a time when professionals were empowered to protect her from harm. In 1986 for the first time sexual abuse was specified in *Working Together*, the government guidelines for all agencies responsible for the safety of children. This was the context in which paediatricians Chris Hobbs and Jane Wynne published that radical research on signs of sodomy in children.[8]

But before and after that moment of radical potential, the files are mostly about managing mess. The brief encounter with Dr Higgs and the professionals' new warrant ended, all too soon. The practitioners who had fought for her were culled. It is no exaggeration to say that the effect of the decision to commission the Cleveland Inquiry condemned Minnie to live her young life in a botch of unhealthy loyalties to her family. 'Looking back on it,' she says, 'my mother should never have been allowed anywhere near me. They knew what she was capable of. It's quite sickening.'

After that she was left with two incompatible narratives and a vacuum where there should have been 'public interest' – a follow-up and monitoring of the Cleveland children. What was she supposed to believe? Her personal experience that she had been saved? Or the national narrative that the children had been harmed by the very professionals who tried to keep her safe, and by the woman she believed was her saviour?

Minnie is the first Cleveland child to share her story and what the records disclosed about her life and about the Cleveland scandal of 1987. She is the ache and howl of this book. It will show that there was a scandal, but not the scandal we were led to believe it was.

In reviewing the files held at the archives in Kew, London, re-interviewing people, both those who were involved and academic and social practitioners, this book will take the reader through the history of Cleveland. It will look at the legacy and its impact on child social care in the UK, compare our record with other countries and make recommendations towards a better future for the Minnies and all the other children who need our protection.

Introduction

In the summer of 1987 I was a journalist about to write about the decline of an iconic coal mining community, laid to waste by the Thatcher government. But a mystifying story made me change tack and head up to the county of Cleveland in the North-East of England.

Police and politicians had protested that in a mere matter of months between January and July, 121 children, from toddlers to teenagers, had been taken from their parents by social workers on the unfounded word of two paediatricians at Middlesbrough General Hospital, Drs Marietta Higgs and Geoff Wyatt who, it was alleged, saw signs of rape and buggery seemingly everywhere, even in babies.[1]

Middlesbrough's MP Stuart Bell led the charge against a social workers coven and 'leftist loonies' who, together with psychiatrists, were 'provoking hysteria under which children were effectively talked into denouncing their parents'.[2] Seemingly healthy children had been crammed into a hospital ward already full of sick children.

This was a fearsome charge – narratives of intimate denunciations were a potent trope before and after the Cold War – hyperpoliticised children accusing parents and neighbours to the Nazis in Germany, to Stalin in the Soviet Union, to General Franco in Spain, to Republican Senator McCarthy in the US; to dictators anywhere.

Except that it wasn't true: the conflict had erupted in the very first case in which newly arrived Dr Higgs and Cleveland Constabulary's favoured police surgeon, Dr Alistair Irvine, examined a five-year-old girl. They disagreed about the medical evidence: reflex anal dilatation (RAD) that had been described in a pioneering paper by Jane Wynne and Chris Hobbs in October 1986: 'Buggery in childhood – a common syndrome of child abuse' in *The Lancet*. 'We have not seen this in normal children', they wrote. The girl had been referred to Dr Higgs by a GP who also happened to be a police surgeon. Dr Higgs found medical signs of sexual abuse. Dr Irvine disagreed with her. Although the girl had also identified perpetrators in her family, the police withdrew. And so it went on: paediatricians identified signs of vaginal and anal rape, the police refused to investigate; social services had to intervene: even in the absence of investigation, it was their statutory duty to protect children – but from whom? Referrals kept coming, resources were stretched, staff were stressed. Dr Irvine went public: Dr Higgs was 'absolutely wrong!'. Stuart Bell announced on TV that he would boycott the hospital, and in Parliament on 29 June he alleged that Sue Richardson and Dr Higgs had 'conspired and colluded' to exclude the police.[3]

But ministers were told the opposite by the health authority and the Social Services Inspectorate: they were acting according to the law and their professional duty, the doctors were competent, the medical signs were credible, confirmed by experts, and now eminent second opinion panels were going to review the cases. There was a crisis. But what was it?

If the paediatricians were right, the medical evidence indicating chronic and current anal abuse challenged conventional wisdom about children, sex, men and the creed that sex with children was rare, that it was imagined or incited by children themselves, and that it didn't happen in bottoms except among queers.

In response to the row, on 29 June the Minister of Health Tony Newton told Parliament that if there had been mistakes he would call an inquiry.[4]

On 5 July he received a confidential dossier by the region's chief medical officer, Dr Liam Donaldson, explaining that the paediatricians' clinical judgement was not challenged, that under 'fierce' interrogation by their managers, 'there was none of the irrationality, inconsistency and erratic pattern of thought' associated with incompetence. Furthermore, they had followed government guidelines on the duty to respond to suspected harm. This dossier was not made public.

Some of the 121 children had identified a suspect; some were silent. Some suspects had previous convictions for sex offences against children; some confessed.

The government reckoned that it had a choice: a national inquiry into the phenomenon of child sexual abuse or – under pressure from Bell – a small, short inquiry into a local problem. It decided not to go national; it went for local and for blame. So, despite his reassurance a week or so earlier that he would wait for the independent experts, on 9 July Tony Newton rendered them redundant by announcing an inquiry into arrangements in Cleveland.[5]

This would be led by the Attorney General's sister, a High Court judge, Elizabeth Butler-Sloss. She set to work forthwith: her inquiry began on 11 August in the Victorian grandeur of Middlesbrough Town Hall and ended on 29 January 1988, when the judge wrapped up the hearings to write her report.

In June 1988 her report was delivered to ministers and discussed in Cabinet, where Prime Minister Margaret Thatcher expressed her strong opinions about injustice to parents, and in July the report was presented to Parliament, almost exactly a year after the inquiry had been announced.

The Cleveland Report was hailed as both magisterial and disappointing. Journalists expected the diagnosis to be discredited. It wasn't. But the inquiry's brief allowed obfuscation: its task had been to address 'arrangements for children who have been abused in Cleveland'. Note, 'had been abused'. But those words drifted … the brief didn't address whether they had been abused. Why not? If the paediatricians were wrong, why not say so? If they were right, why not say so? How could the inquiry assess arrangements if it did not ask whether children had been abused and whether suspected perpetrators had been identified? Could medical 'diagnosis' be a new route to the discovery of hitherto hidden crimes? Was Cleveland's conflict a little local difficulty or a national phenomenon? None of this was addressed.

Yet these were, I thought, the key questions that needed to be asked. They were the focus of my research that became a book: *Unofficial Secrets*, published in 1989 with a new edition in 1997. I thought then that the Cleveland case was a crisis of knowing, how things come to be known – and how they can become not-known. Medical examinations could relieve some children of their secrets; they could clarify the ways that small children's bodies might *show* what they themselves could not *say*, or comprehend.

3

The signs demanded professionals' curiosity, knowledge, empathy and imagination – and a response. The Cleveland case showed, however, that *seeing* – or *hearing* – is not necessarily believing. Even if children could speak, what they said could be made to not matter. Worse, a perpetrator's confession to the police could be made to not matter either.[6]

Simple sums

The Cleveland Report did not engage with these dilemmas. Instead, it offered a stark statistic, alluring because it was simple: of the 121 children, 98 were returned home. The inference that most of the children had not been abused seemed obvious. It encouraged a myth: that the doctors and social workers were 'zealots' who had caused moral panic and miscarriages of justice. The inference was obvious but wrong.

Nevertheless, the myth became a meme, recycled over the years by a sceptical commentariat that, like 'dementors' lying in wait to gust and squall, routinely swooped into child abuse controversies waving 'Cleveland' (see Chapter 11).

In the decades following *Unofficial Secrets*, thanks to the Freedom of Information Act and the National Archives, I have changed my mind. I had thought that the government and the inquiry had decided to not-know. But since then I have discovered secret dossiers and confidential correspondence between government departments, the Department of Health and Social Security (DHSS) and the Treasury, showing that the answer to the key question – *were the children abused?* – has been covered up. Files in the National Archives show that DHSS and the Treasury didn't not-know the answer. *Before* the inquiry's report was presented to Parliament, the Treasury was told by the DHSS that the doctors' diagnoses were 'correct in at least 80 per cent of the 121 cases'.[7] But the Treasury regarded this as 'dangerous territory' because it could attract demands for extra resources. And so it remained a kind of state secret (see Chapter 1). This document is dynamite.

Secrets and Silence revisits what I believe is a scandal. It began not in Cleveland in 1987 but in Westminster a year earlier: in 1986 the government published *Working Together: A Guide to Arrangements for Inter-Agency Co-operation for the Protection of*

Children.[8] Astonishingly, this was the first time that the government specified sexual abuse as something that the state, professionals and the police should prevent. But there was a cynical caveat, headed 'Resource Consequences': 'The guide does not propose any additional responsibilities for authorities' and it should not have any significant overall financial or manpower consequences. This was not an estimate; it was an order.

The 1980s was what I describe as a new enlightenment – by then everyone was aware that thousands of children were suffering, in private and in plain sight. But this new duty prescribed in *Working Together* to do something about sexual abuse was annexed to old, unreformed systems with no new money. Nevertheless, *Working Together* changed everything: practitioners felt encouraged by this new mandate.

Years later, I discovered that in autumn 1986 the leader of the northern region's paediatricians, Dr Bob Nelson, warned the health authority of an impending crisis: 'a juggernaut was accelerating' into the health service; soaring sexual abuse cases were crashing into paediatricians' workloads. Six months later he warned the health authority again that sexual abuse referrals across the northern region had risen by 'several hundred per cent' in a year – that is, since the publication of *Working Together*. 'This was certainly not unexpected,' he wrote, and since it indicated better recognition it was to be welcomed. He added a dire warning: expectations 'cannot be met'.[9] But the health authority had already decided in 1986 that child sexual abuse would *not* be a priority.

And so it came to be: unhappily, Bob Nelson was vindicated – the crisis was inevitable.

However, the Cleveland myth became an orthodoxy that framed policy and public opinion for a generation: the presumption was that the children had not been abused, that the Cleveland doctors were wrong, *and even if they were right they were wrong.* Reputations were ruined, expertise was squandered and children suffered needlessly. Some professionals did not flinch, and some children were saved or saved themselves; survivors' movements, their allies and advocates kept on and on until national inquiries were commissioned; and in 2014 the UK government called an inquiry into historic abuse, the Independent Inquiry into

Child Sexual Abuse. In the context of a swell of new awareness and global alarm about the scale, character and consequences of child sexual abuse, the Welsh Government published a national programme, *Preventing and Responding to Child Abuse: National Action Plan*,[10] in 2019 and in 2021 the UK Government published a national strategy, *Tackling Child Sexual Abuse*.[11]

This new sensibility is a historic opportunity to breach what the French historian Raphaëlle Branche – in another context – calls the 'structures of silence',[12] which suffocated public knowledge of children's suffering. It is an opportunity to excavate the past and to empower the new enlightenment. It is a chance to confront these thoroughly gendered crimes: most men don't rape or assault children, but everywhere it is men who do: 98 per cent of perpetrators are men. It is a time to apprehend why these atrocities are simultaneously condemned and 'condoned'.[13]

It is also an occasion to discover the needs of millions of people who are being, and have been, harmed, to offer redress, recognition and respect, and, in the most uncomfortable political circumstances, to work out what would it take to make society a safe place for children.

The new strategies appeared at a time when governments and international institutions acknowledged a child sexual abuse crisis. This book appears, then, amid an historic opportunity to confront it.

1

A journey through the archives

It was a journey through documents sequestered in musty cardboard boxes and filing cabinets undisturbed for decades, under beds, in garages, in lofts and basements, but above all in the National Archives at Kew in London, and files acquired by Freedom of Information questions, that made me change my mind about the Cleveland case.

In my book *Unofficial Secrets*, first published in 1988 and updated in 1997, I wrote that the inquiry, its report and the government's response to it were ways of 'not-knowing' what had happened to the 121 children who had been removed from their parents.[1]

The second edition was the beneficiary of a confidential dossier by the Northern Regional Health Authority (NRHA) and sent to the Minister of Health David Mellor in October 1988, *after* the Cleveland Report had been presented to Parliament: *Action Taken Following the Report of the Judicial Inquiry into Child Abuse in Cleveland.*[2]

Filmmaker and fellow journalist Tim Tate and I acquired it, separately and unknown to each other – we still don't know who sent it – long after it had been dispatched to the minister. I had thought up to then it was perhaps the most important document in the whole debacle – the only one to declare that most of the children had, in fact, been raped.

Tim Tate's acclaimed Channel 4 documentary, *Cleveland: Unspeakable Truths*, had also followed up some 'innocent parents' who had found many minutes of fame during the controversy. He confronted them with their convictions for child abuse.[3]

This is what *Action Taken Following the Report of the Judicial Inquiry into Child Abuse in Cleveland* said:[4]

- 'It is clear that there was no wholesale error of diagnosis.' Furthermore, 'extremely thorough and in-depth assessments of the children and families' made by 'eminent paediatricians and child psychiatrists from outside and within the region and working in pairs' concluded that 'around 70–75 per cent' of the diagnoses were correct.
- This was 'arguably better than might be achieved in other fields of medicine at the stage of initial observation'. And it would, of course, 'clearly be contrary to general public understanding of the accuracy of the diagnoses'.
- Dr Higgs was admired by colleagues and Dr Wyatt was regarded by patients with 'an attitude of devotion'.
- But continuing to diagnose cases when 'there was insufficient infrastructure seems in retrospect very difficult to justify'.
- Though the paediatricians were not responsible for the management of cases, said the dossier, their referrals had created an infrastructure crisis. Despite their vaunted accuracy and high regard, they were to blame: Wyatt was to be barred from working on child abuse 'for the foreseeable future', and Higgs was not to be allowed to return to Middlesbrough General Hospital: 'neither will work in the child abuse field'.

But the dossier was not allowed to affect 'the general public understanding', or dispose of myths of misdiagnosis and miscarriages of justice, or to vindicate the Health Service as a context for the discovery of hitherto hidden crimes against children – any and all children, of all cultures and classes, not just the purportedly rough and unrespectable who were already in the sights of police or social services. Not because their medical findings were wrong but because of the impact on health and welfare systems. They would take the hit.

The DHSS decided that the document's incendiary contents would not be made public.[5] According to the files in the National Archives, in anticipation of questions in the House of Commons, senior officials were informed that the dossier 'cannot be published at present' while the NRHA was facing legal action by Drs Higgs and Wyatt and possible legal action by some parents. Not only was this information to be kept from Parliament and the general public, it was also to be withheld from legal proceedings in which it would have been not only salient but also perhaps decisive.[6]

At the end of the year, the NRHA issued a public statement about Dr Wyatt's restriction: 'all our information strongly suggests a higher degree of diagnostic accuracy in respect of the child sexual abuse cases than the public have hitherto understood'. But it added that by continuing to diagnose abuse when 'there was insufficient supporting infrastructure seems in retrospect very difficult to justify'.[7]

The notion that children should not have been examined or diagnosed, or that suspected rape of a child should not have been reported because of 'insufficient supporting infrastructure' was surely unethical, not to say unconscionable.

An eerie echo of the sentiment – that identifying a symptom creates the symptom – emerged during the COVID-19 pandemic 30 years later when President Trump notoriously complained that 'testing makes us look bad – when you test you create cases'.[8]

A historic compromise

That 1988 document, *Action Taken...*, was also a historic compromise: a defence of clinical competence and professional duty *and* capitulation to political expedience that allowed the Establishment to rid themselves of these troublesome paediatricians.

By the time Tim Tate and I reported its findings, our society was in the thrall of a child sexual abuse backlash in which the Cleveland Inquiry was implicated and the scandalous secret drifted unnoticed to nowhere. No minister and no one in authority who knew the answer to the key questions rose to the challenge: it was their obligation to the public, I suggest, to dismantle the myth they had helped to make.[9]

Stuart Bell had not gone away: Sue Richardson discovered that he had objected to her appointment in 1995 to lead a community project working with adult sexual abuse survivors in Glasgow, Casa, set up by Scotland's National Children's Homes (NCH).[10]

The London headquarters banned her from participating in Tim Tate's documentary.

The night before filming was due to start, Tate told me, a Yorkshire TV director 'phoned with instructions from the board:

"you are not to produce this film. It is cancelled." More sinister,' said Tate, was what he then discovered: someone sent him the Yorkshire TV board minutes: 'they showed that Stuart Bell had lobbied the board'.[11] The board caved in until a bigger power, Channel 4, stood up to Bell and Yorkshire TV's management, and insisted that the film go ahead. Sue Richardson was forced to leave by NCH.

This was a time when I was chided by one of my commissioning editors on a national newspaper: 'we don't want Bea Campbell banging on about child abuse'. Let me say, of the myriad subjects on which I have written, spoken or made films, not one has elicited that complaint. Banging on about politics, war and peace, or housing or riots or just about anything else was de rigueur; child abuse was not. His rebuke was a sign of the times.

I am positioned, of course: I am part of an activist network of journalists, survivors, parents and professionals nationally and internationally. In my own neighbourhood at the time, Newcastle upon Tyne in the 1990s, we organised conferences and support networks. As a writer I have worked with survivors – adults and children – helping them write their own stories, and I've been privileged to work as Writer in Residence in Prison with men serving life sentences for murder and rape. What I learned from them was that their troubles often began with childhood abuse and violence. Why wouldn't we want to know about this?

The dossier that doesn't exist

For this book, I reread that 1988 NRHA dossier, *Action Taken Following the Report of the Judicial Inquiry into Child Abuse in Cleveland*, and the inquiry transcripts, and searched the Cleveland files in the National Archives to see who knew what and when.

When I asked the Department of Health to confirm the existence and contents of the NRHA's document, a young-sounding press officer came back with the reply that it didn't appear to exist. Oh yes, it does, I said: I've got a copy.

Eventually, requests at the National Archives produced a result and the dossier that didn't exist was delivered to the reading room at Kew. But everything after page 13 – half the document

– was redacted; that is, all the details about the doctors' diagnostic accuracy, their competence and their fate. There seems to be a determination, to this day, to keep the secret. In whose name? The children, who have lived with a national lie? The professionals, whose reputations were ruined? The public, who have been misled?

Nevertheless, the journey into the archives encountered gold in desiccated documents.

The trail begins when the centre of gravity of the Cleveland conflict shifted from Middlesbrough to Westminster at the peak of the crisis, towards the end of June 1987, when Stuart Bell took his protests to Parliament.

By then the police surgeon Alistair Irvine and Stuart Bell had appeared on local television making inflammatory allegations, and the NRHA appealed to the government to encourage a ceasefire – to its chagrin, Bell and Irvine seemed to frame the agenda, while the focus should have been child sexual abuse and what to do about it.[12]

Things were already beginning to settle down: the Child Resource Centre that had been proposed by the county's social services department was up and running within weeks; the police were about to surrender and accept that paediatricians conduct examinations at hospital, rather than police surgeons in police stations; and the health authority agreed to set up eminent second opinion panels to consider the sexual abuse cases.

Newton informed the House on 29 June that if these independent expert panels 'confirm suggestions that there have been significant failings', then the government would call an inquiry.[13] But Newton was trumped by Bell in a *j'accuse* moment: protected by parliamentary privilege, Bell said that 'those women', Dr Higgs and social services' child abuse consultant Sue Richardson, had 'colluded and conspired to keep the police out of the allegations of sexual abuse'.[14]

Several Labour MPs were appalled, but Bell had vocal supporters among Conservatives representing neighbouring constituencies. He provided Labour cover for a Tory government that had landed everyone in a mess: without establishing a knowledge base, it had thrown practitioners into new terrain, without money, a map or a parachute.

Despite the NRHA's plea to the minister, Bell's *coup de théâtre* went unchallenged: it was decided that any ministerial statement 'should be avoided' until the outcome of the independent second opinion panels – expected imminently.[15] The department's senior civil servant, Permanent Secretary Rupert Hughes, briefed ministers that contrary to Bell's tirade there 'had not been indiscriminate diagnosis' and the health authority, 'with some reluctance', had invested in extra hospital accommodation. The health authority's assessment of the situation was accepted, while Bell's allegations were not.[16]

Rupert Hughes warned that there were no national statistics and no additional funding to cope with the massive increase in national sexual abuse registrations.[17] A member of one of the independent expert panels, consultant paediatrician Dr Simon Court, warned the NRHA that if national prevalence estimates were right, then about four thousand children in his catchment area, Gateshead, were being, or already had been, sexually abused. 'Even if that is a gross overestimate,' he explained, 'we would have trouble in coping with 400.'[18]

Smoke signals about soaring sexual abuse referrals had been wafting all over the country for months, but they had scarcely permeated the ministerial membrane.

However, Bell appeared to have found a friend in a higher place: Cabinet minutes show that at the end of June, Tony Newton's boss, Secretary of State John Moore, had apparently already made up his mind: there would be an inquiry and it would be local not national. He informed the Cabinet that the Social Services Inspectorate (SSI) had sent a team to Cleveland and he was expecting a report from the NRHA within days. But Moore pre-empted both. According to the minutes, *before* receiving these dispatches from the front line, Moore told Cabinet colleagues: 'It appears that the Social Services Department had not been following the department's guidelines on child sexual abuse cases.' And so, 'He would probably need to establish an inquiry into the matter.'[19]

The *professional* assessments he received – in contrast to Bell's political crusade – confirm that Moore was ill-informed: the SSI and the NRHA had advised him that clinicians and social workers were, in fact, acting according to the law, the guidelines sent out by his own department and their professional obligations. If anyone was not following the guidelines it was the police. He was also warned that child sexual abuse was a *national* problem. But Moore had already decided that 'he intended to limit the scope of an inquiry into Cleveland cases rather than into child abuse generally'.[20]

Resources: 'a question which could be applied to any other area of health care'

This is what the SSI's Situation Report said: Cleveland was not unusual – national sexual abuse referrals had soared by 137 per cent in less than a year. Cleveland had a particular problem: 'long-standing difficulty with the police'. Unlike other jurisdictions, they were 'not willing to follow up cases which have been diagnosed by the paediatricians and not by police surgeons'. This was turf war. And it preceded the arrival on the scene of the women whom the police sought to blame: it had been 'aired 18 months ago and is still not resolved', reported the SSI. Worse, 'Police have withdrawn from a working party set up to try to draw up procedures for joint police/social work investigations.'[21]

The NRHA's dossier, *Report on Child Sexual Abuse in Cleveland*, was prepared *before* the inquiry had been called, and was dispatched by courier from the authority's Tyneside headquarters to the DHSS on the morning of 6 July. It, too, has not been available to the public until now.

This is what the *Report on Child Sexual Abuse in Cleveland* said:

- 'A particularly unusual aspect of this case is the fact that the clinical judgement of the two consultants is not being challenged; indeed, we know that they are regarded by colleagues as highly skilled and competent.'
- During a long, 'full and very robust discussion' in which the paediatricians had been subjected to a 'fierce' interrogation by the region's managers, they 'gave logical and carefully considered defences of their clinical approach … there was none of the irrationality, inconsistency and erratic pattern of thought which is often associated with cases of clinical

incompetence'. The paediatricians had been criticised for 'administrative shortcomings', but these were 'not uncommon in everyday medical practice'.

- Public opinion was being led to believe that there had been a 'wholesale miscarriage of justice'; public opinion showed 'over and over again' not so much 'denial as disbelief', particularly in anal abuse. The public needed help, more research and information.
- Contrary to rumours, there had been no exodus from Middlesbrough General Hospital.
- The NRHA was acting according to the NHS Act 1977 and the government's 1986 requirement in the *Working Together* guidelines 'to play an important part in the prevention of child abuse'.
- The doctors had followed the DHSS guidelines, and they had also kept parents informed about their concerns.
- Cases had been referred to the paediatricians and they were obliged to respond; they either confirmed the diagnosis or not, but having reached a diagnosis they were faced with 'a child at risk and they could hardly ignore it … they did not admit all cases, but they sought social services help when abuse was "strongly suspected"'.
- Children's confidential records were being shared with the general public by private solicitors; the police surgeon Dr Alistair Irvine had behaved inappropriately when he appeared on television in June 1987 claiming that Dr Marietta Higgs was 'absolutely' wrong. She had felt that it would be unethical to respond, and in any case the children were involved in confidential legal proceedings.
- Should paediatricians make diagnoses, the authority asked, when there were inadequate resources with which to respond? 'This is a question which could be applied to any other area of health care when it is acknowledged that there is substantial unmet need.'[22]

So the Secretary of State and the Minister of Health had been given stark, unequivocal intelligence: the police were refusing to sign up to joint protocols, health and social services professionals were acting properly, child sexual abuse referrals were soaring nationally, and in any area of medicine the discovery of unmet need could confront inadequate resources.

The NRHA's response in this July 1987 *Report on Child Sexual Abuse in Cleveland* is, in one decisive respect, entirely contrary to its position in its dossier sent to the Minister *after* the inquiry, in October 1988, *Action Taken Following the Report of the Judicial Inquiry into Child Abuse in Cleveland*, in which it mobilised 'inadequate resources' and discovery of 'unmet need' against the discoverers to justify disciplinary action. What had happened between July 1987 and October 1988? The inquiry had happened.

The suppression of these documents' contents, the NRHA's first and then its final word on the Cleveland events, kept society in the dark. This, I suggest, is a scandal that shames ministers, mandarins and managers alike.

Censored: 'resources are needed'

This offence is compounded by another act of political vandalism.

We owe this discovery to Dr Wyatt. After the 30th anniversary of the crisis he began talking, writing and researching and came across an undated typewritten draft in the National Archives of what was to be the final Cleveland Report's Part III, Conclusions and Recommendations. On page 7 it states: 'Resources are needed to meet the growing detection of child sexual abuse. Those resources are both material and skills. Since we are unable to assess the incidence of child sexual abuse, we cannot advise on national resources...' He compared texts and saw that this vital but brisk paragraph had been cut from the published Cleveland Report.

It was lack of *resources* that had been used to ambush practitioners – this act of censorship let those responsible for the lack off the hook, and released the government from responsibility to expand the means to meet the growing detection. The Conservatives' third election victory in June 1987 had established Margaret Thatcher's 'exceptional dominance'; her newly invigorated Cabinet advanced the ethos of skeletal state and 'popular capitalism' in public service, the utilities and in health and education. Relations between public, private and personal were being reconfigured.[23] The government embarked on a strategy to implement 'free market' schemes in the health service, piloted by John Moore, a former stockbroker, an ardent advocate of shrinking the state and privatisation – and no friend of the Cleveland professionals. This government was a cold house for the new enlightenment.

'Dangerous territory': the number that doesn't exist

In June 1988 Thatcher's Cabinet received the Cleveland Report – or rather a precis, prepared by Butler-Sloss, as the *Short Version*: it was intended for politicians and press and people whom Butler-Sloss did not expect to read more than 30 pages – certainly not the nearly 300 pages of her full report. Documents in the archives show – unsurprisingly – that right up to the eleventh hour both reports were being amended and finessed.[24]

Ministers and mandarins engaged in intense coming and going on how to manage publication.

Contradictory opinions and speculations were circulating: either that the paediatricians would be vindicated, or that they would not. Records in the National Archives of the Cabinet discussion, and post-Cabinet conversations between ministers about what Parliament would be told are meagre, slight and yet so suggestive – ministers seemed to be spinning the Cleveland Report among themselves. The files signal the government's mindset and, worse, they suggest a determination to mislead. The source for this conclusion is a thin file, 'Chancellor's (Lawson) Papers'. This was released in 2018 and it is a revelation. It contains ministerial comments on what to stress and what to suppress in the speech to be made by Tony Newton introducing the Cleveland Report to Parliament on 6 July.[25]

On 1 July, John Major, the Chief Secretary to the Treasury – later Thatcher's successor as Prime Minister – sent to Thatcher, Cabinet colleagues and senior mandarins a memorandum enclosing extracts from the Cleveland Report that, he claimed, showed that 'press reports which suggested that the paediatricians had been vindicated were inaccurate'.[26] However, he also included its contrary observations about Dr Higgs: 'we have in general no reason to question the accuracy of her clinical observations'.[27]

Major attached a *'Note on the Report's Findings About Whether or Not the Children Were Abused'*, which said:

> The judge has made no findings on whether sexual abuse did or did not occur ... she reviews the medical techniques of diagnoses at some length and notes that in only 18 of 121 was reflex anal dilatation said to be the sole physical sign. She nevertheless finds that the sign was given undue weight by the paediatricians.[28]

On 4 July, Major echoed the criticisms of Nigel Lawson and John Moore: the draft, he wrote, 'did not bring out strongly enough the need to protect children from the horrors of a false diagnosis of sexual abuse'. The prime minister agreed.

But on 5 July, the day before the Parliamentary debate, a Treasury official dropped the dynamite into the conversation: he warned Nigel Lawson and John Major that discussion of the diagnosis was 'dangerous territory for us to get into'.[29] 'DHSS have told us that an independent medical assessment has been made that the diagnoses of sexual abuse were correct in at least 80% of the 121 cases. Comments in this area are liable to be turned back on us later as bids for extra expenditure.'[30] That number challenged everything. Therefore, best not to mention it; better to focus on something else. That is exactly what the Treasury official's memorandum proposed: 'I suggest therefore that you confine yourself to endorsing the Prime Minister's amendments.' These referred to parents' rights, misdiagnosis and training. This gave the minister the opportunity to mention money without steering extra resources to child abuse. Major duly made a plan: he wrote to John Moore that day proposing that the speech should include 'a new specific grant from next year for training in the childcare field'.[31] He also wrote to Tony Newton confirming that no substantial funding changes were anticipated.[32] Major reminded him of that cruel appendix to *Working Together* in 1986: 'there would be no presumption that additional resources would be made available to meet the extra expenditure arising from childcare law reform'.[33]

'And we're going to have to look after an awful lot of children'

The memorandum disclosed that Chancellor Lawson insisted that 'nothing should be said in public about the report's recommendation that a Family Court be created'. Why? There were expenditure implications. The memorandum also proposed that ministers avoid any commitment to the report's proposed Office of Child Protection. It took another 25 years before the UK acquired a Family Court.[34]

These themes circulating around the prime minister were copied to members of the government Cabinet, the Lord Advocate, the Attorney General, the Captain of the Gentlemen at Arms and Sir Robin Butler, Cabinet Secretary and later head of the Civil Service.

If Parliament and the public were allowed to know that the doctors' diagnoses were credible – at least 80 per cent correct – then the political and economic implications would be intolerable to a neo-liberal government determined to shrink the welfare state. The Treasury's imperative was to pre-empt demands for more resources in future.

When I mentioned this document to a member of government at the time (someone who had not been involved in decisions about Cleveland), the former minister said, 'Oh shit! I'm so glad I was never a Treasury minister.'[35] Another former DHSS minister during these events, Edwina Currie, also commented that 'A responsible organisation would ask: what resources do we need? That question should have been asked by Butler-Sloss. Everyone should have been thinking, "We have a serious problem, and there are serious educational implications for the police,"' Currie told me, 'And we're going to have to look after a lot of children, I want a report immediately.'

However, that was not the talk in the DHSS, the former minister recalled: 'the issue was being presented as if the doctors had been wrong ... and people didn't finish the sentence'. People knew that something was wrong, but what was it? A deceptive uncertainty seemed to fill the holes left by the unfinished sentences.

When I read the chancellor's file in the tranquillity of the National Archives reading room, instantly Minnie came to mind, and the other Cleveland children, and the maligned professionals, and all the children and child protection practitioners I know who have been blighted by the cover-up.

Dr Higgs reads the dossier that doesn't exist

I'm ashamed to admit this: it never occurred to me that the main subject of the NRHA's October 1988 dossier, Dr Marietta Higgs, might not have seen it. While writing this book I asked her about it – and I was chastened by her answer: 'No', she said, she'd never had sight of it. Yet it was perhaps the most significant document of her entire career. She is the key person in the events it describes, but no one had the grace to share it with her, not even covertly, via a leak, and not even me. That document might have changed her life. We had first met decades earlier, when Drs Higgs and Wyatt were stalked by the paparazzi, snapped as an unyielding, unspeaking, unsmiling duo who were, in fact, bound to say nothing.

On 16 September 2017, 30 years after the inquiry began, I found Dr Higgs in her garden where she was working on her fruit trees, and presented her with a copy. We were now grey-haired women with gardeners' hands, still fit and still working in our professions. She took the document to her kitchen table, her husband David made tea and she read it in silence, punctuated by an occasional, whispered expletive.

It was a document of which she had had no knowledge, about a character she had long ago left behind, about events that brought the mass media camping outside her home, a posse that her children had to confront every day on their way to school, past people who promoted a stereotype of their mother as a medieval inquisitor, a child kidnapper, a homewrecker. The journalist Anne Spackman reckoned that in those days she 'might have come out near the top in any poll about the most hated woman in the country ... hatred is not too strong a word'.[36]

As she read the 27 pages, David watched, silent, rapt, proud. His eyes never left her face as she reached the last page. 'I never doubted her,' he told me, 'not for a minute. She is a very thorough doctor.'

Like Dr Higgs, the Cleveland children have never been allowed access to this document, yet it is about them too, and their place in the history of childhood adversity. That is a scandal.

Had the Labour MP Hilary Armstrong, later an active peer in the House of Lords, seen this dossier? It was important to her too – she was the only politician who dared tell the House of Commons during the Parliamentary debate on the Cleveland Report on 6 July 1988, that 'the heart of the matter ... lies in the fact that the majority of those children in Cleveland were abused...'.

She was shouted down and reprimanded by Tony Newton. She was not allowed to know how right she was.[37]

'Good God!' she said when I told her about it. No, she had never seen the dossier either, until I sent it to her while working on this book. She told me she was stunned.[38] It is a scandal that she too, like the rest of Parliament, was misled.

2

The inquiry

These documents – the Social Services Inspectorate report, the dossiers from the NRHA before and after the inquiry, the Treasury's confidential memorandum – confirm that before the inquiry was announced and before its report was presented to Parliament, certain key ministers were aware that:

- The clinical findings/diagnosis were well established.
- The paediatricians were competent – most of their clinical findings were estimated to be correct.
- There were long-standing issues with the police.
- Referrals were soaring nationally.
- There was a nationwide resource crisis.
- Reform of childcare procedures was overdue.
- Stuart Bell was known to be unhelpful and inaccurate.
- The police had been uncooperative but were prepared, finally, to concede medical examinations to paediatricians.

All of this begs the question: why set up an inquiry? And why *that* inquiry? Why not create the opportunity for society to think and learn – to become an educated public. Why not investigate prevalence, perpetrators' modus operandi and victims' survival strategies, popular cultures and the implications of sexual abuse for the institutions? We now know, from the archives, that the inquiry was intended as containment: to shut down rather than open up the national conversation.

No such thing as society

The prime minister's position was unambiguous: two days before the inquiry was announced, Margaret Thatcher answered a question in the House of Commons that could be said to have predetermined the outcome: on 7 July 1987 she was asked to 'allocate extra funds to deal with the rising rate of child abuse referrals'. She did not demur, 'No,' she replied.[1]

In September, when the inquiry was well under way, *Woman's Own* magazine published an interview in which Thatcher described the way people were 'casting their problems on society and who is society? There is no such thing! There are individual men and women, there are families...'[2]

That was that. There was more at stake here than Thatcherite political economy: child abuse did not seem to be on her radar. According to Thatcher's authorised biographer, Charles Moore, she was 'not censorious about the private lives of her ministers or acquaintances'. That summer, police briefed her about one of her 'favourites', Chester MP Peter Morrison, and his sexual interest in boys. Afterwards, 'she said something like, "oh dear, well, there we are"', wrote Moore.[3] Colleagues were worried about reputational damage; it seemed that she wasn't. (Morrison's behaviour was later confirmed by evidence from the security service, MI5, to the Independent Inquiry into Child Sexual Abuse.)[4]

At a time when sexual abuse was on society's mind as a *social* problem, she spurned a once-in-a-generation opportunity to challenge predatory sexual culture and to reform outdated, unwieldy child protection processes.

On 8 July, the day after Thatcher's parliamentary 'No', her government was finally condemned by the European Court of Human Rights for its failure to reform overlong 28-day Place of Safety Orders that offered neither parents nor children a right of appeal.[5] The government had lumbered the child protection system with this unwieldy instrument that became a major source of conflict in Cleveland.

Yet Tony Newton deflected criticism with the surprise announcement to Parliament the following day that there would be a judge-led public inquiry into the events in Cleveland – to which he added a brief appendix: 'The House will also be aware, that the European Court of Human Rights, in a judgment published yesterday on five cases from the United Kingdom, has found inadequate our legislation on parental access to children in local authority care.'[6]

What motivated the creation of the inquiry? Was Cleveland being set up? The Opposition spokesperson Michael Meacher suspected so. He spotted a sly manoeuvre to let the government off the hook. Reforms that had attracted all-party support, which 'have been such an issue in Cleveland', had not been implemented. 'We are concerned that this does not turn into a narrow judgmental inquiry confined to one area.' Newton's reply vindicated Meacher's worries: 'We hope we can produce an early report specifically about Cleveland ... we do not want an enormously lengthy report.'[7]

By pre-empting the independent experts' opinions on the Cleveland cases, the DHSS rendered them irrelevant. Tony Newton's colleague Edwina Currie rated him very highly: 'he was utterly genuine' and he 'would want to know "what's the bad news, and what's the really bad news?"' If the really, *really* bad news was that the majority of the children had been abused, 'Then you'd need to ask: "what do we need to do? If the doctors are right, oh God! We need a proper inquiry."'[8]

What if that intelligence was not being provided to the judicial proceedings in the courts? Were children to be victims of sexual abuse *and* miscarriages of justice? Newton insisted that the parallel processes – judicial proceedings and the inquiry – would not be allowed to clash. But how could they not?

Missing the point

The terms of reference were: 'To examine the arrangements for dealing with the care of children abused in Cleveland since 1 January 1987, including in particular cases of child sexual abuse; and to make recommendations.'[9] It was written by Rupert Hughes, the senior civil servant at the DHSS and a master of the memorandum: nothing in his 30-word brief was inadvertent.

The timeline, since January 1987, fixed an ulterior target: it was the date Dr Higgs arrived at Middlesbrough General Hospital. Not April 1986, when the government launched the new sexual abuse duty without new resources, not 1985 when Cleveland Police refused to sign up to new protocols, not 1984 when a committee of MPs, led by Renée Short, urged action on child abuse and the establishment of children's enforceable rights.[10]

This seemed to be a prime example of the 'invention of a scandal': in their book *Scandal, Social Policy and Social Welfare*, Ian Butler and Mark Drakeford argue that 'scandals don't just happen', they are created in moments when pressure for change cannot be reconciled with the 'gravitational pull of the status quo and vested interests'.[11] Public inquiries originate in 'the tectonics of policy development' rather than the events themselves; they create a 'scandal' in the way that facts are reassembled, reinterpreted and retold either to hinder or facilitate momentum for change. Would this inquiry seek the causes of the crisis, or would it control what could be known and thus create a collective memory – what the eminent Irish legal scholar Angela Hegarty describes as a feature of public inquiries: the 'government of memory'?[12]

These were the political tectonics when the lawyers landed in Middlesbrough in August. Holidays were cancelled, childcare arrangements were improvised, witnesses worked day and night gathering their evidence. And children suspected of being abused lost their advocates to the inquiry. The politics of it were personified by the woman appointed to chair the inquiry, High Court judge Elizabeth Butler-Sloss. She had been recommended by her brother, Sir Michael Havers, a Tory MP and Margaret Thatcher's Attorney General, later to be Lord Chancellor. His sister had defied the expectations of her class and generation, that girls would go quietly into marriage to an appropriately upper-class gentleman, by going unquietly and bravely into law at a time when there were few women barristers, and still fewer without a university degree. Their father had also been a High Court judge. She had had political ambitions – in the 1950s she stood as a Conservative candidate in the London constituency of Vauxhall – and she had been an Anglican churchgoer all her life. The Cleveland Inquiry was a great leap for her into national prominence, and she was rewarded by being appointed the first female Lord Justice of Appeal. From 1999 she was President of the Family Division of the High Court until her retirement in 2005, after which she remained an active member of the House of Lords.

A question of culture

A certain Establishment feeling was articulated in an oddly jocular description by Butler-Sloss of her appointment to the Cleveland Inquiry; this might have slumbered in the archives had it not been for her appointment more than a quarter of a century later to lead the UK's second major inquiry into child sexual abuse: the Independent Inquiry into Child Sexual Abuse, launched in 2014. A vigilant Scottish journalist, Fiona Montgomery, discovered a recording of a candid interview with Butler-Sloss at London's Gresham College in 1989. She was asked about the Cleveland Inquiry:

Q: 'Who instigated the inquiry, how did it get set up?'

B-S: 'Well, I think it was my brother actually, who was Lord Chancellor ... the Prime Minister wanted somebody, and she said this has really got out of hand, MPs' questions in the House of Commons and so on, 125 children, and what was going on? And I think it was the sheer numbers, I think, that got the sort of headlines, and together with the MP up there, who made a great fuss, quite rightly. ... So, the Prime Minister wanted somebody, and my brother said it would probably be politic – because there was some Marxist-Leninist feminine ... er ... feminism ... and ... There was a certain element of women against men – and so I think my brother said, "Well I think you'd better have a woman judge." And there were only three women judges, and by a process, I have to tell you, of elimination – the other two were not available – I found myself doing it.'[13]

We learn a lot from this vignette about the Establishment's motives and what bothered Margaret Thatcher: women and radicals getting out of hand.

Why a judge? There were several child abuse inquiries in 1986 and 1987, none of them led by a judge. The appointment of Butler-Sloss, therefore, who happened to be the Attorney General's sister and a Conservative, was, as Butler-Sloss commented, a '*politic*' manoeuvre.[14]

I covered the Cleveland Inquiry in 1987, and the issue of women and blame was in the air: I can say, as a Marxist (of sorts) and a feminist, that I know them when I see them, and none of those 'notorious' women in Cleveland were Marxist–Leninists or 'women against men'. They were all married, and all of them were mothers. If they were feminists of one kind or another, and if they were mostly more or less progressive – they understood the travails of women and children, and they believed in the welfare state and public service – then that was neither unusual or sinister. But it was significant. Of course, gender was omnipresent, but the problem was not 'a certain element of women against men'; rather – as the inquiry would learn – it was the other way round: it was men who shouted and threatened, and who appeared unable to tolerate female professionals.

The suspected perpetrators were male. The sexual acts were penetration. Historically, gendered sex and violence had been patrolled by masculine institutions, the police and the criminal justice system, and during the 1980s all of that was under unprecedented scrutiny.

But from the very inauguration of the inquiry, it became clear that blame would be redirected towards women: Counsel to the inquiry was Mathew Thorpe QC. His task was to harvest the material, organise the witnesses and, crucially, provide a neutral and non-partisan summary. He opened the inquiry on 11 August 1987, and in his closing speech on day 73 (27 January 1988) he recalled that 'at the outset we were, as it were, thrust into a darkened room in a search for light and we fumbled about and by degrees we found the switches and we illuminated the room'. Did they see the light?

The themes were the diagnosis – the role of medicine in not only corroboration but also proactive detection among children of all classes, not merely those children already under the scrutiny of the state; disclosure – what children say, when and if children speak; and how to respond to suspected sexual abuse.

Thorpe had set the scene for a showdown: between cautious, conservative versus proactive and progressive, represented by police surgeons versus paediatricians, and between social workers concerned with protection and police whose priority was prosecution; to some extent, he added, social services were 'naturally inclined to align themselves behind the paediatricians, for their professional lives are devoted to child care'. There was also polarisation between clinicians who regarded anal signs, specifically reflex anal dilatation (RAD), the medical sign so contested in Cleveland, as significant and those who did not; those who argued that it demanded investigation and intervention and those who did not.[15]

And, of course, there was gender. By the end of the inquiry, in January 1988, Thorpe dismissed outright Stuart Bell's cry of collusion and conspiracy, but he nevertheless invoked a coven of powerful women: social services' Sue Richardson, specialist nursing officer Marjorie Dunn, psychologist Heather Bacon and Dr Higgs. There had been no plot, he said, but they 'shared a progressive view' about the need to tackle sexual abuse and 'by fortuitous circumstances ... found themselves in decisively important positions'. They 'shared a common resolve, a common conviction, a common philosophy'.[16] This was something for the inquiry to consider, he warned, ominously.

He represented the conflict as a political schism – between a progressive and a conservative approach – as a 'subjective' choice between the 'search and pursuit' of sexual assault in contrast to 'greater scepticism' that saw the child's interests as prioritising 'preserving the home and the family'.[17]

But Thorpe was surely wrong: professionals were not licensed to act only on their ideological whim – they had obligations that were 'statutory', not 'subjective'. They had a legal duty to protect children from sexual abuse in family homes or anywhere else.

In patriarchal societies, what good were scepticism and traditional values to children who were being abused by their fathers, or to professionals being challenged by dramatic forensic evidence, or to political culture that had been framed by those values? Thorpe's lexicon of conservative, patrician, not to say patriarchal virtue, and the sniff of obloquy attached to 'progressives', infused the proceedings.

The diagnosis

In the beginning, Thorpe hailed police surgeon Dr Raine Roberts, Dr Irvine's supporter in some of the cases, as a source of 'authority and moderation'. She believed that RAD could not be cited as evidence because – unlike the pioneering paediatricians Dr Jane Wynne and Dr Chris Hobbs, who had put medical signs of anal abuse on the medico-legal agenda – she believed 'it is present in some children who have not been abused'. Cleveland's police surgeon Dr Alistair Irvine said he had also noticed RAD among his patients, and regarded it as normal. They were not alone among some clinicians who were outraged at the suggestion that they had missed something. Dr Irvine told the inquiry that he had seen RAD in his general practice, but it could not have indicated sexual abuse.[18] Seemingly RAD had been observed in women, children and gay men – but not, apparently, in heterosexual men (see Chapter 5). There were others, however, who told the inquiry that they had missed it; they had failed to recognise abuse.[19]

Eventually, moderation was exposed as extreme: the eminent Manchester consultant paediatrician, Dr Frank Bamford, warned the inquiry on 12 November 1987, day 52, that if, having seen RAD in a child, a doctor did not record 'consistent with child sexual abuse', then that doctor would 'be open to criticism'.[20] The extreme position was to deny its significance; the mainstream position was to acknowledge it.

The interrogation of Drs Higgs and Wyatt during December 1987 turned on both their competence and the consequences of the diagnosis. Thorpe challenged Dr Higgs: why didn't she seek second opinions from 'eminent people who believed that a good deal of caution should be applied in relation to these new techniques?' he asked. 'I looked to people whom I thought had most experience in the field ... years of paediatric experience do not necessarily help you,' replied Dr Higgs. In fact, Dr Higgs had been trained by some of the country's most eminent consultants specialising in child abuse. She had been mentored by Tyneside's Dr Tina Cooper – one of the first UK specialists to recognise the prevalence and characteristics of sexual abuse, co-founder of the British Association for the Study and Prevention of Child

Abuse and Neglect, and in the 1970s a government adviser on child abuse policy.

Shouldn't she have held back on medical findings?, Thorpe asked. Children were entitled to a diagnosis, she replied: 'what you are faced with is the patient or the child in front of you and you have to give an opinion and make a decision'. That was her job.

Dr Geoff Wyatt was not alone among the Middlesbrough paediatricians for whom sexual abuse had not been a significant part of his clinical practice until Dr Higgs joined them. Once Dr Higgs's expertise became known at Middlesbrough General, referrals accelerated. When Wyatt gave his evidence to the inquiry, Thorpe asked him, why keep a child in hospital, why not follow the practice elsewhere, where 'it is very rare to admit into a hospital ward a child who is sexually abused'. Wyatt replied, 'They had other resources and alternative places of safety.' Another feature of the crisis had been parents' reactions. Did he consider *not* telling parents his thoughts?[21] 'There is an obligation for me to account for myself to the parent,' he replied. Dr Wyatt raised an issue that worried many experienced child protection professionals in Cleveland and elsewhere. Should a consultant paediatrician share concerns with parents about sexual abuse before the protective agencies had been alerted? This worried other doctors who stressed the dangers of sharing information when the perpetrator had not yet been identified and before the child was protected.[22] Herein lay an important dilemma for professionals, which the inquiry never resolved.

The din of battle

By the end of the inquiry, police surgeons who had been hailed by Thorpe, and who had been so persuasive in some Cleveland wardship court cases, were ultimately excoriated. In his closing speeches in January 1988 Thorpe declared his disappointment: Dr Roberts had been 'extremely and unnecessarily critical and contentious', and he urged the inquiry not to 'adopt or accept her views'. Cleveland's police surgeon Dr Irvine 'had the din of battle in his ears'.[23] Eleanor Platt QC, for the NRHA, argued that his behaviour was cause for 'great concern if he is in future to have any role to play in sexual abuse cases'.[24]

This had colossal implications: some individual children's wardship cases appeared to have been 'resolved' on the basis of these police surgeons' evidence.

Nevertheless, Thorpe insisted that he was guided by the outcome of those court hearings rather than the evidence before his own inquiry: 'Anybody who has looked at the outcome of the judicial proceedings as the yardstick has inevitably to conclude that the level of misdiagnosis is in any view unacceptably high.'

Robert Nelson QC, representing the paediatricians, mounted an attack: of the 69 Cleveland cases that had been in court since the summer, few had been 'determined on the merits', that is, actually heard the evidence. So how could they be binding on the inquiry, he asked. In one case, 'Without any hearing of the evidence on the merits, a finding of no abuse was made by a High Court judge.' Nelson was adamant: only those cases in which the evidence had been fully considered should be regarded as binding on the inquiry.[25] Butler-Sloss baulked. 'Forgive me,' she admonished, 'I must accept what the judge said. This is an inquiry, not a court of appeal.'

This was unpropitious: it was not supposed to happen. Indeed, when Tony Newton had announced the inquiry he insisted that it would not happen. The parallel legal proceedings were the fault line of the inquiry, but they gave it a lifeline. The outcomes also provided sceptics with a number: 98 out of 121 children returned home.

But Robert Nelson reminded the inquiry that of the 29 medical experts who gave evidence to the inquiry, 27 considered RAD to be relevant to the recognition of sexual abuse and only two did not: one of them was Raine Roberts.[26]

Neither the assessments by the independent panels, nor the expert evidence given to the inquiry, nor even the testimony of the president of the Police Surgeons Association, Dr Hugh de la Haye Davies, supported the approach of the police surgeons involved in Cleveland. Nelson reminded the inquiry that of the 14 scholarly articles published on anal dilatation since 1945, only one suggested that the diagnosis was invalid. The significance of the medical findings has since been vindicated by an international review and the collective wisdom of the UK doctors' royal colleges.

Nelson directed his fire at Stuart Bell's dossier. Before the judge called a halt – the inquiry was running out of time – Nelson showed that a significant portion of his cases were families that included men who had been convicted, or charged, or identified by children as the perpetrator.[27]

Nelson argued that the police position, that it should be 'left to the child to disclose abuse before anyone took any steps to ascertain whether or not abuse had occurred', was contrary to what was known 'beyond a shadow of doubt': that children were either too young to talk or typically remained silent: 'If you wait for them to talk there is no way that damaging abuse can be discovered.' As we will see, Nelson was right.

This went to the core of Cleveland's dilemmas – to those children who could not or would not speak about their experience but whose bodies spoke volumes. Even 'moderate and sound' evidence to the inquiry suggested that the medical signs justified the 'precise course based on the signs' that the paediatricians had followed, said Nelson, thus 'Where is the error?'.[28]

Disclosure

It was well established before the inquiry that most children never tell anyone about sexual abuse during their childhood (see Chapter 5). But when the inquiry turned its attention from diagnosis to 'disclosure' work – to child-centred techniques to help children share their experiences – it seemed oblivious to that fact. The Cleveland Report was critical: the word disclosure 'suggests there is a crime to disclose', it cautioned. Yet the medical evidence in Cleveland suggested there was indeed something to disclose.

The modernisers were represented by Dr Arnon Bentovim, an eminent and pioneering child psychiatrist at Great Ormond Street, London's celebrated children's hospital. Like many clinicians in the 1980s, he explained, he had been exercised by children's 'sacrificial' silence, their difficulty in speaking out and the courts' difficulty in hearing children's narratives.

The great and the good of child psychiatry made plain to the inquiry their distaste, notably Professor Israel Kolvin and Dr Harry Zeitlin. 'Disclosure work' worried them; it could be 'coercive', said Kolvin, and it 'did not take into consideration the possibility that nothing has happened, or that perhaps we will not know',[29] (a worry shared by several witnesses) – this was, after all, new territory. It had become a crusade, 'It had acquired a mystique', said Zeitlin. Worse, they said, it could be sexualising and abusive.[30] They did not supply evidence for this opinion, which astounded practitioners and some journalists at the inquiry: what were they thinking of?

Their concern received loud endorsement by the only international witness to give evidence to the Cleveland Inquiry. This privileged and somewhat bizarre presence was Dr Ralph Underwager, a burly Lutheran pastor and psychologist from Minnesota in the US, who routinely appeared as an expert witness for the defence. Although flamboyant and foreign, Underwager's service to the inquiry was to give contemporary expression to the elite English discourse of the 'stiff upper lip': there was no good purpose in children talking about sexual abuse, he told the inquiry, 'there is no therapeutic efficacy to the expression of feelings'.[31]

I suggest that Underwager provided coherence to a dissonant medley of critics. As one of the leading defence psychologists on child suggestibility he proclaimed *fortissimo* that children were being brainwashed, literally; that psychologists and social workers were interrogators 'creating' abuse narratives that were not rooted in real events.

His explanation for children's silence in the context of strong signs and symptoms was simple: normal people did not abuse children, children had no difficulty disclosing abuse, they did not minimise, they did not keep secrets, and all that 'stuff about the big secret' was 'pure speculation', he said. If children didn't speak it was because they had nothing to say.[32]

But beware if they do speak, he cautioned; they might have been induced, or worse: brainwashing and false accusations were signatures of the new enlightenment. Underwager was a doyen of US defence expert witnesses. But no one seemed to have studied his full CV, or noticed that his star was waning: he was of 'supreme interest to prosecutors' in the US who commissioned research into his reliability (see Chapter 7).

Underwager insisted that the courts were the 'final arbiter' of truth. Only about 5 per cent of reported sexual abuse resulted in a conviction, hence most allegations of abuse were false: 'for every person correctly identified as an abuser nine innocent people ... are incorrectly identified'.[33]

Underwager was not challenged at the inquiry: he was not invited to provide proof of brainwashing or of his belief that if children had been abused they would readily declare it. He serviced the inquiry's shift from signs to speech, silence and suggestibility. Together with a handful of Establishment psychologists and psychiatrists, he gave the inquiry a conservative critique of efforts to encourage children to share their experiences.

Underwager looked like the proverbial prophet, and reading his testimony 40 years later I wondered if any of us appreciated how prophetic he would be: his words became a template of the looming backlash (see Chapter 7).

Unheard

Who was, or was not, invited to address the inquiry was of great salience, above all to Underwager's wild claims. The inquiry did not hear witnesses on prevalence of child sexual abuse or on research on perpetrators. Yet in 1987 probation officers and social workers in the UK were attending seminars on sex offenders led by the pioneering probation officer Ray Wyre and internationally renowned US expert on abusers' strategies Dr Steven Wolf.[34]

Wolf's work provided early and shattering insights into perpetrators' manoeuvres to take control of a child's environment and world view. He was touring on the inquiry's doorstep, but he was not invited in.

The inquiry did not hear from the UK's premier expert on children's evidence and reliability and on vulnerable witnesses, Professor Graham Davies, whose research was a direct challenge to Underwager: criminal court outcomes were no guide because 'The great majority of children who complain of abuse never reach the judicial system.'[35] The inquiry did not consult the pioneer in the field, Gail S. Goodman, whose studies, beginning with her 1981 paper 'Would you believe a child witness?', unravelled shibboleths about children's capacity and credibility.[36]

Nor did the report acknowledge that there was an international debate about children's testimony, interviewing techniques and what the American psychologist and lawyer Thomas Lyon calls 'a new wave of suggestibility research' that was emerging from the laboratory rather than real life.[37]

It did not invite Ralph Underwager's great adversary, Dr Roland Summit, whose essay 'The child abuse accommodation syndrome' addressed the very crisis that had erupted in Cleveland: the dialectic between traumatic signs and silence. Even if abuse had been disclosed or discovered, wrote Summit, the child typically retained ambivalence, accommodation, 'guilt and the martyred obligation to preserve the family'. Furthermore, 'Contrary to the general expectation that the victim would normally seek help', most victims in retrospective surveys had 'never told anyone during their childhood'.[38]

Least of all, feminist scholars and activists who discredited old orthodoxies about abuse and new orthodoxies that blamed abuse by fathers on mothers' low libido, or depression, absence or busyness; Judith Lewis Herman's 1981 watershed book, *Father–Daughter Incest*, argued that sexual abuse 'is a central and formative experience in the lives of countless women. This disturbing fact, embarrassing to men in general and to fathers in particular, has been repeatedly unearthed in the past hundred years, and just as repeatedly buried.'[39]

It is very hard to believe that these oversights were innocent.

'*All* of them'

The inquiry's only attempt to talk directly with children was undertaken by the Official Solicitor, who had asked 32 of the 121 children (who had been able or willing, or permitted by parents) to talk – not about their childhood experiences, but whether they felt 'content' or 'not content' with the doctors' examination. What seemed to divide the children who were 'content' from those who were 'not content', concluded the Official Solicitor, wasn't 'what happened at the hands of the various agencies', rather it was whether 'they knew what was going on, if they are treated with kindness, and if they were listened to'.[40]

Deborah Glassbrook, Director of the Child Resource Centre that had been swiftly set up at Middlesbrough General during the crisis, provided the inquiry with a unique report on work with Cleveland children.[41] When she appeared before the inquiry,[42] she was not questioned about what she had learned from them. I asked her 30 years later about the children who came to the Centre. She retrieved that report: of 67 children who had attended the Centre, 29 had no discussions about their lives because they were either simply attending the Centre's school, or their parents refused to cooperate with staff, or they were too young to talk. Of the remaining 38 children who had been able to share their experiences, 'all of them indicated sexual abuse', she told me, '*All* of them.'[43] Glassbrook's evidence does not appear in the Cleveland Report.

Intimations of doom

On the last day of the inquiry, Stuart Bell, who had made himself available for only half a day during the public hearings, ensured that he would have the last word: the *Middlesbrough Gazette* reported his warning that people were 'voting with their feet not to use Middlesbrough General Hospital'. He was wrong. The NRHA reminded the inquiry that 'the facts are entirely to the contrary'. During the whole of 1987, and including the months of the inquiry, the number of children attending was much higher than the previous year and is unabated.[44]

It appeared that there was no loss in public confidence. But what was not known at the time was that well before the inquiry came to a close there were negotiations, of the greatest significance, to punish the paediatricians – apparently to appease public opinion. The records in the National Archives include confidential minutes of NRHA meetings showing that as early as autumn 1987 a pre-emptive strike against the paediatricians was planned.

I suggest that the paediatricians were forced to wave the white flag *before* the inquiry finished. If that failed, then it would have been too late, and the authorities, the NRHA, the DHSS and the Home Office, might have been exposed to censure for their responsibility for a national and local resource crisis and failure to reform outdated procedures.

It was not disclosed at the time, but officials had been warned *before* the crisis that there was an exponential rise in sexual abuse referrals. In October 1986 the leader of the Northern Region's paediatricians, Dr Bob Nelson, wrote to the NRHA's medical officer Liam Donaldson and to the Regional Medical Committee that child abuse was seriously increasing paediatricians' workload, and pointing out that increased recognition meant that this was 'likely to increase further over the next few years'.[45]

In May 1987, when the crisis accelerated in Cleveland, he wrote to all the region's paediatricians telling them about a hurricane of child abuse referrals: 'the increase in the past year has been several hundred per cent'. Furthermore, he had kept a record of referrals to himself personally – not a child abuse specialist – and other colleagues at his Gateshead hospital: 'they amounted to an extra five hours' work a week'.

Many other paediatric departments were also experiencing a 'marked increase in referrals for child abuse'. This was 'not unexpected', Nelson wrote, 'and increased recognition was to be welcomed'. However, paediatric departments were already 'stretched by barely adequate medical staff levels. It is also very apparent that expectation cannot be met.' It had been decided to conduct a workload survey of all paediatricians in the region so that by September the region could assess how to manage child abuse.[46]

Before the inquiry was called, the SSI had told the DHSS that referrals nationally had soared by 137 per cent, and that there was long-standing resistance by Cleveland to joint working with health and social services (see Chapter 1).

So the regions' health managers had been warned in autumn 1986. But Bob Nelson was not invited to discuss his written evidence in the inquiry's public hearings. And when Liam Donaldson appeared at the inquiry on day 32 (7 October 1987) and was asked by Eleanor Platt QC, counsel for the NRHA, if he had any indication as to what was likely to happen in Cleveland, he replied that he doubted 'it would have been possible to have known'. He did not tell the inquiry that Dr Nelson had alerted him to soaring referral rates, or that Dr Nelson, on his own initiative, had distributed a survey in the spring to all paediatricians in the region about the impact of sexual abuse on their workload. (Dr Donaldson did, however, mention that *after* the inquiry had been announced he conducted his own survey of 50 paediatricians.)

In a statement made by Donaldson on 20 February 1989 he acknowledged that 'it did not seem at the time that a review of the issue of child sexual abuse at Regional level could be regarded as a priority'.[47]

Was the mooted disciplinary action therefore a pre-emptive strike against Drs Higgs and Wyatt, a tactic to deflect blame that could land on both regional and national officials? 'Probably,' confided an inquiry insider. But there was a problem: there were no medical grounds to suspend the paediatricians under their disciplinary code, Circular HM(61)112 (see Chapter 4).

Nevertheless, it was decided that something had to be done – if they could not be dismissed then they had to be forced to surrender. No one told them this. On 8 December the agency chiefs met to plan how those 'who had been prominent at the inquiry should be encouraged to withdraw voluntarily from the area of child sexual abuse for the time being'. Code for a purge. Lawyers urged the paediatricians to do a deal. Submit! Save yourselves!

The deal was done on the day before the inquiry's final speeches, on 27 January 1988:[48] Dr Higgs would be redeployed temporarily to specialise in neo-natal care in Newcastle; Dr Wyatt would return to his job, but he would not be 'involved in the management of child abuse cases'; and Cleveland's child abuse consultant Sue Richardson and social services director Mike Bishop were made aware by their County Council employers 'that we had to find somewhere to flee to'.[49]

'No wholesale error'

It fell to the NRHA's counsel, Eleanor Platt QC, to signal the deal. The NRHA's difficulty was not the diagnosis itself but 'management' of the response to it, Platt explained in her concluding speech. Unjustifiable punishment of the paediatricians 'would send entirely the wrong indications to professionals'. They had been subjected to criticism 'of a savagery beyond that which any person should be expected to endure. We consider that they have conducted themselves with dignity and professionalism,' she said. Nevertheless, 'It is quite clear that the names of Dr Higgs and Dr Wyatt and, we believe, those of other key workers in

Cleveland are at present adversely and inextricably linked in the public mind with the crisis. In our view, that is likely to remain so for the immediate future.'[50]

However, I believe that a temporary tactical compromise turned into ruinous destruction of professionals' reputations, and the loss of a historic opportunity to take the side of children, not just in Cleveland, but everywhere. That is a scandal.

3

Two reports

Before Tony Newton presented the Cleveland Report to Parliament, an early draft of his speech, in the National Archives, explained:

> Action in some cases was taken too precipitately, with insufficient attention to the weight of the evidence, the interests of the child and the parents, and the possibility of taking action falling short of removing the child from home.
>
> *Nevertheless, many children no doubt received protection that was needed.* [italics added] Although handling of the cases fell short of best practice, not least in failing to adequately recognise the needs and interests of parents, it is clear that in all such cases the needs and interests of the child must be paramount...
>
> When the evidence supports a conclusion that action is needed to protect the child against sexual abuse, that action need not always be precipitate.[1]

During the week of haggling over the contents, senior politicians argued that there was not enough emphasis on parents' rights. So by 6 July Newton's speech to the Commons became:

> 'The whole House will be united in its condemnation of sexual or other abuse of children, and in its support for proper action to protect children from it, but it will be no less united in insisting that this must be

achieved in a way that does not trample on the rights of parents and inflict unnecessary distress on the very children we wish to be helped.

It is clear from the report that this balance was not achieved in Cleveland during the period in question, *even though many children received the protection they needed* [italics added]. The House would wish me to express the deep regret of all of us to those who have suffered as a result. It is perhaps hard to imagine the shattering effect on those parents who were innocent and on the children.'[2]

Newton, regarded by his colleagues as an honourable man, was under immense pressure. So his serious – if critical – assessment metamorphosed into condemnation: in a speech of 1,203 words, only nine referred to the children.

The speech did not acknowledge that:

- The 'diagnoses of sexual abuse were correct in at least 80% of the 121 cases'.
- The government would not release extra resources.

In the week beforehand, Newton had conferred with the Leader of the House, John Wakeham, about another unmentionable: Stuart Bell's disgrace. The report had condemned his 'intemperate and inflammatory' remarks and commented that it was 'sad' that he had not withdrawn or modified allegations of conspiracy and collusion and empire-building that he could not substantiate. It had criticised the media too, which had tended to be one-sided and steered 'a degree of hysteria'.[3]

It was a delicate matter. In the event Bell was safe: Newton told the Commons in a carefully crafted formulation, 'the Honourable Gentleman has earned the respect, and will receive the thanks of those of his constituents who feel they have suffered so much injustice.'[4] Even though Bell had been repudiated in the report, with Newton's commendation his reputation was intact and, Professor Nigel Parton, a veteran social work theorist, comments, his allegations 'continued to frame and dominate the agenda'.[5]

MPs on both sides of the House delivered accolades for Butler-Sloss and what Opposition spokesperson Robin Cook called her 'exhaustive and authoritative report',[6] until the adroit intervention of the aforementioned North West Durham MP Hilary Armstrong (later baroness), a former social worker who had followed the controversy closely,[7] broke through the congratulations: 'At the heart of the matter', she said, 'lies the fact that the majority of those children in Cleveland were abused, and ...' She was not allowed to get to the end of her sentence before she was interrupted by growling protests. She persisted: 'I am interpreting what I understand from the Report.'[8] Newton wouldn't have it: 'I am not quite sure on what the Hon Lady based ... her remarks,' he snapped. His comments were based, he said, on 'the *Short Version* of the report and that states: "We understand that out of the 121 children ... 98 are now at home."'[9] His inference was apparently obvious, and wrong.

They were referring to different documents: Newton, like Cook, was quoting from the 21-page *Short Version Extracted from the Complete Text* distributed to the Prime Minister, the Cabinet, MPs and the media. But Armstrong was basing her remarks on her knowledge of the case and a close reading of the 320-page *Report of the Inquiry into Child Abuse in Cleveland*, known as the Cleveland Report.[10]

Newton wouldn't listen: 'I hope that the Hon Lady will not make judgements as clear-cut as the one that she implied in her remarks.' What no one knew, of course, was that his own department had told the Treasury that the figure, 'at least 80 per cent' of the diagnoses, was correct. His admonishment prevailed, but Armstrong was right.

Two reports

The *Short Version* was given ardent attention by Butler-Sloss because it was intended for mass consumption: the MPs were not expected to read the 320-page report. Butler-Sloss told me 30 years later in my interview with her in 2018 for this book, 'The majority of people who mattered would not read the full report'. Particularly, politicians, 'you'd never get politicians to read 200 pages.'[11] So what the *Short Version* said and did *not* say was purposeful. It was amended three times in the weeks before publication, on each occasion strengthening the focus on Newton's number: 98 children out of 121 back home.

It provided politicians with their political compass. Here is what it didn't mention:

- The censure of Stuart Bell was inflammatory and inaccurate.
- There was consensus about the diagnosis among 27 of the 29 expert witnesses at the inquiry – the medical signs were endorsed by the Police Surgeons' Association and the Royal College of Paediatricians.
- The paediatricians' clinical observations were not in doubt.
- There were no grounds for disciplinary action against the paediatricians.

No reason to doubt

The full Cleveland Report commented that 'an honest attempt was made to address' sexual abuse, but 'in Spring 1987 it went wrong' because of management misunderstandings about agencies' different functions and lack of communication.[12] Was it misunderstanding or disagreement? This was not answered.

'Tensions came out into the open with Dr Higgs's appointment' and with her view that 'physical signs' could help to identify sexual abuse.[13] We now know this was not a radical position. There was 'no reason to question the accuracy of her clinical observations'. Furthermore, 'many of the comments' about Dr Higgs 'apply equally' to Dr Wyatt. Thus, there was also no reason to question *his* clinical accuracy either. Nevertheless, everything that followed was cauterised; the inferences and implications were burned off.

In a perverse rebuke, Drs Higgs and Wyatt were condemned for following 'prescribed practice'; they caused some children to suffer 'harm after they were removed from home whatever may or may not have happened to them previously'.

By that killer judgement – unsupported by evidence aired at the inquiry – the report reprised an old notion that the reaction to sexual abuse was more damaging than the abuse itself. It also shielded the government from blame for 'prescribed practice'.

The report commented that social services should have focused on cases already in the system rather than children from any and all social classes who were not under scrutiny.

'Disclosure work' was to be discouraged because it was 'inherent that there is something to disclose': out went anatomically correct dolls to help children identify body parts and to show – if they couldn't say – what might have been happening; out went 'facilitative' activities', playing, drawing and asking open or hypothetical questions. This wounding judgement on the Great Ormond Street team was compounded by the report's affirmation of Dr Harry Zeitlin's 'cautionary words' that disclosure work could be almost coercive, a notion that was 'strongly endorsed by Dr Underwager – who claimed that in the US some interviewers "'lie, threaten, fabricate'". Underwager's outrageous allegations, inexplicably and inexcusably, were recited as if he was enunciating common sense.

Neither report referred to Deborah Glassbrook's evidence from the Child Resource Centre, nor to the well-established research showing that, far from being rare, not telling was typical; neither cited the aching observation made by Canada's compendious commission of inquiry into sexual offences against children that what the victims feared most was the disclosure of what had happened, that children and young people were unlikely to turn to children's services or police, and that 'only a few victims of sexual offences seek assistance from the helping services'. Official information systems on services were 'virtually worthless in serving to identify the reported occurrence and circumstances of child sexual abuse'.[14]

Neither Cleveland report addressed the crisis created by the government's decision in the 1986 *Working Together* guidelines to allocate no new resources. Parton notes that 'as with previous child abuse reports, a lack of resources was not seen as causing the crisis in Cleveland'.[15] Of course it was not known that the need for extra resources had been edited out.

What if...?

Each version, inevitably, locates the crisis in Dr Higgs's arrival in Middlesbrough in January 1987. A caricature of Dr Higgs as inscrutable and implacable and Dr Wyatt as excitable and impressionable was encouraged. But what if the calm, clever woman and the impulsive young man had recognised signs of sexual abuse that had been missed and stopped it? This, it seems, was an unbearable inference.

Social services' Sue Richardson and the paediatricians were blamed for not solving the problem that didn't belong to them: an intransigent and ignorant police force.[16]

Neither document explored the specific challenges of sexual abuse and the nub of the controversy: how could children be protected if there were medical signs of rape and buggery but no narrative and no confession?

Neither report considered what would help practitioners to manage the risk that haunted everyone: to act or not to act on reasonable suspicion, as the law required them to do. Neither report had anything to say about how to help children who were controlled, body and mind. Perpetrators, their 'conducive contexts' and the 'structures of silence' were the lacunae of the inquiry.

The discussion of 'arrangements' was confined to the etiquette of administration: when, and if, suspected child sexual abuse should ignite intervention. But of course this ignored the absence of discretion: practitioners had a statutory duty, not a 'subjective' choice, to act: The General Medical Council in 1987 confirmed an unequivocal policy: 'if a doctor has reason for believing that a child is being physically or sexually abused, it is not only permissible for the doctor to disclose information to a third party, but it is a duty of the doctor to do so'.[17] But this was not endorsed by the Cleveland Report.

The report reiterated the importance of using the authority of the law and of keeping parents informed – despite the judge's view that this alerted possible perpetrators and risked undermining investigation, and despite the challenges to Drs Higgs and Wyatt during the inquiry's hearings.

Professor Nigel Parton comments that this resulted in 'strengthening of the rights of parents and making more explicit the move toward identifying the law itself as the crucial mechanism for informing decision-making and resolving disputes'.[18]

'There may be rare occasions when a child does not choose to tell'

The Cleveland Report urged caution – that was hardly contentious; but I suggest that the cumulative effect of the inquiry's fatalism, cemented by subsequent statements by Butler-Sloss herself, left professionals in a quandary: if they could not act on physical signs, if they could not offer interim respite and if they could not encourage children to share their experiences, what could they do? *Not do their duty?*

The answer was yes. Both reports contain a pernicious codicil to the statutory duty to act – permission to *not* act: 'The danger of false identification ought not to be forgotten. Therefore, when a suspicion arises the professional may elect to take no further action.'[19]

Without any basis other than Ralph Underwager's egregious testimony, the reports restored legitimacy to the 'suspicion' that had always impugned children's testimony.

It got worse: 'There may be rare occasions when a child does not choose to tell...' and that 'adults should respect that'.[20] That perverse word 'choose' denied the context and crux of child sexual abuse: the exercise of domination by adults that extinguishes consent or choice. What could 'choose to tell' mean for a child of two or four or ten? Far from being 'rare', it was typical for a child of any age to tell no one. These words appear in Chapter 12 – the liturgical chapter of the Cleveland Report: whatever else social workers took from it, they had to live by Chapter 12.

Unnoticed, the Cleveland Report reverted to the prehistory of the new enlightenment, by relying on the least likely event: children choosing to tell. Those few words quashed all hope for vulnerable, loyal, scared and snared victims.

What is 'whatever'?

'Whatever had happened before' alluded to the suspected rape and buggery of 121 children whose average age was eight, referred to paediatricians in the Middlesbrough General Hospital outpatients department between January and July 1987.

What function was served by this term? It filled the vacuum of that unanswered question: were the children abused? It emptied the Cleveland narrative of the gravity of the suspected crimes against the children, and of the need to answer the questions: Why had the children been referred to the paediatricians and social services? What if the doctors weren't wrong? What might make intervention less of a crisis? These questions were not on the inquiry's agenda. Its interpretation of its brief avoided the implications of suspected *real events*, and instead allowed it to *imagine* institutional harm that it had not measured.

On day 73 of the inquiry the judge had announced, 'I will go through every single one of the 121 children', she would cross-reference each with the second opinion panels and the police surgeons: 'I have to form my own view in the end.'[21]

Would the public be enlightened? The short answer is no.

4

Whatever happened to ...?

The children: out of sight, out of mind

Everything seemed to be designed to keep children out of sight and out of mind, beyond our empathy.[1]

The random, brisk fragments that follow come from the agencies' summaries given to the inquiry. They are the children the Cleveland Inquiry was supposed to have in mind:

Children K

Three girls and a boy were examined after the boy told their mother that their father had been touching all his sisters. He was a registered sex offender. No physical signs were found on the girls, but RAD and several other signs and scars were found on the boy. He told his mother that anal penetration had happened 'about 12 times'. The father was arrested, but not charged. Outcome: 'No further action'.

Child T

An 11-year-old girl, solitary, unhappy, with several physical signs, including anal abuse. She told a social worker that her stepfather had been touching her with his hands 'and something that she found difficult to say'. This had been happening for two years, every Thursday – her mother's night out. Dr Raine Roberts did not confirm the medical signs. The police schedule noted, 'dubious allegations'. Outcome: 'No further action'.

Children A

A ten-year-old girl was examined after her stepfather had been arrested and charged with indecent exposure to several girls. At school she was 'unhappy, withdrawn, always frightened'. Dr Higgs identified RAD and other medical signs, confirmed by the independent second opinion panel. The girl told a woman police officer that her stepfather had been exposing himself to her and her friends. Her brother was 'treated by other children as if he was not there'. Dr Higgs examined him and found RAD, confirmed by the independent panel. The stepfather was convicted.

Child J

A five-year-old girl was referred to the police by social services. Her father had previous convictions for sexually assaulting girls. Her grandmother raised the alarm about the child's sexualised behaviour. A police surgeon noted genital injury. During the examination she screamed. Dr Higgs confirmed medical signs of sexual abuse. The girl told a woman police officer what her father was doing. The police officer 'had no doubt the father had sexually assaulted child, but with the *"present policy"* [original italics] she was unable to charge him'. Her mother wanted it to be known that she had 'nothing but praise for Dr Higgs'. The father was arrested and released unconditionally.

Children S3

A two-year-old girl was taken to casualty following convulsions; also her bottom was bleeding. Dr Higgs examined the child while the mother watched.

Thirty years after the Cleveland Inquiry the mother meets me for a cup of tea in Marks & Spencer in Middlesbrough. She looks better than the last time we met in 1987, although nothing has been easy.

She is the mother of three girls, all now grown up. She remembers that day in 1987 when Dr Higgs examined her youngest daughter and saw anal dilatation: 'it totally astounded me'. Over the next few days the girls talked about secrets; there were more examinations indicating chronic abuse, and finally the two older girls told their mother what their father had been doing to them. The oldest girl told the police what had happened and who had done it: it was rape and buggery. By now it was June and the chief constable's moratorium on investigation was in force. The police took the father into custody, but even though he was identified as the perpetrator, they wouldn't charge him unless he made an admission. He didn't. The medical evidence was confirmed by the independent second opinion panel. On 29 July he killed himself in prison.

He left no message for his wife or for his children. The court proceedings and the child protection services died with him. 'That was it. No services.' She was virtually alone with three children under the age of ten. 'I hated him for leaving me with the children, but I didn't hate him for what he'd done. I was puzzled.' What troubled her was that 'He never left a note, he made no admissions, nothing. He left me without any answers.'

Over the years she worked in school meals, took care of the children, participated in the church and contained her own feelings until after the girls had grown up and left home. Then, 'My focus had gone' and, for the first time, she grieved. Still, she didn't hate him. Why not? 'My daughter asked me the same thing', she said. Her daughters didn't want to talk about it; they didn't want the stain and stigma. And they still didn't understand her stance.

She tried to explain: there had been no prosecution, no public recognition and no justice. It would have been better, she said, 'if it could have gone to court and the jury could have decided, rather than me'. As a devout Christian, she believed in forgiveness: 'That does not mean we think what he did was right or acceptable.' That adjudication belonged to a higher, heavenly court, she said. Justice on earth, however, 'is a confirmation that you were believed'. There was no justice in his last act: he left his children with blame, they lost him, they lost righteous indignation and the community's recognition. Their mother believes that they didn't get justice or recognition from the inquiry either.[2]

Child C: a Cleveland child?

Child C was not a Cleveland child, according to the Cleveland Report and the *Short Version*, but he should have been. I suggest that the situation at Saltergill special school in North Yorkshire, which, according to Butler-Sloss, was resolved, was in fact managed and minimised. This is exemplified by Child C, as he came to be known.

Child C was 15 years old in April 1987 when the head teacher at Saltergill had alerted social services to sexually abusive activity by two boys; he had been in and out of local authority care since he was two years old. But he did not come to the attention of Dr Wyatt, who had examined the boys referred to him and found signs of anal abuse in both, confirmed by Dr Higgs, and offered to examine the other 25 or so boys resident there. The school is cited – unnamed – in paragraph 44 of Butler-Sloss's *Short Version*: This is what it says: 'In the event the situation was dealt with by the Education Department.'

However, 'in the event' it wasn't really dealt with at all. Butler-Sloss told a lawyers' conference later that owing to the paediatricians, some things had gone right for some children. More things might have gone right for more children had Dr Wyatt's invitation been accepted.

One of them was Child C. He had been moved to Saltergill where, since he was 11 years old, his 'housefather', Myles Brady, who had been appointed to provide 'fatherliness' to the boys, had been raping him – in the school, outside the school, anywhere. Brady introduced him to prostitution.

Dr Wyatt's offer had been declined and so Child C came to no one's attention. He was unlucky – he was hidden in plain sight. A medical examination might have called attention to Brady's regime and Child C might have learned that he wasn't alone; he might have found solace and solidarity.

Early in 1988, as Child C approached his 16th birthday and was due to leave Saltergill, he took his chance: he told a member of staff about Brady. The housemaster's modus operandi had been classic: he invited boys into his room, he had favourites, whom he abused, to whom he gave presents, and ingratiated himself with parents.[3] Brady was reported to the police, charged, prosecuted and acquitted at Teesside Crown Court.

Ten years later Brady was exposed in journalist Mary Raftery's television series *States of Fear*, a watershed investigation into endemic brutality and sadistic sexual abuse in Ireland's residential schools. Brady had been a devout Catholic, a drinker and a sadist.[4] After his conviction and imprisonment, a torrent of lawsuits hit the Catholic Church. Revelations about the 'Irish gulag' became uncontainable.

Child C decided to sue the local authority – for the decision to put him in Saltergill and for their responsibility for Brady. He lost his case. He appealed in 2004 and lost again. No one doubted him: Judge Paul Collins said that Brady had been 'unjustly acquitted'. But the courts' decisions turned on technicalities about liability and a statutory time bar.[5]

In 2008 the bar was lifted. Child C tried again, and this time he succeeded and was awarded redress.[6] It was 20 years after he'd left Saltergill.

What if...?

It all might have been so different. What if the boys living at the school had top-to-toe medical examinations as part of routine well-being assessments? What if the inquiry had been interested in the perpetrators' strategies and the sacralised status of fathers and father figures, and the needs of boys who needed protection from men?

These themes were relevant to the Cleveland children: they didn't all live with their families, some were in care 'homes' and residential schools, and some were being exploited in prostitution.

But children's homes, residential schools and the streets were not in the inquiry's mind. It did not address arrangements to manage what children were up against – exiled in militaristic regimes run by barely regulated or trained staff, weakly scrutinised, if at all, where the word of a trusted adult is valued against that of a troubled child, and acknowledgement of abuse is resisted by the owners' insurance companies.

'In the event' the sexual abuse situation at Saltergill had not been 'dealt with', and at least one child rapist was freed (and who knows how many more?).

A decade after Cleveland, the Social Services Inspectorate chief inspector Sir William Utting published his report, *People Like Us*,[7] drawing attention to 'serious and systematic abuse' amid 'continuing contraction, fragmentation and stress' in residential care. Utting warned that 'it would be intolerable if the next century brought revelations of widespread abuse in some children's homes now'.[8]

The ink was scarcely dry on the Cleveland Report before Myles Brady was tried and acquitted by the Crown Court and Child C began his long journey for justice. There were many more victims too, year after year, fellow travellers, until they finally ignited the second great child abuse tribunal, the Independent Inquiry into Child Sexual Abuse, in 2014. Utting had been right – the intolerable had been tolerated.

Don't! Do not follow up

The decisions that were taken ensured that the world would *never* know what had happened to the Cleveland children, never know the impact of intervention and never know how they fared thereafter: it was decided that there would be no follow-up, there would be no one designated to keep a weather eye, no one appointed to think about how life would be for those children who had, after all, been participants in historic events.

So far, it has been impossible to ascertain who made and then enforced that decision. Filmmaker Tim Tate recalls that a Cleveland official made contact after receiving 'a memo from the Department of Health in which the destruction of the records of the children as a group' (this is the vital bit) was ordered. The children's individual records were not, of course, ordered to be destroyed: just the records of them as a group. Why does this matter? Cleveland was split into four separate local authorities; there was no independent follow-up of the 121 Cleveland children and to the best of my knowledge no one has found out what became of that group of children.[9]

It is known that at least a fifth of the cases swiftly came back to the statutory services – they were re-referred. Those children had not been protected. Any suggestion that the Cleveland case be monitored or revisited was met with total resistance.

Tink Palmer was a specialist social worker, she was a guardian *ad litem* (specialist representatives of children in court proceedings, appointed by and answerable to the court). In around 1990 she became Cleveland's Principal Child Protection Officer. Thereafter she became a prominent manager and campaigner for children being abused and exploited.

She was a well-known independent practitioner in the region, she'd been involved in many of the Cleveland cases as guardian *ad litem*, and she was not above criticising some of the professional practice she encountered. As Principal Child Protection Officer, she was informed of all Cleveland child abuse referrals. 'Any referral of a child suspected of being abused, and any strategy meeting planned for that child, came across my desk. I picked up name after name from the inquiry. How did I know them? Because there were 19 children for whom I had been the guardian *ad litem*.'[10]

She knew that what she was seeing was important. She raised it with the management. 'I said, "This is key." Children who'd been sent home were now being re-referred. I said, "this needs collating". I was told not to touch it: "you do not!" That is what I was told. So, I just I kept it in my head.' And she told anyone who would listen, 'I have said it publicly, I have said it in government committees. I said it to the management.'

Furthermore, in strategy meetings, she would urge that these children's needs were the priority, not embarrassment about the past or muddle about the Cleveland chill effect, not resources: 'I'd say, when child protection plans were drawn up, "we need to meet the needs of the children you are considering". It seems obvious, doesn't it?'

But it wasn't obvious.

There was a new director of social services, David Behan, and Tink Palmer asked him about monitoring. As she told me:

'I remember getting a message from David Behan saying: the policy should look at what resources we have and fit the needs of the children within those resources. My riposte was: and what if we don't have the resources? I felt two things: 1. This was ethically wrong; 2. How are you going to find out what the children need? How are you ever going to find out what resources you haven't got?'

David Behan eventually became the chief executive of the Quality Care Commission in 2012. I asked him to comment on the decision to not follow up, and to discuss the policy and resource arrangements for which he had been responsible in Cleveland. He declined to be interviewed, but he wrote, 'I can recall no special or different treatment being given to these children or their families. Each referral or re-referral was given appropriate consideration. They were assessed and if they had needs which could be met by the Social Services Department, we made arrangements for those needs to be met.'[11] Evidently, Tink Palmer was right.

No follow-up meant that it would never be known whether the children suffered or thrived, whether the intervention had harmed or helped, how many children had been returned home to alleged abusers, whether suspected abuse stopped or resumed and whether engagement with the services was for good or ill. There would be no monitoring of the consequences of anything. That decision ensured that the children's stories would be entombed in individuals' memories. Among those too young or too troubled to remember, their experiences would be lost; or their narrative would be the adults' version of events. What were they to make of some adults' claims that their symptoms were merely the result of playground knocks, falling into bushes or falling off bikes? How many sought their personal records, only to retrieve bulky catalogues, undisturbed for decades, that splattered everything they had been told by their parents and the mass media about themselves and their families? How were they to think about the system that exculpated abusive adults, and about mass media that made celebrity 'victims' out of perpetrators?[12]

We can only speculate about what they might have felt about a society that barged in on their intimate life, but found the experience so unwelcome that the 'powers that be' didn't want to know them, and left them with institutional lies about their childhood.

We know from other calamities and inquiries, from the Aberfan disaster to the Hillsborough football stadium crush,[13] that survivors feel no pride in being there, in surviving but being mired in fright. It therefore behoves the state to support the conditions in which social suffering can be contemplated and translated into public knowledge.[14] The determination to *not know* whether the children's lives got better or worse, is not only inexcusable, but it also guaranteed that the question – were the children abused? – could never be answered.

When I reported that no-follow-up decision to one of Britain's pre-eminent child psychiatrists many years later, the response was a gasp, 'No follow-up! That needs to be exposed, that is shocking. Longitudinal study is what's required; this obfuscation is very serious.'[15]

Thus the case became a site of shame: the authorities and above all the government couldn't bear it, and gave their shame back to the children.

The professionals

Purged

Even before the lawyers had packed up their bundles, the social work and health professionals were discovering that their work on child sexual abuse had no future; they would have to fight for their professional lives. The paediatricians would be forced to capitulate if they were to have a job to go back to. But what at the time appeared to be a tactical compromise turned into ruinous defeat would ricochet across an entire era of child protection.

Social workers: scapegoats

Before everyone went home for Christmas in 1987, the omens were palpable. Sue Richardson recalled that even their representatives and supporters 'made it clear to us that we had to find somewhere to flee to'.

The lawyers were mindful of the antipathy towards the women and proposed a formula that appeared to neutralise it: if it was conceded that there had been a serendipitous confederacy of powerful women, then it could not be argued that any individual was to blame. But the women thought this reduced their male colleagues to mere ciphers who had been haplessly mesmerised. There was a mighty row. However, resistance was futile.

After the report was published, Middlesbrough councillors convened a group to respond. They imposed a vow of silence: everyone would be banned from speaking about the crisis, including the councillors themselves. Sue Richardson was to be sacked. Late one night a distressed chief executive called her at home to deliver the verdict. She wasn't home, so he told her husband. 'It was extraordinary,' she told me later; she was a senior professional, but her business wasn't her own and serious, confidential information was popped into her home as if it were a Christmas card.[16]

Her trade union negotiated a deal that allowed her to remain until the beginning of 1989 and to retrain. The council even assigned her to a careers consultant, 'to help me to find a new identity, to go away, to be somewhere else'. She was offered to be seconded to any social services department that would have her, anywhere, salary paid in full. There were no takers. She became an independent psychotherapist – not the career she had wanted – and finally, in 1995, the children's homes charity NCH appointed her to head up an adult survivors' service.

In 1997, the tenth anniversary of the Cleveland Inquiry, Yorkshire Television commissioned a documentary about the case (see Chapter 1). NCH warned her not to participate. She did. NCH forced her to leave. Wherever she went, to work or study, managers would be alerted. 'It was relentless,' she told me, 'it stopped any of us having a role. Even well-meaning people completely underestimated the ruthlessness of our enemies – we all did.'[17]

Social Services director Mike Bishop, by general accord, was a decent manager who had stood by his staff and had taken initiatives that relieved health services staff. The minister and the DHSS had been well aware that Mike Bishop and Sue Richardson had risen to the occasion.

But Bishop was not to be forgiven. The new Health Minister, David Mellor, focused and strident, wrote to the county council in autumn 1988 to complain that it had not taken disciplinary action against Bishop and Richardson. He said he wanted to 'welcome and commend the action' of the health authority, but, he warned, this could 'accentuate his dissatisfaction with the County Council's approach'.

Bishop was doomed, humiliated and disempowered: when some councillors encountered him in the corridor they turned their backs and shunned him. It was unendurable. Before the year was out, he was out.

Doctors: doomed

The numbers attending Middlesbrough General's paediatric department were, according to the NRHA, 'much higher than in the previous year' – if anything, it seemed that many parents thought that these professionals were not fighting *against* them but *for* their children. Public confidence was not the problem. Yet if the professionals felt that they had survived obloquy, they were wrong. They had to be made to surrender. There was no time to lose. According to the health authority's confidential minutes released in the National Archives, during the autumn of 1987 it discussed its options: it was not possible to 'do nothing' but it had to be 'demonstrably fair'; it had to have good cause. The doctors had to be forced to wave the white flag, but there were no *medical* grounds: according to the health service consultants' disciplinary code known as Circular HM (61)112, disciplinary action or dismissal was only warranted by professional misbehaviour, clinical judgement or consultants' personal behaviour, typically 'undesirable behaviour' – drunkenness, assault or abusiveness, theft or fraud.

So Circular HM (61)112 did not apply: the paediatricians had acted according to the letter of the government's guidelines. They may have been committed, clever, exasperating, pesky or passionate, but they weren't mad or bad. There had been no evidence of clinical incompetence. If anything, their crimes were political naivety and professional integrity. How could the 'powers that be' put an end to all this? The condition of their return was to do no sexual abuse work for the time being – until the dust settled, it was said. The deal was done before the closing speeches began on 27 January 1988, when the inquiry was told that Dr Higgs would be dispatched temporarily to Newcastle to an interim post as a neo-natal specialist and Dr Wyatt would return to Middlesbrough General Hospital, where he would be 'low key'.

On day 72 of the inquiry, Eleanor Platt QC closed the health authority's case: there was 'no prima facie case of incompetence or professional misconduct'. Unjustifiable punishment 'would send entirely the wrong indications to professionals', she said. The doctors had been subjected to scrutiny and criticism 'of a savagery beyond that which any person should be expected to endure. We consider that they have conducted themselves with dignity and professionalism.'

Despite no evidence of a parents' boycott, the professionals' names 'are at present adversely and inextricably linked in the public mind with the crisis'.[18]

Ambushed

Documents in the National Archives show that by then officials had parleyed with the health authority almost exclusively about what to do about the professionals – not what to do about sexual abuse. The consultants didn't know it, but plans were being laid in the autumn for an ambush.[19] Confidential minutes of the meeting held on 27 October 1987 reported that a group would be convened to discuss the paediatricians' future roles. Confidential minutes of the 24 November 1987 meeting explained that arrangements had to be made *before the final report of the Inquiry* (italics added). They were summonsed to a meeting with the health authority on 18 October and told for the first time that disciplinary action would be taken against them.[20]

Dr Higgs fights back

So, a year after she'd arrived at Middlesbrough General Hospital, Dr Higgs was to leave colleagues with whom she'd felt 'on the same wavelength'; it had been 'the most exciting time in my life, intellectually', she told me: 'It was when we thought we could *do* something.' Talking to her almost three decades later was awkward, not because *she* was difficult, but because she was far away from the case and its aftermath; it seemed to elude her memory, as if it had been packed up, disposed of. She had kept everything, her lists, notes, letters and files, but she wasn't sure where. That was somehow symbolic, as if for her it was a different time; it was over.

But in October 1988 the minister, senior civil servants and NRHA managers fretted about disciplinary action, what to say and who would say it; the NRHA warned that if there was any hint of criticism of the health authority they would go public, and 'thus the Department would be exposed and embarrassed'.[21]

The deed was done: the paediatricians were informed of their fate. Instantly, they appealed. The department and the NRHA were adamant: a DHSS note declared that 'there will be no negotiation. Dr Higgs will *not* be staying ... though no information yet about where she will end up!' That probably meant nowhere. At the end of October, the NRHA sent the minister its report, *Action Taken...*, which the DHSS decided would not be published.[22]

Tyneside colleagues had already provided a temporary lifeline for Dr Higgs, and the eminent neo-natal paediatrician Dr Edmund Hey offered an interim post.

But by October 1989 the NRHA decided to end that secondment. She was to be cut adrift. Dr Higgs's lawyers launched legal action against 'constructive dismissal'.

Dr Higgs's loyal mentor, Edmund Hey, was pessimistic: she couldn't win, she wouldn't be allowed back to Cleveland, 'no way ever, under any circumstances'. On New Year's Day 1989 Dr Hey sent her a handwritten letter warning that the situation was unfair; the health authority's problem was of its own making, as it had not found a way of standing up for a sexual abuse service. 'Everyone knows', he told her, that, 'the police, social services and the legal division all shared responsibility for the way cases were managed.' But there would be no justice; she would never get her job back, and 'you can't *make* them', he told her. Her legal action worried him: she could end up unemployable.[23]

A group of 11 paediatricians in the area signed a letter to *The Guardian* on 18 February 1989 – a few weeks before her appeal was to be heard.[24] It was the paper's splash that day: 'The overwhelming majority – possibly over 90 per cent – of the 121 Cleveland child sex abuse diagnoses were correct.' The paper reported that this letter was 'the strongest indicator yet of medical unease about the treatment of Dr Higgs'. The paediatricians wrote: 'Over the past 18 months we have watched with a mixture of helplessness, incredulity and despair the way the crisis in Cleveland has unfolded.' The doctors could only have defended themselves by releasing their evidence to the public, but this, the paediatricians said, 'they are restrained from doing for ethical reasons'. Consequently, the public had been misled. 'As a group we jointly have access to much information about events in Cleveland which we have studied carefully.'

They confronted the Cleveland Report's bare figure of 98 out of 121 children returned home: this failed 'to reflect the number of children returned home with the agreement of social services and the courts because the perpetrator had been excluded'. This could have been revealed in the Cleveland Report.

Commenting on cases in which judges emphatically dismissed the diagnosis, they wrote: 'They were usually acting on a preference for the medical evidence of the police surgeons. We believe that some genuinely abused children have been wrongly returned home by the courts quite possibly to suffer further abuse.'

There had been problems of process, they acknowledged, but a myth had been created that was both 'unjust' to abused children and 'unjust' to courageous paediatricians and social workers. Their views were based on a professional consensus, they wrote, and a close reading of the Cleveland Report itself. Signatories to that letter have told me that they had got their figures from sources at the centre of the inquiry and from health authority managers who had confided to colleagues around the region that the figure was 'between 70 and 90 per cent'.[25]

That *Guardian* letter caused uproar in Westminster. It was decided that each of the signatories would be contacted personally and warned that there could be consequences.[26] But they stood firm.[27]

Memoranda and briefings swirled between senior officials, the minister and the health authority to work out what to say. By then, of course, the NRHA had sent the minister its October 1988 dossier that estimated a high level of diagnostic accuracy.

A senior official suggested that should the minister 'have to say anything' he should merely refer to ongoing legal proceedings. The department's line was that 'as far as we are concerned the paediatricians have no new information available that was not considered by the Butler-Sloss inquiry'. But, of course, the paediatricians were not saying the information was *new*.[28]

Neither the NRHA or the DHSS was prepared to acknowledge what they did know:

- The NRHA: 75 per cent of the diagnoses were deemed correct and the doctors' initial diagnostic accuracy was higher than would be expected.
- The Treasury official R.B. Saunders memo to Chief Secretary John Major, 'Confidential Butler-Sloss Report', 5 July 1988: 'at least 80 per cent of the diagnoses were correct'.

Reinstate her

Dr Higgs was now represented by Brian Raymond, the ingenious and intrepid solicitor who had represented the feminist gynaecologist Wendy Savage and whose cases had included some of the great controversies of the decade.[29] After the High Court rejected Dr Higgs's case against dismissal she appealed, and in October 1989 she appeared before the Master of the Rolls, Lord Justice Donaldson. It was a moment of high drama in the torrid aftermath of Cleveland, as well as in Donaldson's career. Lord Justice Donaldson was a Tory who had presided over some of the most notorious miscarriages of justice in Britain in the 1970s.[30]

At the end of the first day of her appeal, Dr Higgs's team emerged from court 'worn out and dispirited', recalled Brian Raymond. They expected the worst when they arrived the next day, only to be utterly taken by surprise. 'What took place was an extraordinary mingling of the legal and the political,' Raymond told Dr Higgs.[31] Brian Raymond wrote a long letter to Dr Higgs outlining his impressions of the hearings: 'The first day was legal, with a flavour of the political and the second day was political with a flavour of the legal.' The court believed that she had the disciplinary code HM (61)112 on her side, and the decisions cooked up between the DHSS and the NRHA amounted to 'the clearest possible case of constructive dismissal'.

The panel of judges had recognised that Dr Higgs faced 'professional death'. But the remedies available to her were paltry. Raymond believed that the Master of the Rolls had taken 'a political line', and even though 'he is renowned for doing this ... that morning's events were remarkable even by his standards'.

Donaldson had ordered an adjournment in the hope of sorting out 'a settlement which he feels would be morally (and politically) right but is beyond the power of the courts to impose or secure'. Raymond believed that the NRHA had handed her critics the argument on a plate, more out of 'muddle and ineptitude than malice'. The 'unrestrained and unanswered political invective' against the Cleveland professionals had left a 'near indelible mark on the public consciousness', and it was that mark, Raymond believed, that made the Appeal Court's volte-face on the second day, that adjournment, 'really astonishing'. The outcome had stunned Brian Raymond.

Seize the time, he urged Dr Higgs; there might not be another chance. The Appeal Court had been unequivocal: find this woman a job. Raymond counselled: do a deal. She agreed.

The NRHA then hawked Dr Higgs around other health authorities, and even appealed in vain to the minister for help. But Gateshead, across the Tyne from Newcastle, welcomed the offer. 'I just asked my colleagues,' recalled Dr Simon Court, 'and they said "yes, sure".' They made the offer, and in April 1990 got Dr Higgs – and a new registrar, too.[32]

Dr Court was familiar with the whole Cleveland saga. He had been a member of the expert second opinion panel, and he had written to Liam Donaldson during the peak of the crisis to say that the Middlesbrough figures weren't unusual.

Dr Higgs went to Gateshead, and after a few years moved to the Scottish border town of Dumfries and finally to the south of England – at the invitation of one of the first consultant paediatricians she had met on her arrival in England.

The ban on child abuse work did not apply. But something happened to change her resolve to do it, she told me many years later. 'A boy had been brought to me by social services – he had 76 bruises. The parents said he was accident prone. It went to court. I gave evidence. The judge referred to Cleveland and my reputation.' That was irrelevant, of course, but it was made to matter. 'It was not accepted that this was a case of non-accidental injuries.' This normally serene woman froze; it was hopeless. 'What was going on in that court was nothing to do with the child or the evidence,' she recalled. 'What was going on was to do with me and my history', and that didn't help a boy with 76 bruises.[33]

Dr Wyatt: banned

Every morning, Dr Wyatt recalled he would wake up in bed 'thinking of another woman, not my wife'. He loved his wife, but he entered the day with Marietta Higgs on his conscience. It was survivor guilt, he told me nearly three decades later.[34] He had gone back to his old job; she hadn't.

Tamed, the ebullient Dr Wyatt had returned to work only to discover that his tactical surrender might never be enough. The NRHA was in difficulty: technically, it had no grounds for disciplinary action, but he had already conceded temporary restriction, and that allowed the employers to pile on the punishment and deliver a public rebuke without going through the proper process.

The NRHA feared that Wyatt might resign: it didn't want him to quit because it was aware that he had a considerable reputation and he had strong support among parents. It acknowledged that the 'issue of professional competence' concerned only sexual abuse, and in any case 'turned less on the question of accuracy of the initial diagnosis, than on the influence of that diagnosis...'. What it had first wanted from him was that he curb his enthusiasm, not only about child abuse, but everything – that he not run away with new ideas and not campaign. What they wanted by autumn 1988 was to deliver what should be regarded as a *serious* reprimand, and to extend the restriction and review it from time to time.[35] What had happened? 'Serious' was new. And why no disciplinary process? What had happened was DHSS pressure: the new minister David Mellor to be seen to be punishing the baddies, while presenting the NRHA as goodies.

The NRHA invited Dr Wyatt to come and talk. What about? He, like Dr Higgs, had not been allowed to see that 'enormously confidential' October 1988 dossier sent to the minister. In December 1988, only after intense pressure, the authority allowed him to have sight of it. But by then it was already too late. Wyatt had accepted restriction and lived in hope that it might get better. It didn't. He had been checkmated.

Ironically, when the authority announced the 'severe reprimand' and restriction, its public statement simultaneously acknowledged for the first time that clinically Dr Wyatt might not have been far wrong: 'all our information strongly suggests a higher degree of diagnostic accuracy in respect of the child abuse case than the public have hitherto understood'. Though 'he did not have responsibility for management' of the cases, some of the children had been 'disadvantaged by the intervention, whatever may or may not have happened previously'. He had worked 'far beyond the call of duty in caring for his young patients' and he 'demonstrated a commitment to the wider advancement of child health in his health district which contains some of the worst areas of deprivation'.[36]

Eight years passed. There seemed to be no hope of release. In July 1996 he took his case to a panel convened by the health authority – now the Health Trust – backed by fulsome testimonials from doctors in the region. Meanwhile, the professional context had changed: most suspected abuse cases were referred to community paediatricians in multi-disciplinary teams. The panel unanimously affirmed his skills as a doctor and proposed to 'fully rehabilitate him' through a three-year programme of training, counselling and mentoring.

Another eight years passed: there was no mentor and the restriction remained.

In 2006 he took his case to the National Patient Safety Agency. It decided that irrespective of Dr Wyatt's practice the Cleveland saga could be mobilised against him – so the restriction should remain. His employers resolved that it should be lifelong.

So, two decades after the inquiry there had been no proper disciplinary process, no annual reviews, no mentor and no change. In 2007 he appealed. The Trust found another weapon: Dr Higgs. To this day, Marietta Higgs doesn't accept that the diagnosis was wrong.[37]

By implication so would Dr Wyatt. The Trust would not expose itself to that risk, so the restriction would remain. He appealed again. He was told he must reconcile himself to the restriction for the rest of his career. If Dr Wyatt had been referred to the GMC – though he never was – restriction might have lasted up to five years. His calvary endured for 21 years. In 2010 he replied that he would not accept the ban. He was summarily dismissed.[38]

The judge: Butler-Sloss explains

Almost 30 years after the inquiry Lady Butler-Sloss agreed to meet in the House of Lords tea room. She had retired from the bar and was now an admired and vigorous cross-bencher.

A clue to her thinking had been aired at a Medico-Legal Society meeting in London's Wimpole Street in 1989 at which she was challenged by an eminent health care lawyer, Bertie Leigh. He put to her that the question of abuse had not been answered by the inquiry, but that it had been 'answered in the wardship proceedings on the basis of evidence which was incomplete', compared with the evidence put to her own inquiry.[39] His question addressed the fault line of the parallel proceedings – judges making rulings in care proceedings without the benefit of the collective expert intelligence given to her inquiry, and sometimes, as Robert Nelson had argued, not on the merits of the case. She replied, 'One of the important elements about the wardship cases was that they were very largely compromised.' She did not elaborate at the time.

I asked whether this meant that the courts had been less well informed than the inquiry. Not at all, she said. 'At no time did we deal with individual cases ... in none of the cases did we give a ruling.' That had not been her task, which was to 'assess, discuss, advise on processes and procedures'. So, although 'we knew a lot' about the cases, she said, in none of them did the inquiry 'make a determination of any sort ... consequently we were on the sidelines.' Thus, she added, 'nothing we did touched on the decision-making processes of the judges trying the cases'.

What did she mean when she described the wardship cases as 'compromised'? She explained that she was not referring to the different evidence bases of the wardship judges and her own inquiry, but the child protection process itself: the consultants had 'jumped the gun', she said, 'there was probably quite a lot of evidence, and by jumping the gun, they destroyed the credibility of other evidence'. This did not mean that they were wrong clinically, but they had shown their hand.

In the context of the guidelines at the time, and the vigorous parents' movements that insisted on being informed and consulted by professionals, hadn't the paediatricians done what was expected of them, share what they had seen with parents and other professionals?

She believed that this meant that they had pre-empted investigation. But even if a child named a perpetrator, that had not necessarily inspired investigation. Even if there had been 'sufficient evidence' to trigger investigation, she parried, cases 'were ruined by premature removal. The children shouldn't have been moved.'

This was not a commentary on the evidence as such, she explained, but on the process laid down at the time. 'What the doctors did was basically ruin any other evidence that might have come, because they took the children away too quickly.' Many professionals agreed: they felt that the doctors should have stayed shtum, kept a watching brief and lived in hope that a child might be able to talk at some point.

'The middle class go to lawyers'

In practice the dilemma was bypassed: if sexual abuse was one aspect of an abusive, neglectful, violent childhood, then other reasons, such as physical violence, might be found to justify taking cases to court. That was unlikely to work in middle-class families where the children were well fed, clothed and educated, and where, it was assumed, wrongly, that the power of a perpetrator did not rely on the fist.

Butler-Sloss was alive to the impact of social class: the Cleveland children were not all from 'known' families. 'One of the problems with middle class families', she said, 'is that they are very difficult to manage; they are articulate, particularly defensive, and almost certainly they go to lawyers.'

She was convinced that if (following the guidelines) children were admitted to hospital, or to foster care, on the basis of suspected sexual abuse, without a child's statement or a confession, there would be trouble: 'If you take a child away too quickly and you haven't got enough evidence, the children go back to what is potentially an abusive situation.' Nothing could protect the child.

Butler-Sloss always insisted that no one could ever know how many of the children had been abused. There were three groups, she explained: some were 'perfectly obviously abused'; some 'perfectly obviously should never have been taken away from home. The doctors should have waited.' In other children, 'there were signs but not enough'. That group prompted 'real concerns', but if 'you don't have enough evidence there is no point in taking the children into care'.

She vividly recalled a professional family in which the children showed physical signs of sexual abuse. She had watched the videos of interviews with the children – 'far too many interviews' – and the most that the children said was that their mother 'needed them at home, she couldn't cope, and they never said a word. All they said was "mummy needs us, we must go home..." nothing except "please can we go home". They were very worried about mummy all the time, it was tear-jerking.' They should never have been removed: 'there wasn't enough evidence to keep them away, so they went through the most ghastly experience'.

If there was physical evidence but no narrative, 'you have to be brave and decide you shouldn't take the child away', because as soon as 'you've taken the child away the parents will be wary'. Not even to hospital? 'You don't move the children against the wishes of the parents unless you've got some evidence, ever!'

In Cleveland, she added:

> 'The children were moved early. If there was no other evidence and they had to go back to a potentially abusive situation. If they had not been moved, then were staying in a potentially abusive situation but they haven't had the trauma of being taken away. And there are different sorts of trauma.'[40]

She was adamant, 'if you haven't enough evidence, never take the child away, hold off.'

Then there was the elephant in the room: the police. One inquiry insider recalled that they were regarded as 'hopeless, absolutely hopeless, completely out of date, unbelievable'. Butler-Sloss was very critical of the police, but she held the challenging opinion that 'these are not really police cases'. In intra-family abuse cases in Cleveland, she believed 'the police had no role to play'. Not even if there was suspected rape and buggery? 'I don't think the police had any part to play at all.'

'That's not what we said'

Her report had provided a figure of the final outcomes – not of findings of abuse, but of children who returned home: 98 out of 121 children. Most commentaries inferred that the diagnosis was wrong, that the children had not been abused, 'Oh,' the judge replied, 'that's not what we said.'

Oh, but that's what people thought. She seemed surprised.

She said she had always insisted that 'I do not know how many children were sexually abused in Cleveland … and nobody will ever know. It was not my job to find out.' However, nothing much should be inferred from this determined not-knowing. Careful reading of the Cleveland Report and of her speeches shows that Butler-Sloss *never* said that the differential diagnosis was wrong; she never said that the signs and symptoms were a figment of mad minds.

Asked about the NRHA's estimate that 75 per cent of the diagnoses were correct, she replied, 'I didn't know about that.' But in any case, 'it would not have changed my mind. The children shouldn't have been taken away.'

What did she think professionals should do about the crux of Cleveland's crisis: strong physical signs but little or no narrative? She was candid: 'I don't know.'

5

A new enlightenment

What was so threatening that it made some professionals and police officers lose their manners and made ministers mislead Parliament? The Cleveland controversy belongs to the history of how things come to be known and not-known: how adults' sexual interest in children has been 'common knowledge' and yet periodically becomes 'anathema'.[1]

For more than 2,000 years medical scrutiny of children's bodies, dead and alive, has been concerned not only with disease but also with harm and justice.[2] Hippocrates (460–377 BC), established semiotics as the study of symptoms – signs that stand for something other than themselves.[3] Since signs do not speak for themselves, it is the work of medicine to interpret the ecology of bodies – it is, therefore, never neutral; it is always political.

European forensic science was established as a field in the 19th century, founded in the investigation of epidemics spread by social intercourse, sex, trade and industrialisation, and in the investigation of bodies in morgues, constabularies, courts, mines, factories and the homesteads of the modern metropolis.

I venture that signs of child sexual abuse are to be found in the very moment that forensic medicine emerges as a new field in the dark heat of 19th-century capitalism and mass migration to the cities: it is there, with sewerage, pollution and the great diseases that exercised the public health movements that participated in the creation of the modern welfare state. Forensic medicine was potentially the scientific partner to the testimony of women and children. But as we shall see, that relationship was contingent – unstable, intermittent and ad hoc. Doctors were periodically the friend and the enemy of the victims.

Heroic Auguste Ambroise Tardieu

France was the hub of the new science, where the pioneering medical examiner Auguste Ambroise Tardieu exposed injuries to children in mines, slums, factories and families. He has a special salience in our story because he was the first to recognise the scale of children being mistreated at home.[4] He published 'a classical description of the battered child syndrome' a century before it was 'rediscovered' in the US.[5] And he was the first to describe the signs of sodomy that exercised the Cleveland controversy. Tardieu's great *oeuvre* on sexual offences, *Etude medico-legale sur les attentats aux mœurs*, untranslated into English but available in French in the British Library, reports 616 cases of sexual violence, mostly against children, 339 of whom were victims of rape or attempted rape. A third of the text is devoted to child abuse and physical signs of sodomy, including anal dilatation, in girls, boys, women and men. Such was its impact that another six editions were published.[6] However, this new field swiftly became politically polarised: some physicians sympathised with women and children, while others joined the ignoble repudiation of victims.

Fanny and Stella

Tardieu was familiar to England's emerging forensic medical examiners in the 1860s. The historian Louise Jackson discovered court cases in Victorian England in which 'anal dilatation was seen as crucial sign' of the abuse of boys.[7] Tardieu's work made a dramatic entrance in 1870 in the florid trial of two young London clerks, cross-dressers Frederick Park (Fanny) and Ernest Boulton (Stella), habitués of London's theatreland, where they were 'ravished' – and paid – by eminent men.

A young police surgeon had examined them at Bow Street police station, and recognised anal dilatation because he'd read Tardieu's manual.[8] In the criminal trial, Tardieu was cited in a medical report by Alfred Swaine Taylor, the father of English medical jurisprudence.[9]

The affair was reported in the press with lavish innuendo. So, a century before Cleveland, readers were rather well informed about the medical signs of sodomy.

Repudiation and reinterpretation of signs

The second half of the 19th century was a period of obsessive regulation of bodies, ideologies of gender and the meaning of sexual acts, and the participation of forensic science in sexual politics was inevitably contradictory – simultaneously exposing and endorsing patriarchal practices.

Tardieu was 'unable to convince the physicians of his time of the prevalence of the maltreatment of children in their own family', comments the Canadian paediatrician Jean Labbé, and child victims were 'condemned to suffer abuse and neglect for another century without the support of the medical community'.[10] Forensic sensitivity to child abuse as a crime of the family dissolved.

Historians of sexual politics have mapped a 'conceptual shift' in the 1880s, from the perception of sodomy as a masculine act, part of men's penetrating repertoire, to a specialism of homosexuality.[11] Anal dilatation became established in forensic medicine as *proof* of homosexuality, and Tardieu's legacy was weaponised against gay men: sexual activity with children was claimed as something queer men did to boys; the habitat was presumed to be streets, arcades and public toilets, and the schools of the elite, not the home, except when it was the predilection of paupers or village idiots.[12]

Skewed statistics and new knowledge

This brief chronicle of the discovery, disavowal, reinterpretation and rediscovery of medical signs found its echo in the response to speech: there was respect for, and simultaneously recoil from the testimony of victims. Harvard professor of psychiatry Judith Lewis Herman writes that clinicians, historians and survivor movements have exposed 'a vastly elaborated intellectual tradition which served the purpose of suppressing the truth about incest'.[13] The classic case is Sigmund Freud, founder of psychoanalysis, who in 1896 believed the cause of traumatic symptoms of his female patients was sexual abuse by men in their families. Within a year he retracted. Herman identified Freud's discomfort: 'if his patients' reports were true, incest was not a rare abuse confined to the poor and mentally defective but was endemic to the patriarchal family'.[14]

The historian Linda Gordon's great study of family violence from 1880 to 1960, *Heroes of Their Own Lives*, showed that the movements to expose and prevent child abuse that began in Europe and the US in the 19th century were sustained politically when women's rights movements were confronted family violence. Awareness grew when 'feminism was strong and ebbed when feminism was weak'.[15] After feminism was marginalised towards the end of the 19th century, child sexual abuse as a crime of the home was reinterpreted and refocused on the street, the stranger and the pervert.

In the 20th century 'incest was de-emphasized' and the culprit became not the adult, but the child. The criminologist Carol Smart has analysed child abuse as a 'history of ambivalence and conflict' over the meanings of 'child' and 'harm'.[16]

'The bones tell a story'

It was when the invention of radiology and its widespread use in public health services after the Second World War transformed what could be seen that Tardieu was restored to the study of child abuse. This inaugurated a second revolution in the awareness of violence against children that can be called a new enlightenment.[17] A team of eminent physicians, led by C. Henry Kempe, published 'The battered-child syndrome' in 1962 and duly acknowledged the debt owed to Tardieu.[18]

The impact on child health services was profound. In the US, the Child Abuse Prevention Act of 1974 promised a new infrastructure of research, mandatory reporting and care. There was close contact between the US and doctors and children's societies in the UK, particularly the British psychiatrist Dr Arnon Bentovim and his team at Great Ormond Street Children's Hospital in London.[19] Britain's relatively well-developed welfare state and its National Health Service enshrined the principle of universal entitlement and an ethic of moral duty, a belief that children were owed the forensic attention of their doctors. When these pioneers put sexual abuse on the agenda, they were challenged both by children's 'self-sacrificial behaviour' and the courts' seeming inability to engage with children.[20]

It was in the context of the new enlightenment that scholars used new sociological methods to measure prevalence; that is, the proportion of the population that had experienced abuse. Crucially, they asked participants about specific sexual acts and they analysed their meaning in the minds of victims. Traditional research methods had failed to access people's secrets, ambiguities and complications, and the 'social construction' of sexual culture. There was nothing less than an epistemological revolution: childhood experiences had never been accessed in this way before. Research established that between a quarter and a fifth of girls would experience rape or sexual assault.

In 1979 the American sociologist David Finkelhor published the first national survey, *Sexually Victimised Children*. It confirmed that 'the more detailed and sensitive the questions' the higher the figures. Finkelhor found that 19 per cent of female students and 8 per cent of male students had been abused in their childhood by relatives. The majority had told no one: 'for a great number our survey was the first mention they had made of it.'[21]

In the 1980s, the psychologist Mary Koss published several groundbreaking studies that changed how the victimisation of girls and women could be understood. *The Unacknowledged Rape Victim*, published in 1980, exposed the asymmetry between official data and what actually happened: only a quarter of women who had ever experienced an act that was legally defined as rape described it as rape. 'Acknowledged rape victims are women who have experienced forced sexual intercourse and view their experience as rape. Unacknowledged rape victims have suffered the same experience – forced sexual intercourse – but who for various reasons do not conceptualise their experience as rape.'[22]

In 'victimisation terminology' they were deemed a 'safe victim'; that is, someone unlikely to implicate the man. Koss and her colleagues specified acts and avoided using the word 'rape': 27 per cent had experienced what would be legally defined as rape, but only 23 per cent acknowledged it if it had involved an acquaintance.[23]

In 1984, Diana E.H. Russell published her pioneering study, *The Secret Trauma: Incest in the Lives of Girls and Women*. Russell concludes that 38 per cent of women reported at least once experience of sexual abuse within and outside the family before the age of 18.[24]

In 1985 Gail E. Wyatt, and a civil rights activist and the first African-American woman to be licensed as a psychologist in California, published the first major study of Black and White women: she found 52 per cent had experienced sexual abuse by people known to them.[25]

In the UK a more conventional – and limited – survey conducted by the market research company MORI in 1985 found rates of 12 per cent among girls and 8 per cent among boys. The psychiatrist Tony Baker and psychologist Sylvia Duncan, who led the research, extrapolated that about 4.5 million people in Britain had been sexually abused in childhood.[26]

This radical research ignited tough debates about methodology: studies of virtually any other crime 'raise barely a ripple of concern', comments Professor Bonnie Fisher, but not so with sexual violence and abuse.[27]

Wynne and Hobbs's terrible discovery

This, then, was the context of the next great convulsion in the 1980s. British consultant paediatricians Chris Hobbs and Jane Wynne had attended thousands of children in the northern city of Leeds. Their collegial approach to sharing knowledge encouraged referrals by carers, nursery staff, schools and mothers of young children and even babies, and the city became one of the most aware in the UK.

Referrals of suspected sexual abuse rose from zero in 1979 to 50 a year in 1984. The city was then jolted by an enormous quake that prefigured the rediscovery a decade later of organised child sexual exploitation across the country: 11 sex exploitation rings were discovered in a single neighbourhood, with 175 child victims aged from under a year to 15. In 1985–6 the police and social services in Leeds identified 608 children thought to have been sexually abused.[28]

In 1986 *The Lancet* published Wynne and Hobbs's paper 'Buggery in childhood: a common syndrome of child abuse'.[29]

Wynne and Hobbs stressed that the medical examination should be relatively brief: The dynamic sign of reflex anal dilatation would appear in less than a minute: if the internal sphincter had been weakened or stretched, it could only briefly be supported by the external sphincter, and the anus would open. They advocated swift reaction to the medical evidence; it was, after all, indicative of a clear and present danger.

Everything about this was a shock. The sign had been well established in forensic pathology, but as a signature of homosexual not heterosexual men. This discovery disturbed the orthodoxies about sex, who does what to whom; what I called, in *Unofficial Secrets*, 'the politics of the orifice'.[30]

Their research showed that medicine could be a resource in the discovery of child sexual abuse in all classes, not just impoverished social services clients. The frisson of their work captured the precise cruelty of child sexual abuse: the medical evidence announced chronic trauma as a symptom, not a story. Furthermore, if penetration ceased the anus healed swiftly, and that, too, was decisive in the diagnostic process.

The symptom seemed to be a physical analogue of the psychological responses to the discovery of abuse described in a poignant essay by Dr Roland Summit, a community psychiatrist in Torrance, California, 'The child sexual abuse accommodation syndrome'. Children's agency in the non-disclosure of it was expressed not in the fantasy and fabrication hypotheses of sceptics, but in entrapment and accommodation.[31]

The Wynne and Hobbs paper in *The Lancet* attracted protests by a few doctors who had not noticed the sign, or thought it meant something else, or meant nothing at all. But Wynne and Hobbs had history on their side: they brought the medical evidence back to where it began – with Tardieu, patriarchy, the family and public health.

On 30 October 1986, a few weeks later, Childline was launched, a national telephone helpline for children living with neglect, abuse and cruelty. The phone lines were jammed.

New enlightenment versus new world order

By now no one could be unaware that child abuse was big, very big. This moment synchronised with growing international political recognition that children should have enforceable right

– soon to be inscribed in the 1989 United Nations Convention on the Rights of the Child.

In Canada, under pressure from Indigenous activists, feminists, child abuse survivors and professionals to reform sexual offences legislation, the government had commissioned medico-legal scientist Sir Robin Badgley to lead a committee of health, welfare and justice specialists to investigate. Badgley organised exhaustive research into child sexual abuse, child prostitution and child pornography. The committee analysed 10,272 cases, sought the stories of both victims and perpetrators, and tracked the conditions in which assaults were disclosed and to whom. Unlike the Cleveland Inquiry, the Badgley committee was prompted by a need to know, not a need to blame. It tunnelled into institutions' archives and found that sexual menace had been and remained ubiquitous. Its discoveries synchronised with revelations of endemic sexual abuse everywhere: in families, in Canada's Catholic schools and in the residential school system in which thousands of Indigenous children had been interned in a strategy of cultural genocide.[32]

Its report, *Sexual Offences Against Children* (two volumes, 1,341 pages long), revealed that half of women and a third of men had been 'victims of unwanted sexual acts' – 10 per cent involving penetration – and four fifths of these during childhood; '98.8 per cent of the suspects were males'. The report analysed acts of abuse and also associations and contexts: between a fifth and a quarter of assailants were family members, and a third were friends or acquaintances. It demolished the notion that 'sexually abused children are more likely to be harmed by the bitter reactions of their parents or the harsh exposure to legal proceedings than by having been victims of sexual abuse'. It was alarmed that neither the acts nor the associations determined intervention strategies: 'victims of more serious offences were as likely to be left in their homes', while Indigenous children were typically seized from their homes and families and removed to institutions where abuse was endemic. And it noted that 'only a few victims of sexual offences seek assistance from helping services'.

The report was the subject of much debate and criticism, but one of its great achievements was to exhume criminal justice records that showed the highs and lows of society's interest in sexual abuse across a century: convictions peaked in the 1870s and early 1880s, coinciding with feminist activism among Black and White people in the US and Canada, and dipped until after the First World War, peaked again in the 1920s (another period of feminist activism) and declined steadily to a low point in the 1960s.

None of this inspired governments to confront the desolate conclusion that few victims informed anyone. The new enlightenment was threatened on all fronts: there was panic in government offices about a tide of referrals that synchronised with the wielding of the neo-liberal axe: welfare was being restructured and restrained. In both the UK and US public childcare was unusually underdeveloped – and privatised – compared with the rest of the industrialised world. Roland Summit had warned in the early 1980s that in this inhospitable climate, the explosion of interest in abuse created new hazards: 'it increases the likelihood of discovery but fails to protect the victim against the secondary assaults of an inconsistent intervention system'.[33]

Dr Richard Krugman, a leader of paediatric opinion in the US, director of the C. Henry Kempe Center for the Prevention and Treatment of Child Abuse and Neglect, lamented the political decline of concern about child abuse. The US Advisory Board on Child Abuse and Neglect, set up to research the phenomena, had conducted 'dedicated, daring, collegial and public spirited work'.[34] But it was no longer welcome: the Clinton administration (Democrat) and a right-wing faction of the Republican congress ultimately destroyed the Board. With it went a great deal of momentum. Krugman warned that the child protection system was 'fragmented, underfunded, overworked, episodic'. Unsurprisingly, some discouraged clinicians 'have deliberately followed a pattern of civil disobedience' by not reporting abuse.[35]

Resources, professional practice and ideologies about sex and power, public and private, met vehement resistance and a clash of paradigms between traditional family values, sexual modernism and the rediscovery of child sexual abuse thwarted by the difficulty of disclosure and detection.

Social scientists Janet Newman and John Clarke write that the looming Cleveland crisis in particular, and child abuse generally, profoundly unsettled the thoroughly patriarchal norms of the professions, bureaucracies and state structures. They had assumed the 'normal' family 'as the focal point of state welfare'.[36] Child abuse required fundamental realignment of the professions and public service to be ready, and trusted, to put their skills at the disposal of children.

Thatcherism imagined national re-formation in the 1980s not as a new deal between the public and the state, but as privatisation, for profit, and the public to be reincarnated as clients and customers. But there was no consensus about the 'public' and whether the concept included children, and how a child could be conceptualised as a 'client' or 'customer'.

So the new enlightenment required reconstruction of the welfare state at the very moment when the neo-liberal project inaugurated its deconstruction. As previously noted, Margaret Thatcher famously declared that people were 'casting their problems at society. And who is society? There is no such thing. There are individual men and women and there are families.'[37] Thatcherism had no interest in exposing the interior of family life as 'not necessarily an intimate and tranquil haven', and it did not recognise the family as the *main* realm that both produced and concealed child sexual abuse.[38]

This was the political conjuncture of the *Working Together* consultation. The chief civil servant in the Department of Health and Social Security, Rupert Hughes, had been given a wide brief to rationalise the legal 'hodge-podge' and he aimed for a draft that would attract cross-party support while setting a wider threshold 'for compulsory state intervention in family life'. Hughes was regarded as a 'heroic figure', diplomatic and adroit, just the man for the job.[39]

Meanwhile, practitioners took the mandate in *Working Together* to heart – this was the zeitgeist. But they didn't stand a chance. Sexual abuse referrals were rushing into old ideologies and systems that officials already knew weren't fit for purpose. Cleveland was the first casualty. The 'civil disobedience' predicted by the US paediatrician Richard Krugman, I suggest, was to become not only a bad habit in the UK but also public policy.

6

Parallel lives

Two cases in the UK and Canada exemplified both the new enlightenment and the contrasting national contexts. Both cases involved multiple perpetrators, trails of connections, cruelty, perhaps pornography, perhaps prostitution, weird rituals – and certainly lifelong sexual abuse across generations.

In England, the Broxtowe case was contemporaneous with, and in some respects also a consequence of, the events in Cleveland. It was the UK's biggest case of abuse in an extended family, and the social work practice received a commendation – most unusually – by Margaret Thatcher in the House of Commons in 1989. In Canada, following the Badgley Report, the acclaimed Project Jericho found hundreds of victims in Prescott, a small town in Ontario. These cases, and others in the UK, show the polarised political reactions to exemplary professional practice.

Broxtowe: a 'fabulous job'

In 1986 a Nottinghamshire senior social worker brought a fresh eye to an extended family on Nottingham's Broxtowe estate, well known to professionals and the police through generations. So much time spent to so little effect. She considered that 12 children, now teenagers and adults, and 23 grandchildren, ruled by a patriarch – the grandfather and his adjutant, his wife – were at risk of inheriting his legacy of poverty, neglect, sexual abuse and sadism. The family included convicted sex offenders (including the grandfather himself) who did their time, returned to the family and circulated around satellite systems of sexual abuse among their friends and relatives.

In 1987 the social workers were, like many in 1980s social services departments, using what they had learned in the new enlightenment about children and about sex offenders. They consulted probation officers, experts on perpetrators, doctors, psychiatrists, the National Society for the Prevention of Cruelty to Children, lawyers and senior public officials, locally and nationally. They mapped the risks and adopted what can be described as a 'perpetrator-challenging' approach. Possibly because the family was known and criminalised, social services interventions were likely to be supported by the police.

Everyone was being careful – Cleveland was in the news. Judith Jones was, like Sue Richardson in Cleveland, one of the newly appointed national network of specialist consultants, following Louis Blom-Cooper's *Lost in Trust* report. At her welcome meeting, Judith was told by the then director 'now we don't want another Cleveland here'.[1]

The social workers' review of the family prompted Nottinghamshire County Council to ask the wardship court for permission to remove the children, aged between 3 and 14, from their parents to assess them while they tried to work with some of the mothers who had already shared their own fears. The court agreed. They went to live with experienced foster carers, and the court regulated every aspect of their children's lives.[2]

No interviews!

'Disclosure work' – judged so pessimistically during the Cleveland Inquiry – was out. The wardship judge ruled no interviews with the children and decided that instead the foster carers should note down their impromptu sayings and doings. Their records, known as the 'diaries', were passed to the social workers and then to the police. Medical examinations identified serious, chronic sexual and physical abuse, confirmed by the mothers. The determined stories in the 'diaries' were corroborated by other children in the extended family, also in care, with whom they now had no contact.[3] Highly controlled access to the parents was organised until an abusive incident put a stop to all contact. That was when the children really began to talk.

Three months after the children had been removed, the parents, who were well aware of the allegations, were arrested. The police said they found no material evidence of abuse. Of course not. When I made a TV documentary about the case in 1990, neighbours confirmed that the parents set bonfires in their back gardens before the arrests. Adults involved – including one of the convicted perpetrators – confirmed that they had disposed of evidence, 'well of course, most of the evidence was destroyed before the arrests, because we knew they were going to happen', one commented.[4]

What the children told their carers is the closest version that exists of their experiences. They were describing not only sadistic sexual abuse, but also something 'ceremonial' and strange. They also began to identify participants outside their families.[5] The case travelled successfully through the wardship, appeal and criminal courts. According to the wardship judge, Mrs Justice Booth, the children's narratives suggested a 'wholly exceptional' context and culture that she described as 'often accompanied by strange and obscene rites'.[6] According to the Director of Social Services at the time, David White, she 'took the possibility of children being involved in satanic rituals very seriously'. He repeated her comments: 'In the Broxtowe case the offences against the children were often accompanied by strange and obscene rites.' She concluded that she could not resist the finding that the children had experienced 'dreadful and ... satanic nonsense'.[7]

On 19 July 1988 – the same month as the Cleveland Report was published – three Appeal Court judges endorsed her conclusion, and added that the children 'had been subjected to gross sexual abuse at the hands of adults, sometimes at parties, where full intercourse had taken place in the presence of a number of adults and other children'.[8] White accepted the definition formulated by the Nottinghamshire social workers of severe sexual abuse in a context 'linked to symbols, or activities that appear to have religious, magical or supernatural significance ... used to frighten, intimidate and confuse the children'.[9]

The response of another wardship judge, Morrison, J., in June 1990, to claims that a foster carer in another case had 'led the children or put ideas into their heads', was curt: the foster mother's evidence was 'the most eloquent testimony I have ever heard or seen. … It has been suggested that she led the children or put ideas into their heads. I find that is ludicrous.'[10]

In 1989, ten adults, including two women, were jailed after being convicted of gross cruelty and sexual abuse. Two appealed in 1995, claiming that the prosecution would have been discredited had the criminal court been given access to the children's bizarre allegations. But it had all been available to the court and to the defence, and the appeal was refused.[11]

Locked in

Social workers' warnings that other children outside the family were still at risk were repudiated by the police, who – reminiscent of the Cleveland Police – were often emotional, angry and brutal: one officer locked the door of his office and told a senior social worker that he would not let her out unless she agreed with him.[12]

Although the case had been acclaimed as a model of good practice, the social workers and foster carers became the focus of an unending counter-attack in the media. The synergy of the police resistance and the excess and extremity of the Broxtowe case excited huge resistance.

The Chief Constable and the Director of Social Services set up a Joint Enquiry Team (JET) to review the work. Its report contradicted the judges, condemned the carers and social workers, and rehearsed old fables – children lie, they fantasise, they are contaminated by horror videos or by frightened, fabricating adults, sometimes Christian zealots – and added new dogma: professionals were *creating* children's implausible narratives and spreading the contagion at conferences.[13] This version was promoted by Nottinghamshire Police and the mass media, particularly the broadsheet *Independent on Sunday* and the tabloid *Mail on Sunday*.[14] The sceptical commentariat did not consult anyone directly involved: the carers, social workers, managers or the mothers who corroborated what the children said.[15]

Social workers and carers themselves wondered whether children had actually witnessed events or had been made to think so. Had something been performed for a video? Had they been given drugs? Were more children at risk? This last question was left unanswered – except by the police and the JET, whose answer was simply 'No'.

The JET Report was leaked onto the internet by the authors despite legal action by Nottingham County Council.[16] An example of its staying power, and its utility as a backlash dossier, was its reincarnation a quarter of a century later in a BBC Radio 4 *Analysis* programme presented by David Aaronovitch – again, without interviewing anyone directly involved in the case – to discredit the entirely unrelated historic abuse allegations that prompted the 2014 Independent Inquiry into Child Sexual Abuse.[17]

Few days in her life without abuse

In the early 1990s I interviewed one of the convicted mothers in prison. She had returned from a home visit troubled and fearful about her impending release, and decided that she wanted to share her story, just in case. I have never revealed her identity or the details of her narrative, and nor will I do so now, but it feels important to share a little of what she had to say for this reason: like the Cleveland children, her children were bequeathed a fictional account of their lives in that family. It was bad enough for them to have lived that life; it is gratuitous and cruel that they should also live with a lie.

Here is a vignette of that woman in prison in 1993. She had finally got the spectacles she needed – but never possessed – as a child, and had her teeth fixed. She was wearing a blue suit that she had sewn herself – in the style of a lady's costume with a Margaret Thatcher bow. She smoked, drank tea and ate Jaffa Cakes while we talked.

'When I was a child my parents talked about the devil all the time. They said I was "born for the devil".' When she herself was a mother, there were parties at home, as the Broxtowe children had described, confirmed by neighbours, and at other places, also described by the children, where the adults dressed up and 'Dad was the devil'. They went to various locations (identified by the children), houses, caves and tunnels (the city is built on caves and tunnels); events were videoed, costumes were hired from a shop in the city, and they had others at home: 'they were at my Dad's house'. Why didn't the police find any of this, I asked her? 'Well, of course, most of the evidence was destroyed before the arrests. We knew they were going to happen. We had a bonfire.' During a home leave visit in 1991, accompanied by a police officer, she had been taken to look at some of the houses identified by the children. The police 'said to me "don't give me this!" About porn, the videos, witches, devils, dead babies. ... That's what they said.'

When she had her own children, 'my Mum and Dad said, "they're not children to be loved ... they're an ornament to be messed with"'. Her role in the family had been to control the children – everyone regarded her as frightening. She described getting pleasure from, and being aroused by, the pain that she inflicted on the children – she liked seeing it, she said. This woman talked often in prison with her probation officer and a prison psychologist about the pleasure of that power. Indeed, according to the professionals who worked with her, the only experience of power she had had in her life was when she abused children: 'Before entering prison she has experienced a life which has been totally defined in terms of abusive experiences', commented one of them. 'There will have been very few days in her life that have passed without some form of abuse.'[18]

Safe to speak

How did the Broxtowe story become so contested? How did some versions seem so attractive compared with others that were nearer to the original sources? Why was it so important to repudiate these rites and practices? Why did some groups and individuals with no apparent involvement in the story seem so excited by it that they had to be *in* the argument?

The courts – unlike the mass media – were given all of the available evidence and the arguments. No court supported the JET narrative. No carers or professionals who were alleged to have poured horrific (and therefore abusive) narratives into the minds of children were ever disciplined. I suggest this is because no one close to the events really believed the hypothesis. The Director of Social Services, David White, delivered his final word on the children's narratives in November 1990 – ignored by sceptics: 'I find it difficult to believe that the stories were imprinted in their minds by foster carers and social workers. Even if the children have not suffered each incident physically, they have been made to believe that they have.'

White agreed with the social workers' opinion that 'the significance of ritual overtones is not that it is necessarily linked to a belief system but rather it provided a mechanism for manipulating vulnerable children'. It would be unwise, therefore, not to accept the possibility of 'ritualistic elements in this case', he said.[19]

Unnoticed, 30 years after the event the director told the Independent Inquiry into Child Sexual Abuse that a 'fabulous job' had been done protecting the youngsters.[20]

Ironically, the Broxtowe strategy, founded on a successful 'perpetrator-challenging' approach, had been influenced by the response to events in Cleveland: children were not interviewed formally; they spoke when they – like Minnie – were given clean sheets, warm baths, good food and kind words, and when they knew they were safe. While so much of what they said was corroborated, including by adults, it was denigrated by the police.

The strategy directed by the court, and evidence accepted by the courts, did not immunise those closest to the children from attack. On the contrary, they became the source of what appeared to be a homegrown backlash, a portmanteau of notions: suggestibility, contamination, horror videos, fairy stories, brainwashing, naïve and zealous workers, feminists, empire builders, Christians. Social workers and foster carers did not recognise themselves or their thoughts in a mass media that rarely, if ever, consulted them.

By the time the Broxtowe children had grown up, they might tell their story differently. 'More mature narratives might contain insights to which they had no access as children', Judith Jones reflected years later. 'They might have compared notes with brothers and sisters. They may have been told that their "memories" were false, they had been implanted. The fact is, however, that whatever had happened to them, the records of the foster carers were *their* story, as it was told and as it was heard.'[21]

Project Jericho: 'this is what a good community does'

Did the Badgley Commission make a difference in Canada? Did the new knowledge change professional paradigms? Initially yes, and if any single case exemplified the new times it was Project Jericho.

Like the Broxtowe case, there were physical signs in very young children, transgenerational transmission, long tangles of perpetrators–cum-victims, children and adults, diverse scenarios from banal sadism to elaborate and bizarre brutality. However, Project Jericho identified chains of discrete or disorganised connections, from poor people to the powerful.

The testimony of very distressed young children after they had been taken into care from filthy, violent homes was supported by adult victims and perpetrators' admissions. The perpetrators were 'known', but it was a new political mandate, a new generation of professionals that changed the meaning of *normal* and acceptable *harm*. The case exemplified what can happen when scale and complexity is matched by collegial co-operation and solidarity, and above all by the investment of huge resources and positive interest by the state.

The case began in 1988 when a social worker visited a home that was filthy, with flies everywhere, excrement on the stairs and in the cupboards, food on the floor, children wild or subdued who could barely speak. Medical examinations revealed chronic penetration of the children. They were removed and settled with foster parents. Only then did they begin to show what had happened to them, first in fragments – terrors, sleepless nights, screams, vomiting – and finally with words: they described elaborate sexual violence against many children by many people in strange scenarios. 'So much of what I was hearing was so bizarre and emotional, I found myself in some respects backing away', said Pam Gummer, children's services team leader, 'I was saying we need to corroborate this, we should be very cautious'.[22]

Notorious networks of abused and abusive families were revealed as theatres of sadism linked to scores of other perpetrators and victims. Was it ritual abuse, the professionals asked themselves, was it organised, was it diverse scenarios and genres occurring at the same time?

A child told social workers about groups of adults dressing up, playing 'monster games' in a basement, filming them, killing animals; and talked of a baby called Joshua.[23] When the children described locations, social workers found what the children said they would find. By October 1989, a joint investigation had uncovered many new cases. A family associate admitted to abusing more than a dozen children and named several other perpetrators.

Soon, 'We had physical evidence, medical evidence. They were able to describe the places where they were abused, and we went there and we found what the kids said we would find,' said Gummer.[24]

Rocci Pagnello, a member of the team, had been a young social worker in Prescott in the early 1980s: 'It's a pleasant place, and pretty conservative politically,' he told me. 'Between 1982 and 1985 I'd done almost all of the sexual abuse investigations myself – one person. So you can tell the numbers we were dealing with.' The Badgley Report 'was a watershed', he said.[25]

He became the supervisor during Project Jericho, and because of the great interest in the case 'we developed a team funded by three different agencies: Solicitor General, Attorney General, and the youth services. We had very good officials who'd come and see us; they'd say "what are you thinking … what do you need?"' They acquired their own building – crucially, he added, the police worked on social services' terrain. Support was organised for victims and witnesses and mental health services for the children: 'It was the largest multi-victim/multi-perpetrator investigation in North America.'

Ultimately, they concluded that whatever the various cultures of abuse, they were designed to terrify and silence, and the abusers were not organised so much as *connected*.

Between 1991 and 1994 there were several trials: 119 suspected perpetrators, of whom 65 were charged, and a remarkable conviction rate of 91 per cent.[26]

The community did not flinch. When the case was about to go public, the mayor Sandra Lawn was warned to expect intense questioning about some known and prominent figures in the town: 'the police chief, a very dear friend, indicated to me the day before what was about to happen', she explained. 'The media will inundate our town, he warned me.'[27]

Lawn was an experienced politician who knew her way round family law; she had spent time learning about sexual abuse, and now she thought hard about what needed to be said. The media were interested in 'scandal' and 'prominent individuals', she told me; she didn't want to discuss that as 'it would be a diversion', so she decided instead to talk about the work and the diligence of the investigations. 'What I said was that as mayor I was so proud of our departments because they had rescued these children.'

She regarded her community as 'highly competent', a place where 'we could bring thousands of people together'. And she used her power to do that, to bring people together to explain what was going on, to engage the community in the protection of the children. Unlike in Cleveland, which was encouraged by its political leaders and the police to resist the discovery of abuse, and then to feel ashamed, the town of Prescott was encouraged to feel civic pride about the way it had confronted a catastrophe. An astounding one in four of its children had been affected by the investigation, but they no longer suffered in silence, and they no longer had to believe that hell was how the world was.

A community enhancement strategy accompanied the prosecutions: the poorest and most stigmatised part of town was targeted, families who were marooned in isolation were engaged, the library and local media, the schools, churches and neighbourhood institutions were enlisted to try to build a healthy, educated culture. There were regular meetings between the Attorney General, the mayor and the specialist workers. They went into the schools and public meetings and educated the town. 'The thing I'd be proudest of', said Pagnello, 'was how the community came together and accepted that it happened.'

'The mayor was heavily involved in that', he said, 'and she was instrumental in developing a community response so that people recognised it and accepted it.'

Lawn reckoned:

> '[There were] people who didn't understand how widespread this thing is, and didn't like the light it shone on the community. But I thought that was beside the point. The point was that children needed

to be rescued. There was very little resistance to that, and children were rescued. A good community does that – yes, that's it, a good community does that.'[28]

Project Jericho is little known beyond Canada, and despite its scale and the extremities of abuse, it has not entered the 'clusters' of sexual abuse myths recycled by cynics. Perhaps this is because none of the professionals – and notably the police – broke ranks; no one deemed the unusual or implausible to be impossible, and above all the state and political leaders invested in the children's well-being and in enlisting the entire community to raise its collective awareness. It was simultaneously successful, pioneering and yet, in the outside world, unnoticed.

7

Backlash

Wherever the media discovered sexual abuse the discussion switched almost immediately to 'major scandals about false allegations and inappropriate interventions',[1] reckoned media scholar Professor Jenny Kitzinger: Cleveland was typically cited in the UK as a historical caution – not as an invitation to think, but 'a rhetorical full stop'.[2]

Kitzinger shows how Cleveland became the classic case that 'outlived the actual events'; it became the template that cued the reader to thinking about very different events that, by association, explained each other, the 'dominant analogy' that framed new cases.[3] Thus Cleveland lost meaning in and for itself and became a magnetic pole for a repertoire of hypotheses – mass hysteria, moral panic, moral entrepreneur, moral crusade, witch-hunt.

Unlike the response to child deaths, which attracted none of these tropes, it was as if there had been no real event, only fantasies and fabrications. 'Common knowledge' of these events that were, after all, assaults directly experienced by perhaps 20 per cent of the female population,[4] and known and lived with by many more, was thrown into a 'black hole', a dense space of violent containment, fizzing with mighty but lightless energy that spiked everything – it was always there, in the dark.

How did the resistance work? What were the ways of thinking amid these dissonant medleys? They didn't have to come together as valence, the bonding chemistry of a unifying idea; they bundled into what the Australian scholar Chris Atmore has described as strange alliances in shared discursive terrain:[5] libertarians and civil rights advocates broke bread with conservatives, literary critics, evangelical Christians, pornographers, paganists, feminists, antifeminists and angry men's movements. Contradictory beliefs and interests converged as suspicion, always in the service of denial and deflection. For a while they were hegemonic.

The backlash happened almost instantly when mental health and child welfare professionals were working out how to treat survivors of sexual violence 'often by trial and error,' and suddenly they found themselves 'under very serious attack', writes Judith Lewis Herman, therapist and theorist of abuse and trauma.[6] Abuse does not 'languish for lack of scientific interest', but provokes such controversy that 'it periodically becomes anathema'. She warned that professionals were unaccustomed to 'threatening phone calls, pickets in front of our homes or offices, entrapment attempts, or legal harassment', but they had to get used to it.[7] Of course, the exposure of these condoned crimes confronted pleasures and powers that were not to be relinquished without a fight.

Is there or isn't there a backlash?

David Finkelhor, doyen of sexual abuse research, was optimistic: child protection would hold up, fortified by the women's movement, by public support for child protection and the child welfare professions. He believed that members of a new generation of professionals were 'the real assets of child protection advocacy' and they would 'resist erosion'.[8] Finkelhor was right, they did resist; but he was, I suggest, also wrong.

Law professor John Myers, a children's rights advocate in the US, cautioned that recognition of widespread sexual abuse was 'tenuous, half-hearted and grudging' and backlash would be encouraged by the weakness of child protection services that were confronting herculean responsibilities, and, of course, mistakes. Society was, he thought, 'on the brink of a new era of disbelief'.[9] Myers was right.

Moral panic

In both the US and the UK, government offices in the 1980s reacted to the discovery of an ocean of unmet need with panic: it was a time when the welfare state was being restructured and restrained by the neo-liberal strategies of President Ronald

Reagan in the US and Prime Minister Margaret Thatcher in the UK.[10] Myers reckoned that if child protection professionals were 'out of control', it was not the result of 'irresponsible rampage' but rather that systems were 'so overwhelmed that control is precarious'.[11] Criticism of bureaucratic intransigence, unreformed procedures, incompetent – and competent – investigations mingled with indolent cynicism about dawn raids, diagnoses, 'disclosure techniques', video nasties, mass hysteria, moral panics and witch-hunts.

The award-winning US journalist Jason Berry, who in the 1980s had exposed abuse in the Catholic Church, noticed how swiftly it could happen: 'Newsrooms turned on a dime. *Time*'s cover pictured Freud as a disassembling picture puzzle. National coverage shifted from bishops concealing predators to "false memory", fueled by the suggestibility of young victims, faulty investigators, quack therapists, and a court system hard-pressed to safeguard presumption of innocence.'[12]

Big Daddy

Research published by sociologist Katherine Beckett in the 1990s found a similar switch. The US mass media did not have access to children, but it did have sad or angry adults claiming to have been falsely accused. In childcare cases in the 1980s suspected abuse was met by claims of 'children's propensity to lie' and 'suggestive interviewing techniques', and by the mobilisation of an accused adults' movement, Victims of Child Abuse Laws. Later, the emergence of relatively uncontested adult survivors' stories was 'short-lived' and superseded by the dramatic impact of the False Memory Syndrome (FMS), which captured the majority of media reports in the mid-1990s.[13]

The big daddy of the backlash was Dr Ralph Underwager who, with his partner Hollida Wakefield, was associated with extreme discourses: the false accusations movement that impugned children and professionals in the 1980s and its successor in the 1990s, the false memory movement, whose target was adults and therapists.[14]

When he had been welcomed to the Cleveland Inquiry in 1987, lawyers in the US were so concerned about his allegations that children were being brainwashed 'precisely, exactly, and in detail' as in dictatorships, that prosecutors commissioned research on his credibility.[15] The psychologist Anna Salter, who had worked with both victims and perpetrators, published her findings in 1992: she had discerned a pattern of distortion and inaccuracy in his writing that was 'uniformly' in the service of strengthening their case against children. Underwager harassed and sued Salter until he was banned from using litigation to block scientific controversy.[16]

Underwager got into deep trouble in 1993 following an interview with a Dutch paedophile magazine, *Paidika*, in which he proclaimed that paedophiles should 'boldly and courageously affirm what they choose … as a theologian I believe it is God's will that there be closeness and intimacy, unity of the flesh, between people. A paedophile can say: "This closeness is possible for me within the choices that I've made."' The interview caused great embarrassment to the False Memory Syndrome Foundation that Underwager had helped to found in 1992.[17]

FMS movements soon flourished in the UK and Australia: just as 'innocent parents' assailed by professionals had been fielded in the Cleveland crisis, now parents accused by their daughters were embraced by a mass media that appeared to be sick of child abuse and entranced by a new victim and a new phenomenon.[18]

Fiona Reay: life and death in the courtroom

In 1994 the movement in the UK scored its first courtroom triumph in a historic childhood rape case against the father of Fiona Reay, a care assistant in the north-east of England. Her story of violent tyranny was supported by her husband, relatives and her medical records: the father's defence team persuaded the court to exclude all of this from the hearing. Summing up, his barrister told the court about the 'worrying phenomenon' – not mentioned in the trial – of 'phantom memories' created by counselling. The jury took 27 minutes to acquit her father.

When I put to the father's lawyer that he must have known that 'phantom memories' were not sustained by her medical records, and were therefore not relevant, he replied, 'Did I say that it was?' It seemed that in the court, like the media, the words merely needed to float to become – if not a reality – a brand. Fiona Reay's doctor told me, 'Her tragedy was that she had never forgotten.' It had been the police who had persuaded Fiona Reay to pursue the case: 'I'd decided the child was going to be protected by me going in there as a woman,' she told me, 'using my make-up as a mask...' After her defeat, she felt 'I killed her by not seeing justice be done.'[19]

Memory wars

The groundbreaking challenge to conventional wisdoms about children's testimony at the beginning of the 1980s immediately provoked the renewal of hostilities against narratives of abuse: allegations of children's suggestibility, false memories and brainwashing rounded on the new enlightenment.[20]

In 1985 the psychologist Richard Gardner proposed Parental Alienation Syndrome (PAS) – *syndrome* connoting science – in child custody cases: children were being brainwashed, bribed and programmed, usually by mothers, he claimed, into making false allegations. Gardner also argued that paedophilia was universal, 'considered the norm by millions of people in the history of the world'; it was a creative contribution to human fertility by encouraging sexual arousal in childhood.

Like Underwager, Gardner was associated with the false memory movement: FMS is represented as a disorder of young adults, primarily women, PAS is a disorder of childhood, he wrote. What they had in common was 'a campaign of acrimony against a parent'. Arguing that allegations of sexual abuse against a father post-divorce and during custody disputes were largely a result of mothers coaching their children, Gardner gave evidence in hundreds of custody cases and in criminal cases.[21]

PAS was not recognised by scientific organisations and the concept and the practices flowing from it were repudiated by the World Health Organization in September 2020; mention of it was withdrawn from the International Classification of Diseases (ICD-11).[22] The European Parliament rejected it on 6 October 2021.[23] But Gardner's syndrome enjoyed a posthumous renaissance 20 years after his death, when his PAS (minus the syndrome) became currency in family proceedings in the

US and the UK, with draconian outcomes for (mainly mothers) and children.[24]

In the US the 'parental alienation' effect has been dramatic: Professor Joan Meier, a pioneering advocate in the US Supreme Court, mapped a trend in the family courts based on all published judgments over a decade: if parental alienation was invoked to counter mothers claiming abuse of themselves and their children, it was usually successful; in only 15 per cent of such cases did courts accept mothers' claims; typically mothers lost custody of their children.[25]

In the UK it was increasingly invoked in the family courts, and in some notorious cases children were instantly and brutally removed from their mothers, who were denied any access to their children unless they submitted to therapy regimes recommended or managed by controversial and sometimes unqualified court-appointed experts.[26] Yet research by a team led by Dr Julie Doughty found 'a dearth of robust empirical studies' to back up the concept and no reliable data on its prevalence,[27] lack of agreement on definitions, difficulty in assessing what is outright alienation and what is justifiable estrangement arising from a parent's behaviour as perceived by the child, and lack of data on longitudinal outcomes of interventions.[28] In the absence of any evaluation of 'treatment' in alleged parental alienation cases, children were forcibly removed from their mothers and forced to reside with ex-partners. In a radical departure from the Children Act, courts dismissed the duty to take into account children's 'ascertainable wishes and feelings' and 'best interests' on the grounds that 'parental alienation' made them unascertainable.[29]

Scholars became alarmed by courts' focus on the purported harm of parental alienation rather than the impact of intimate partner violence and poor understanding shown of gender bias; sometimes 'draconian orders' were being made against children whose wishes were not heard, or dismissed.[30] Professor Linda Neilson found a reliance on a 'single controversial issue' as opposed to 'detailed scrutiny of children's best interests'.[31] 'We might contrast the absence of expert scrutiny of domestic violence claims and associated parenting and safety issues with the fact that in 62 of the 142 domestic/family violence cross-claim cases a parental alienation evaluation was ordered or considered by the court. Indeed, in some of these cases, despite the domestic violence or child abuse claims, courts expressly ordered evaluators to restrict their evaluations to assessing for the presence of parental alienation.'

Professors Elizabeth Sheehy and Simon Lapierre brought together eminent researchers across the world to assess the use of parental alienation, its (poor) basis in science and the impact the theory was having on women and children who had experienced family violence.[32] 'Playing the parental alienation card is proving more powerful than any other in silencing the voices of women and children resisting contact with abusive men', warned Dr Adrienne Barnett.[33]

Laboratory versus real life

Where Gardner and Underwager had brought hyperbole to the backlash, the psychologists Professors Stephen Ceci and Maggie Bruck brought prolific scholarship to the 'memory wars'. Best known for their 1993 book *Jeopardy in the Courtroom*, their reviews of research concluded that though most allegations of sexual abuse were probably correct, some children were vulnerable to suggestion, bribes, threats and loyalty. Bruck appeared as a defence expert in a UK libel action in which children's injuries and testimony had been accepted in the civil court, but accused adults had been acquitted in the criminal court. The adults were exonerated by the judge, who said: 'What research has thrown into stark relief is quite simply that very young children do not appear to have the same clear boundary between fact and fantasy as that which adults have learned to draw.'[34]

Professor Elizabeth Loftus, an expert witness for the defence in hundreds of alleged abuse cases in the US, proposed in 1995 that entire events could be planted in the minds and memories of otherwise healthy adults.[35]

These memory researchers hailed the superior virtues of scientific experiments over clinical research. Their critics insisted, however, that these laboratory experiments could not replicate real-life experiences of assault and trauma, or testimony about sexual abuse. Lawyer and psychologist Thomas D Lyon subjected what he calls a 'new wave in children's suggestibility research' to exhaustive scrutiny. These researchers tend to assume that highly suggestive interviews are the norm, says Lyon, despite little empirical evidence; the focus is victims' allegations rather than perpetrators' denials and thus the new wave neglects the characteristics of child sexual abuse that render false allegations less likely and failure to detect abuse more likely; claims that science is value-free may mask value judgements: the researchers' belief, that 'professional lore' affirming children's reliability had no empirical basis, also lacked its own empirical base, Lyon concluded, because they could not reproduce actual abuse or trauma or threats in their laboratories.[36]

Eminent psychologists in New Zealand reiterated that laboratory research 'does not and cannot represent the complexity and severity of sexual abuse'.[37] In the UK, distinguished professors Bernice Andrews and Chris Brewin argued that the 'powerful combination of deception and pressured suggestion' was the 'main driver of false memories in the laboratory', even though this has no analogue in the therapeutic context.[38] Nevertheless, 'memory error' now dominates psychology research at the expense of a previous consensus about 'memory being essentially accurate'.[39] Expertise and eminence is no protection against vitriol: Andrews' and Brewin's work had been subjected to errors and misrepresentation, amounting to an attempt to suppress debate. Objections to their work, they commented, 'appear to be more about the implications of the data than the data themselves'.[40]

Psychologists Suzanne Blackwell and Fred Seymour, who, like Andrews and Brewin, had given expert evidence for both the prosecution and the defence, noticed in the 2000s an exponential rise in applications to admit expert evidence in New Zealand's courts – almost exclusively in child sexual abuse trials and 'most commonly by defence counsel'.[41]

The belief in suggestibility and memory error appeared to have acquired settled status in courtrooms, and seemed to have merged seamlessly into the Cleveland discourse even though no evidence whatsoever was adduced in the Cleveland Inquiry that any of the children had succumbed to implanted memories or suggestion or described events that could not have happened to them. The dilemma exercising the Cleveland Inquiry primarily concerned the credibility of signs on children's bodies, not the words that came from children's mouths.

However, the Cleveland Report's criticism of 'disclosure' continued to reverberate. In an important case in 2019, Mr Justice MacDonald deplored that 'very few of the professionals, police officers and allocated social workers who gave evidence in this case had heard of the Cleveland Inquiry, much less were aware of its recommendations'.[42] And so, 'much of the accumulated institutional memory of how to deal in an assiduously open minded, procedurally fair and forensically rigorous way with allegations of child sexual abuse has been lost'.

Citing Ceci and Bruck, he reiterated the belief that it is possible to induce false memories in children who can speak 'sincerely and emotionally', in ways that are difficult to detect, about events that 'did not in fact occur'; memory is prone to error, and children's accounts are susceptible to influence by suggestive questions, repetition, pressure and threats.[43]

Witch-hunts

The 'memory wars' provided contemporary ammunition to the older 'witch-hunt narrative' about sexual abuse.[44] Conspiracy theories flourished in the 1990s, sometimes stranger than the phenomena they criticised.[45] In the US, the McMartin day care case in the 1980s was invoked as a template for what sceptical journalist Debbie Nathan dubbed 'junior McMartins' in her book *Satan's Silence: Ritual Abuse and the Making of a Modern Witch Hunt.*[46] Cleveland and McMartin became witch-hunt archetypes, endlessly recycled, that worked by repetition and association. Nathan's hypothesis – like Stuart Bell's representation of Cleveland as another Salem – claimed that respectable communities had been convulsed by the whiff of the devil and witch-hunts. This often focused on childcare settings, with multiple victims and alleged abusers. Nathan's version of events was subjected to forensic critique by Roland Summit and by the political scientist, Ross Cheit, who delved into vast numbers of documents, original records and court proceedings to assess the evidence.[47] Finally, Cheit wondered why 'an allegedly national wave of witch-hunts is routinely illustrated by stories about the same handful of cases?'.[48]

In the UK, likewise, sceptics recycled a mere handful of cases involving multiple perpetrators, which, though very different, were complex contexts that did not respect the fictional frontier between intra- and extra-familial abuse, and produced shock at what children might say, or show. Investigations were disoriented by the strategies and resources of perpetrators, by the age, sex and ethnicity of both victims and perpetrators, and not least by sheer savagery and scale.

They were typically cited by reference to Cleveland as further evidence of mass hysteria and witch-hunting. The largest European study of organised abuse cases, published by Bernard Gallagher, Beverley Hughes and Howard Parker in 1996, found that, in fact, ritual abuse comprised only 8 per cent of organised abuse cases, and only 0.2 per cent of all child sexual abuse referrals.[49] Although there were no typical cases, there were similar characteristics: multiple perpetrators, sadism, entrapment, exploitation – often involving pornography. Extreme and bizarre allegations did not initiate these investigations, however; they emerged only *after* several 'troubling' features had led to children being removed. The sheer scale needed surveillance and huge resources, rarely available, and thus investigations were vulnerable to being 'prematurely terminated'.[50]

Gallagher's research began in the early 1990s as a joint project with anthropologist Jean La Fontaine, an expert on witchcraft in Africa, but they diverged over their different research methods and conclusions. Professor La Fontaine's book *Speak of the Devil* argued, contrary to Gallagher, that the children's narratives were remarkably similar. She found no cult and concluded that children were pressurised to make false allegations that were altered or interpreted by foster carers, social workers and evangelical Christians, who were part of a powerful social movement that had parallels in medieval witch-hunts.[51] La Fontaine argued that social workers 'transformed the evangelical campaign against satanism by associating it with child protection'.[52]

Worried by the apparent consensus that workers were driven by 'spurious influences' and poor practice to manipulate children into making impossible allegations of ritual or occult abuse, Gallagher returned to the data and the debate, and in 2001 published a definitive study of 20,000 files in eight regions.[53] He had found only six ritual abuse cases; the workers involved were not zealots, manipulators and brainwashers, but on the contrary, 'invariably exhibited caution' and were 'almost without exception circumspect'. They 'very rarely' raised suspicions of ritual abuse and there was no evidence that workers had manipulated children. By the end of these practitioners' assessments, Gallagher added, they were more concerned about children's mental health and less about issues to do with ritual abuse. 'These results suggest that there should be more confidence in the ability of agency workers ... to respond to cases of alleged ritual abuse.'[54]

What was going on? There is a significant pagan subculture in both the US and the UK. It would hardly be surprising if some sexual abuse cases involved occultists (no more surprising than if the perpetrators were Christians, athletes or trainspotters). The Orkney case at the beginning of the 1990s seemed to suggest a new phenomenon: not Satanist abuse, but sceptical excitement and myth-making. The journalist Sarah Nelson, who covered the case, noticed a 'puzzling scent of organised media manipulation' that, as an experienced chronicler, she had never come across before. The intensity was alarming: 'journalists seemed to lose their normal critical faculties', she commented.[55] Campaigners had disparaged Orkney professionals for representing the case as 'ritual' or 'satanic'. But they hadn't, and it wasn't. A commission of inquiry, led by Lord Clyde, delivered a curt – and unnoticed – rebuke: the Orkney Social Services Department had described the case as organised abuse; the term ritual abuse was not used in the Department.[56]

Children's homes: 'collective ingratitude'

The witch-hunt narrative then migrated to children's homes. The writer Richard Webster, whose interest in sexual abuse had been roused by Cleveland, proposed that there was a witch-hunt that had its origins in an unexplained 'California model' that billowed across the Atlantic to Clwyd in Wales.

His 714-page tome, *The Secret of Bryn Estyn*, drew inspiration from Norman Cohn's history of millenarian cults and collective delusions in medieval Europe. His erudition proved to be alluring despite – or perhaps as well as – his excess: there had been hundreds of miscarriages of justice, 80–90 per cent of suspects were 'completely innocent', he protested, and the allegations amounted to 'one of the most terrible instances of collective ingratitude which is to be found in our recent history'.[57]

Webster devoted himself to defending convicted sex offenders who, the Waterhouse Report on widespread abuse across North Wales, *Lost in Care*, concluded, had 'grossly poisoned' the miserable lives of children in the area's children's homes gulag. Gripped by a kind of cruel virtue, yet unable to engage with victims of sexual violence all around him, Webster conjured instead 'a million' falsely accused 'victims'.[58] He became part of a campaign alleging miscarriages of justice that exercised the Parliamentary Home Affairs Select Committee enough to hold special hearings. Webster, with his co-campaigners David Rose and Bob Woffinden, gave evidence to the sympathetic committee, which declared: 'It has been suggested, and we believe it to be so, that a new genre of miscarriages of justice has arisen from the over-enthusiastic pursuit of these allegations.'[59] However, the committee was unpersuaded: it did not support their proposals that proactive investigations be banned, nor did it agree that the Crown Prosecution Service (CPS) simply believed the word of complainants – not so, the committee commented: 'the CPS rejected a staggering 79 per cent of institutional child abuse cases'.[60]

The witch-hunt hypothesis was floated in one of New Zealand's most prolonged child abuse controversies after childcare worker Peter Ellis was jailed for sexually abusing children in a Christchurch creche in 1993. His first appeal failed. His second appeal in 1999 – in which Ceci and Bruck provided evidence for the defence – also failed. An independent inquiry by former Judge Thomas Eichelbaum in 2001 reviewed the children's evidence, consulted independent experts to assess the interviews and considered practices and inquiries elsewhere – including the Cleveland case. He concluded that interviews with the children had been 'of a high standard for its time'. They had been 'traversed in detail' by seven judges, and after the 'most thorough examination possible' Ellis's case 'should now be allowed to rest'. But it remained undead. The writer Lynley Hood published a 650-page book, *A City Possessed: The Christchurch Civic Creche Case*, alleging a witch-hunt against Ellis. It became a bestseller. The witch-hunt imprimatur invoked by Stuart Bell to describe Cleveland's local crisis, *When Salem Came to the 'Boro*, had gone global.[61]

Moral panic or moral protest?

Moral panic, moral crusade and witch-hunt shimmer with allusive potential, connoting mysticism, zealotry, careerism, snake oil traders and evangelical holy rollers cashing in on sin or misfortune.[62] They all bustle in the Cleveland tombola.

What is moral panic? It's mob rule, isn't it? It's when child abuse is 'a national obsession',[63] mass hysteria and media frenzy.

There is a certain hauteur, not to say contempt, among some advocates of these notions, who present themselves as objective, disinterested observers of other professionals causing havoc or losing their marbles. But this was not the focus of the pioneering theorists Stanley Cohen and Howard Becker, whose work has been invoked in these child abuse controversies. Cohen's *Folk Devils and Moral Panic* was written in the 1960s in the context of Establishment anxiety about class, sex and race. Cohen proposed 'moral panic' as a conservative and disproportionate reaction to new, exaggerated and episodic cultural phenomena. He tried to explain the orchestration of panic by powerful elites against the unruly activities of the lower orders – specifically the sporting face-offs between Mods and Rockers on scooters at English seaside resorts, episodic pageants that were magnified as general threats to public order.[64] The book was a foundational text on how 'subcultures' were demonised.

Sociologist Howard Becker theorised deviance as an *ascription*, not an *act* but a label 'constructed' by rule-makers. Becker conceptualised 'moral entrepreneurs' as mobilising on behalf of established power against purported deviance or social evils.[65] Like Cohen's theoretical framework, Becker's meaning got 'lost in translation' when it was deployed to critique not imaginary bogeymen, but mainstream, popular, purported irrationality.

Cultural studies scholar Chas Critcher, who with Stuart Hall adopted Cohen's moral panic theory in a groundbreaking analysis of the demonisation of young Black men in the 1970s, interrogated its relevance to the Cleveland case: it didn't apply, and in fact the response to Cleveland 'appeared to set back recognition of child sexual abuse in the family' for decades.[66]

In time, sexual abuse scepticism troubled Cohen so much that he felt provoked to repudiate the misuse of his work. In 2002, in a new introduction to *Folk Devils and Moral Panic*, he condemned a 'wilful refusal' to take public anxieties seriously. Sexual abuse scandals revealed not panic 'but a chilling denial', and worse, 'repeated waves of denial, exposure and denunciation'. Social workers had become 'folk devils', he warned, and Cleveland was the case that 'marked the peak of this period and condensed its themes'.

But not even the 'master' theorist Cohen could stop the misuse of his work. In fact, 'wilful refusal' was fortified by another theory of knowledge: social constructionism, the study not of *real* events but of *representation*. Thus children and child abuse were not things; they were ideological inventions, discursive creations.

Even after Cohen's distressed revision, scholars who should have known better carried on regardless. The sociologist Professor Ken Plummer described mass protests in India against rape, and 'One Billion Rising' against sexual violence,[67] as 'global moral panics'.[68] But these events were not examples of Cohen's 'moral panic' theory; they were mass protests against real, pervasive and sanctioned sexual violence against women and girls. It seems that whenever people take sexual abuse seriously and do something to stop it, their protest is traduced as panic.

'Constructing' children: a moral crusade

When the US philosopher Ian Hacking threw himself into child abuse debates in 1991, it was 'not to understand this evil, child abuse, it is not to explain it or discover its causes ... my purpose is not that of the social historian curious to explain the sudden prominence of child abuse in America in the 1960s and its subsequent evolution'.[69] You might ask, why not and why bother? Hacking explains in *The Making and Molding of Child Abuse* that his interest is in how characters are created in public discourse: what is this thing, child abuse, he wonders? 'The very idea of child abuse has been in constant flux'. Of course he is right. So what counts as abuse changes over time. Right again.

But he infers that, therefore, it becomes unknowable; in a sense it is made up.[70]

'I have no interest whatsoever in fostering scepticism in general', he insists. 'But here it may be worthwhile.' Why? He believed that 'We have been almost unwittingly changing the very definitions of abuse.' Unwittingly? Hardly: social scientists had *studied* their way to challenging and changing definitions. Hacking complains that the more we know about abuse leaves him wondering, 'Is there then nothing that we can know about child abuse?' The answer, surely, is that we know more. He asks, 'What counts' as sexual abuse? The answer is that it changes, *and* is indeed knowable, and it counts. I suggest that this intellectual vertigo, which became de rigueur in the 1990s, masks more important questions. How can society think? How can an educated public be created? How can knowledge be expanded, revised and shared? How can 'common knowledge' be made to matter? And finally, what should be done about child sexual abuse and how can we stop it?

The US historian of religion Philip Jenkins represents abuse as merely a transient concern, a created category that serves conservatives and feminists (always feminists): a 'nightmare of recent construction'.[71] British sociologist Frank Furedi rehearses the familiar Cleveland template and elaborates a constructionist disinterest in real events. He shares an aversion to child abuse activism and feminist sexual politics, and he proposes an alternative vision: a moral crusade is promoting an apocalyptic fear of the future; loss of faith in established order reaches out to a glowing icon of hope – the child. Children are therefore sacralised and sequestered under the perpetual surveillance of paranoid parents afraid of everything. Like Jenkins and Underwager, he relies on the gap between reported sexual offences and prosecutions and estimated prevalence to argue that there is no hidden crime of child sexual abuse; there is merely peril imagined by moral crusaders.[72]

His argument also echoes the massively influential French philosopher Michel Foucault and his apocalyptic vision of 'a society of dangers' in the 1970s when he and a crowd of intellectuals in France petitioned for the abolition of the age of consent.[73] Decades later, in 2021, a former friend accused him of sexually exploiting children when he worked in Tunisia in the 1960s; he recalled that Foucault would throw money at little boys and propose night-time sexual rendezvous at a local graveyard. For all Foucault's theoretical concern with the question of power, his own power over Tunisian boys as a White, adult male, privileged professor, eluded him. The Tunisian writer Haythem Guesmi located Foucault in a long history of predators 'viewing the (neo-colonial) subject as a disposable body'.[74]

What is a child?

In the wake of the Cleveland controversy, in the 1990s, criminologist Carol Smart interrogated the history of ambivalence about child abuse: she presents the criminal justice system and legal practice as 'the most important and the most problematic sites' for reform.[75] Acknowledging Hacking, she argues, however, that while the meaning of childhood has radically changed – not least by universal education and the regulation of sexual acts – knowledge of, and worry about, adult–child sex and harm is not in fact new; rather, it is contested.

'It is shocking and depressing', she writes, to find that feminist campaigners in the early twentieth century already 'knew what we think we discovered' in the 1970s and 1980s. There was already-existing 'common knowledge' that was not simply silenced or invisible; it was always there.[76]

The philosopher David Pilgrim's riposte to the 'constructionist' case against child sexual abuse agrees that, yes, understanding of the phenomenon has changed over time: 'In Ancient Greece man-boy sexual contact may have been a norm but so was slavery.' These days, 'we do not condone that habit or the coerced prostitution of young girls or push small boys up chimneys'.[77]

Sociologist Ken Plummer suggested in the 1990s that childhood is not a biological category; it is a process of becoming that is not attached to biological age. Thus, the categories of *adult* and *child* are not fixed; they are so fluid that there is 'a potential to suggest that the child is an adult and the adult is a child'. [78] (Plummer has since been obliged to rationalise his relationship to the Paedophile Information Exchange; 'I am saddened', he said, lamely, to think that 'it may have been used to justify child abuse'.[79]

But dismantling the categories 'child' and 'adult' has theoretical effects: the meaning of molestation is destabilised. If we don't know what a child is, if there is no such thing as a child, then there is no child abuser; he is merely a 'nightmare of recent construction'.[80]

These theories resonate, I think, not because of science, or 'common sense', but because – whatever their intentions – they narrow the aperture through which childhood is conceptualised and children's experiences recognised and addressed. Curiosity has been battered by cooked-up conspiracy theories about witch-hunts and moral panics allegedly promoted by social workers – hitherto pragmatic, humane and mostly secular – or foster carers poisoning children's minds with quasi-religious hallucinations. These hypotheses synchronised with cynical resistance – then as now – that relies on the gap between prevalence rates, reported sexual offences and low rates of detection and prosecution – a crevasse that contributes to the lack of consensus about sexual abuse.

David Pilgrim has described 'knowing cynicism' among some critics, and points out that child abuse doesn't have to be invented, 'it is there already'. However, its existence is questioned, its scale deemed beyond evaluation or exaggerated.[81] And there is pleasure in denial: cynics bubble with what the Australian criminologist Michael Salter describes as the joy of 'scorn and contempt' that pulls us away from anathema.[82] The resilience of the myths of Cleveland, mass hysteria, moral panic and moral crusade is also that they are easy: they are spectral, they can't be measured; they are, as Kitzinger suggests, 'rhetorical full stops'.[83]

8

Damned and vindicated

The orthodoxies reinstated in the aftermath of Cleveland shadowed the interpretation of medical signs and their impact on the courts thereafter. Quietly – and unnoticed in the mass media – in 2014, an international consensus was finally established. The British pioneers were vindicated.

The physical effect

'I was at Piccadilly Circus, standing by a railing – it was the meat rack – and I was speaking to a punter. He walked off and then a man came to up me and said, "You are arrested for importuning for immoral purposes…" He took me to Bow Street police station and asked what I was doing at Piccadilly. Of course, I didn't tell him. I was strip searched, asked to bend down and part my cheeks, and the police officer turned away and said, "you're a rent boy."

Then he said, "get back home, we don't want to see you around this area again." He showed me the door, no one was making sure I got somewhere, no chaperone, nothing. That was the system. The point was not to deal with child prostitution, it was to get it off the streets. There wasn't the slightest thought that you were a victim, you were the problem.'

Nigel O'Mara was 13 years old and living in a children's home when he was arrested.[1]

It was a time in the 1970s when the West End was under constant surveillance – by punters looking for boys and by the police, also looking for boys: all of them shared recognition of anal dilatation as a signifier of buggery. Bow Street police station had been inspecting the bodies of gay men for a century.

By the 1980s O'Mara was living in a flat in London with other young men, and discovered another way to live: 'I saw an advert in the local paper in Earls Court.' It described Streetwise, a project formed in 1985 by gay activist Richie McMullen, to support young men exploited in prostitution.[2] 'There were about six of us in the house, all young men, and we decided to speak to them. Somebody was actually interested in us. I don't think any of us had thought anyone was ever interested in us. On 13 June 1986 I decided to change my life, I've never forgotten that day!'

Together with Richie McMullen, he became a founding member of Survivors UK, a helpline for sexually abused men. Then the Cleveland controversy broke:

> 'We had massive discussions about it. We thought the way the doctors were treated was outrageous. We understood the issues then – as did the police. There is a physical effect of anal penetration – it ruptures part of the sphincter, it's just a medical fact. It's something all gay men have if they have been penetrated, it's what you'd expect. It was part of my experience. It is unambiguous. We understood it at the time – so did the police.'[3]

The backlash against the diagnosis

O'Mara's experience showed how sodomy had been interpreted as proof of homosexuality. Internationally, it remained a sign that was invoked as proof in forced examinations and prosecutions of gay men in societies where same-sex relationships were criminalised.[4]

But in the new age of child sexual abuse awareness the sign breached the historical polarisation of gay and straight masculinities: in the 1980s signs of sodomy were revealed as a *male* thing, not a *gay* thing. This, apparently, was intolerable.

Although the Cleveland Report recommended further research of RAD, none was commissioned in the UK, and it remained the site of a merciless, transatlantic affray after US paediatricians mobilised in the 1980s against the medical evidence. A fable reigned: that the Cleveland Report discredited the medical evidence. It didn't. But it took a quarter of a century before an armistice was declared, the medical signs affirmed and Tardieu was vindicated – together with the British paediatricians.

Elizabeth Butler-Sloss told me that she retained vivid recollections of the day in 1987 when the inquiry was shown forensic photographs of RAD from research by Dr Chris Hobbs and Jane Wynne:

> 'We had photographs up in Middlesbrough Town Hall on a huge screen, floor to ceiling, on which were shown the back passages of children. The press didn't like it and went away.
>
> The photographs showed the moment before opening, the moment of it opening, the moment it was open – you could see right through to the rectum. It was an extraordinary sight, astonishing.'[5]

There was a similar occasion in autumn 1987 in a parliamentary committee room during the inquiry that was initiated by Nottinghamshire and West Midlands child protection officers to show that Cleveland was not alone. It was a salutary event: while most MPs present were interested, and riveted by Dr Jane Wynne's presentation of forensic slides, Stuart Bell's coterie shuffled papers and fidgeted.[6]

While the Cleveland controversy flared, the contested themes of diagnosis and disclosure were also exploding in California: marathon trials about alleged abuse in the McMartin daycare centre ran from 1987 to 1990 in the affluent town of Manhattan Beach. Several McMartin workers had been accused but ultimately acquitted of child abuse charges.[7]

The seeming extremity of the abuse, the reputation of the McMartin daycare centre, the high social standing of the families, the numbers of children alleged to have been abused, the children's testimony and the medical signs indicating gross abuse were alarming. And if it could happen in Manhattan Beach, it could happen anywhere.

In fact, it *was* happening: two leading researchers, David Finkelhor and Linda Meyer Williams, identified 270 daycare centres where allegations of sexual abuse had been substantiated between 1983 and 1985.[8]

McCann and Voris: 'it's normal'

In 1989 Californian paediatricians Dr John McCann and Dr Joan Voris dropped a bomb into forensic science. They had the medical evidence in McMartin in their sights and they were also suspicious of Dr Wynne's and Dr Hobbs's research. They organised a study of the 'normal' anatomy of non-abused children.[9]

Their findings were electrifying: 'In 49% of the children there was some dilatation of the anus, which opened and closed intermittently in 62%.' Medical examiners should therefore be cautious about 'rendering an opinion as to the significance of medical findings'.[10] So abnormal signs were the new normal. For decades Dr McCann was unchallenged by any US research.

In an interview with me in 2016, Dr McCann explained that in the 1980s he and Dr Voris 'began to worry about reports in the media about child abuse'. They suspected that 'there was over-interpretation in the McMartin case – doggone it, you don't want to err on the side of over-stating'. So they decided to 'look at children who we felt reasonably comfortable had not been sexually abused. We solicited – terrible term – girl scouts going to camp.' But how could they know whether or not the children in this cohort had been abused? That was the 'major, major problem', he admitted.

> 'We were seeing children who were obviously abused – they came with tears and lacerations, though they were few and far between – and we excluded them from the study. Those who fell into the "suspicious" category we dropped from the study and those kids were put through an interview process with social services. We felt they were pretty well screened. But we recognised the probability that it wasn't pure.'[11]

Dr McCann and his colleagues began sharing their findings at seminars before finally publishing their paper in 1989.[12] By then, Drs Hobbs and Wynne had produced their third study, and they were all published in the same edition of *Child Abuse and Neglect*: parallel research, opposite findings. Dr McCann's paper became hegemonic in the US. But the methodology and the excessive findings roused disquiet among scholars and paediatricians elsewhere: the US researchers had used the knee-chest position – a child kneeling with his or her bottom in the air – for many minutes, 'sometimes up to eight minutes', Dr McCann told me. This approach horrified British paediatricians, who examined children using the 'left lateral position' – a child lying on his or her side – for anal examinations that lasted less than a minute. Timing and position was everything.

What had been so striking to Drs Wynne and Hobbs was the appearance of RAD within one minute, almost instantly, not delayed or intermittent, not opening and shutting over many minutes. 'There was a bit of a furore about the Americans' mode of examination', commented an eminent paediatrician in England. Children might have been abused in the knee-chest position, and 'eight minutes, that's a very long time – if not abusive, then it's not good practice.'[13]

In the UK, it was regarded as simply not credible that half of non-abused children had bottoms that opened almost immediately and wide enough to see down the anal canal. 'We used different techniques', Dr McCann conceded. There was another significant difference: Wynne and Hobbs had conducted all the examinations themselves. 'The major difference is the examiner', acknowledged Dr McCann; he himself had not performed the examinations: 'We had women doing the examination and they were able to get the children so relaxed – some fell asleep. ... The staff who did ours were so good, children relaxed and a fair number dozed off.' He also agreed that 'the longer that we kept a youngster in the knee-chest position, the findings change'.[14]

So not only the findings but also the research methods, the examiners and the timing were not directly comparable. 'We never truly resolved this, the question of timing – the length of time in that position,' said McCann. 'We did find by examining them over an extended time that the whole pelvis relaxed. That's the major difference. We were really castigated for that.'[15]

Dozing off… British paediatricians were aghast. These differences were decisive. In the US, Dr McCann's findings seemed to be regarded as if they were unimpeachable common sense. But the findings were not replicated elsewhere. Were they followed up? They were not. 'That's correct,' Dr McCann told me. 'There was no significant follow-up.'

Had there been a muddle, I wondered, not to say cognitive dissonance, about the methodology and the findings, about the meaning of 'injury' and the difference between chronic and acute signs? McCann agreed: 'This is the major bone of contention.' His team concluded that 'In terms of the children we knew had been abused, it was because they had an injury.'[16] Not signs of adaptation. So the differences involved everything: methodology, consistency of examiners, examination technique, timing, acute injury versus chronic adaptation and finally, follow-up – or, in the US, the lack of it.

Changed minds: 'it never has any significance'

Dr Astrid Heger was a high-flying paediatrician when she became one of the main McMartin medical examiners. She later became a doyenne of children's services in Los Angeles. McMartin had been a gruelling experience. After being in the eye of the storm, she repudiated some of the clinical signs on which she had relied. In the early 1990s she published *Evaluation of the Sexually Abused Child*, which became a standard in the field.[17]

She appeared in the UK as an expert witness in the family court. She could become fierce and very 'adversarial' – 'I can become very impassioned', she told me in an interview in 2016. Furthermore, 'My advocacy is strongly for being conservative.' Dr Heger went down well. She was an unyielding critic of Hobbs and Wynne. 'RAD is so common in the normal population that it is of no significance,' she insisted, following McCann. 'It *never* has any significance.'

Like Dr McCann, Dr Heger did not share the distinction between chronic and acute symptoms. 'Normally the only abnormality is acute injury', she said. She led a study of

2,384 children evaluated for sexual abuse, and reported that only '4% of all children referred for medical evaluation of sexual abuse have abnormal examinations'.[18]

Interviews with the children with medical signs (68 per cent of the girls and 70 per cent of the boys) reported severe abuse defined as penetration. Dr Heger was surprised: she had expected that 'penetrating assault on a pre-adolescent child will likely result in significant trauma and discovery'.

But it didn't always, or even usually. Dr Heger appeared in British courts over the years to vanquish British experts. In one case, citing McCann against Hobbs, she told the court that 'Research into normal anal anatomy in children reports that reflex anal dilatation occurs frequently in children selected for non-abuse.' No research, she added, that compared abused and non-abused children supported RAD 'as a sensitive or specific finding for sexual abuse'.

Mr Justice Holman noted – and excused – her 'impatience and briskness of manner' in the court as 'a consequence of, not the cause of, her own firm opinions'. If Dr Heger had a dogma, said the judge, 'it is the dogma that doctors should be conservative [her term] and not dogmatic in the diagnosis of sexual abuse'.[19] Paediatricians noted these comments too, and wondered: wasn't expertise supposed to be based on evidence and not emotion?

In a case before Justice Crispin Masterman in 2006, he noted that 'There is no doubt that she has an enviable reputation and has been at the forefront of research in this field'; Dr Heger 'told us that 20 or more years ago she was taught things that are now known to be untrue'. It appeared that Dr Heger's mea culpa added value to her evidence. He reported Dr Heger's opinion 'that the UK took a wrong turn' and had been overtaken by other Western nations. 'She and her colleagues differ from the approach of Hobbs and Wynne. She feels there is a tendency in the UK for paediatricians to over-diagnose.'[20]

He continued:

> [Dr Heger] would have hoped that specialists in this area would have kept up with US research (the UK not having had the funding for research that the US

has had) and be working to their standards. She said
the US research, which is to a high standard, is already
making a big difference to the teaching in the UK.[21]

It was indeed making a difference, but not because it was of
a higher standard: the McCann/Voris research had not been
followed up or confirmed by other research *anywhere*.

Still, Dr Heger reigned. Her evidence relied not only on
McCann, but also on Dr Joyce Adams, whose review, *Approach to
the Interpretation of Medical and Laboratory Findings in Suspected Child
Sexual Abuse: A 2005 Revision*, was cited by Justice Masterman
as representing the views of 'leading child abuse specialists in
the USA today'. The Adams paper had this to say about anal
dilatation: 'no consensus exists currently among experts as to how
this finding should be interpreted'.[22] It cited no British specialists.

Normal to be normal

Dr Adams was a leader in the profession; she created the 'Adams
Classification System', reviewing medical evidence over many
years in the hope of building a professional consensus. When
I interviewed her in 2016, she told me that she is retired from
clinical practice and now reviews cases for other medical
professionals, in addition to writing and giving lectures. She also
reviews cases for attorneys, and testifies when she has been called
to court. These reviews are mostly requested by attorneys for the
defence: 'I don't think someone should be sent to prison solely
on the basis of incorrect interpretation of medical findings in
a child.'[23]

Her first direct exposure to sexual abuse was 'a presentation put
together by Astrid Heger in the 1980s', during the McMartin
case. 'I was looking at the magnified photos for the first time and
trying to correlate what she said and what I saw.'[24]

Furthermore, McMartin 'was at the very beginning of using
medical assessment. People were very disappointed that no one was
convicted. There was a strong feeling that the kids would not make
it up these allegations – why would they?' It was a conundrum.

Dr Adams had been so impressed by Dr McCann's presentations
that she moved from Kansas to California to work with him. 'He'd

show these amazing magnified photographs and he'd talk about his surprising finding of anal dilation among the non-abused children when they were in the prone, knee-chest position. The children were sometimes in this position for up to three minutes, and the anus would dilate as time went on.'[25]

After the McCann study, anal dilatation 'was not thought to have any proven association with anal abuse'. In 1994 she published her landmark paper, 'Examination findings in legally confirmed child sexual abuse: it's normal to be normal'. Medical signs were rare, and among children alleging abuse, she wrote, 'it's normal to be normal'.[26]

The British research had established that medical signs were indeed rare, that anal dilatation, too, was rare *and* that (in the absence of other causes) it was indicative of abuse. McCann's study said it was so common that it could not signify abuse.[27]

The contortions and conflicts could not have been more extreme.

Then the Norwegian paediatrician Dr Arne K. Myhre went to California to collaborate with Dr Adams.

Nicer in Norway

In the 1990s public health professionals in Norway had organised a consensus conference on medical criteria for evaluating abuse.[28] Paediatricians in Trondheim in the north of the country had received sexual abuse referrals from a nursery in Bjugn, a small rural community where the alleged perpetrator was a young man, a nursery assistant. Some of the children described what had happened and doctors identified medical signs among several of the children, based on criteria that, according to one of the paediatricians, Arne K. Myhre, were somewhere between the UK and US.[29]

Paediatricians from Oslo were consulted and they interpreted the forensic photographs differently. At the criminal trial in 1994 the suspect was acquitted, but in civil proceedings evidence of abuse was accepted.[30]

Talking with Myhre decades later, he explained that, on reflection, he was not sure that Bjugn was clear-cut: 'Our knowledge was insufficient, it was a new field, people like Chris

Hobbs had only started to do this around the mid-1980s, and we only had one study of normality. I don't think we'd have made the medical findings today.' He reckoned that 'Today I would say none of the children had medical findings – all were non-specific.' At the time, however, 'the relation between the children's stories and the medical findings perhaps resulted in the medical findings being regarded as very important, more important than they were'. Yet there was a strong sense in Bjugn – even among critics – that something had happened at the nursery. But what?

Myhre did not regard the Bjugn trial as a setback because it had got people thinking: 'something creative came out of the conflict'. The doctors weren't pilloried, unlike in the UK or US: 'we have conflicts but it's not like we hate each other. We behave quite well. We don't have these big scandals.'[31]

In 1995 Norway's paediatricians developed a classification system, and Dr Myhre researched 350 five-year-old preschoolers. They were examined in both the prone knee-chest and left-lateral positions for approximately 30 seconds each. Anal dilatation was 'significantly more common in the knee-chest position', and once again, 'the finding of total anal dilatation was rare'.[32]

This was the first large study of 'normal' children's anatomy that compared the different examination positions used by US and UK clinicians, carried out by the paediatricians themselves, for a standard, short period of time. Myhre confirmed both the rarity of anal dilatation and its significance. His project became his PhD, and he defended his thesis before none other than Dr Joyce Adams, 'my best opponent'.[33]

No disagreement

Myhre and Adams embarked on a joint study of more than 1,000 cases in California. They confirmed that anal dilatation was 'found to be significantly associated with anal penetration'. They reported a 'very high' level of agreement with each other, '100 per cent in fact', said Dr Myhre: 'amazing'. Dr Adams was more restrained. 'I wouldn't say we were amazed, but we were surprised', she told me. These findings threw down the gauntlet to the Americans. Dr Adams updated the classification guidelines and included a radical revision. 'Using the McCann study findings to discount anal dilation in a child examined in the lateral position is not a fair comparison,' she said.

But there was still resistance in the US: 'Many of my colleagues still think that anal dilation has too many other causes to be listed even as possibly associated with anal abuse.' When I asked her to confirm that *no* research supported Dr McCann, she was unequivocal: 'You are correct that no research has ever confirmed the figure of 49% of non-abused children having anal dilation.' So the McCann study that had been weaponised against the British pioneers was decommissioned. The knee-chest position, too, was discarded, 'No one does that in clinical practice any more', Dr Adams added, 'so the figure is meaningless'.[34] After decades of dissent and havoc, this was 'amazing'.

British doctors vindicated

Before Dr Chris Hobbs retired – by which time his great collaborator Dr Jane Wynne had died – he wanted to follow up that eternally 'controversial' sign for which they had been famous. Despite the Cleveland Report's recommendation, and the health authority's plea to the government to support more research, it had never happened.

Dr Hobbs's final paper included a poignant sentence in small print: the study 'received no specific grant from any funding agency in the public, commercial or not-for-profit sectors'. Not one agency had contributed to this research on one of the most contested themes in children's health. Dr Hobbs's study was unique: it was based on the records of a huge number of children – 19,785 children had been examined in Leeds between 1990 and 2007 because of child abuse concerns. Of these, 3,119 were diagnosed as likely to have been sexually abused; they were compared with a control group who had been referred to the hospital but among whom there were no suspicions of sexual abuse. These were the only cohorts to have been examined by the same team of doctors using the same methods over nearly three decades. RAD was recorded in 22 per cent of the abuse cases, but in none of the 'controls'. These findings were confirmed by studies in Asia, Scandinavia and Europe.[35] The new research torpedoed the critics of Wynne and Hobbs.[36]

Even though its salience was self-evident, it took three bewildering years for Hobbs to find an academic publisher. Why? His study had been completed at the very time that the Royal College of Paediatrics and Child Health was undertaking a global literature review, with the intention of publishing new guidelines. By the time Dr Hobbs's paper finally appeared in 2014, it was deemed to be too late to be included by the review – a perverse and cruel outcome. Of course, its exclusion rescued the medical establishment from admitting that Drs Hobbs and Wynne – and the Cleveland paediatricians – had been right all along.

The *Purple Book*

In 2015 the Royal College, in collaboration with the American Academy of Pediatrics, London's Royal College of Physicians and the Faculty of Forensic and Legal Medicine, published revised *Physical Signs of Sexual Abuse*, known as the *Purple Book*.[37] Its *most* revised chapter was 'Anal abuse'. 'There'd been close collaboration with the American Academy', explained Dr Geoff Debelle, consultant at Birmingham's Children's Hospital. Their collaboration was anchored 'in the evidence base for all physical signs of sexual abuse in children', he said.[38] That made it momentous. The *Purple Book* finally breached the cleavage between the Americans and everyone else. As one eminent consultant put it, they hoped this would stop defence lawyers saying, 'let's get experts from the US to give evidence we like to hear'.[39]

The *Purple Book* is unequivocal: 'Dynamic anal dilatation or total dilatation of both internal and external anal sphincters in the absence of stool is associated with anal abuse.'[40] The *Purple Book* marked the end of the war. What, then, had been so 'controversial' about that 'controversial' sign? Its significance was physical and social: reflex – or dynamic – anal dilatation was an effect of aggressive intrusion so chronic that over time it disrupted the anatomy's functions.[41] If penetration stopped and a child was being protected, then the symptom would be expected to resolve. The symptom died in the process of healing.

After a lifetime of experience, Dr Hobbs reflects on the decades of dispute, forensic semantics – particularly the meaning of 'diagnosis' – the significance and also the limits of signs: 'The term diagnostic crept in when physical evidence was being considered in child sexual abuse cases. There was a wish by courts to apply the "finger print" approach to making a finding of fact secure. But child abuse is not a medical condition, illness or disease process of the body,' he commented; it is a relationship:

> 'It is the way that a child is treated. What we as health and social care professionals seek to do is to identify when this has occurred, we seek evidence widely from different sources. The legal process then dissects and analyses the results. We look for possible consequences of ill-treatment in the child which may be physical, psychological, social, developmental, behavioural. We try to listen to what the child attempts to communicate to us.
>
> Physical evidence is notoriously and inevitably absent in a great many sexual abuse cases. Studies have shown that there is an unreasonable emphasis on this kind of evidence by the legal/criminal process which leaves one feeling that this is thought to be the only truth worth having. The term "diagnostic" undermines the value of the process by which information and observations contribute to a competent and comprehensive assessment of a case. We are back to the idea of a jigsaw again: all information needs to be put together to reach an opinion in a case conference or a court room on whether the child has probably been abused or not. Identifying the abuser or abusers is another matter altogether.'[42]

Silent witness

Forensic science is interested in law, crime and its causes, in both victim and perpetrator; it excavates the crime scene for traces of the criminal, for what the forensic scholar Paul L. Kirk called the 'silent witness'.[43] It is as much art as science: Forensic photography aims to preserve the crime scene – in this instance, the body. But the image of the body depends on context, imagination and interpretation. I suggest that reflex, or dynamic, anal dilation is the body's memory of the event. The police surgeons' tradition had nominated the sign as proof of homosexuality: the body's adaptation had been interpreted as *co-operation*. Its disappearance from the archives of childhood adversity *camouflaged* the perpetrator. During the Cleveland controversy, everyone was being challenged by the forensic evidence and the politics of the gaze: what was being *seen* and imagined with whom to identify and sympathise, victims or perpetrators? And what to feel – excitement or sorrow?

The life and death of Poppi Worthington

Poppi Worthington's happy photo – her smile, her baby teeth and fluffy red jacket as she sat in her yellow and red ride-on, hand on the steering wheel – joined the gallery of children whose deaths have haunted the political history of childhood for half a century. Their family album photos became icons of martyred infants whose deaths changed the way that professionals were supposed to think about children at risk of harm. Poppi Worthington's death early in the morning of 12 December 2010 brought something else to this mournful gallery. Her case was dynamite: it was about sex and death, dangerous men and vulnerable women.

It was the first case rehearsed in public that reprised the contested diagnosis in the Cleveland crisis and the failure to address the motives and modus operandi of perpetrators in families. It also exemplified Dr Hobbs's observations about signs signifying social relationships and about 'ways of seeing'.[44]

Poppi Worthington's life and death illuminated a child protection system in crisis after decades of political bad faith, child abuse scepticism, denigration of professionalism, rationing of resources and not least the potentially lethal intersection of predatory masculinity, gender and class, abuse and exploitation, loss, grief and economic stress.[45]

Her case also attracted both admirable practice and abject indifference; police non-investigation and an incurious inquest that lasted only seven minutes was followed by the ardent attention of family court proceedings, two inquests and a serious case review. I attended the public hearing of the medical evidence – a rare occasion, allowed by Mr Justice Jackson – that was dense with conjecture, science and drama, in this long-running case in which the judge and the coroner had to manage uncertainties and make meaning out of seeming mystery.[46] The stakes were high: children's lives and a man's liberty were at stake. Was her father – the suspect – a danger to her sisters and brothers, and to his young partner? He had other children with whom he had no contact whatsoever, and despite his huge responsibilities to his partner, the relationship was 'off and on'. He was a man who would come and go.[47]

Jumping to conclusions

Poppi Worthington lived in the county of Cumbria in the north-west of England in a crowded household with her parents and five brothers and sisters. She was healthy when she was taken to her cot to sleep by her mother on the night of 11 December 2012. Her father was in the parents' bedroom: he watched the sports results and some pornography, while the mother slept downstairs on the sofa.[48]

But she was dead when he rushed downstairs with her limp body at around 5.45 next morning. Her mother called the ambulance and she arrived at hospital 15 minutes later, where ten professionals worked until 7 am to resuscitate her.

Her sudden death seemed inexplicable. Yet, contrary to their guidelines, the police failed to preserve the scene of crime or forensic evidence – blood, clothes and nappies, computers, fingerprints – and decided not to investigate.

The pathologist conducting the autopsy, Dr Alison Armour, called Cumbria police not once but three times – including on Christmas Eve – to alert them to the child's injuries, a bleeding bottom and a broken leg, and the implications: sexual trauma that preceded or precipitated her death early that morning. The police dismissed her alerts. Dr Armour was 'rash', she had 'jumped to conclusions', they said – the very accusations that were later made against the police themselves in a scalding report by the Independent Police Complaints Commission (IPCC).[49]

When Dr Armour's final report appeared nine months later, it described leg fractures, revealed by a skeletal survey, that could only have been caused by 'considerable force'. But the child had not been taken to a doctor.

Dr Armour reported a cluster of signs, including a dilated and bleeding anus, tears and a pattern of bruises suggesting penetrative sexual abuse. Although swabs had been taken from her father when the child died, they had not been sent for analysis. When they were belatedly examined months later the child's DNA was found on her father's penis. That might have meant something or nothing, but none of this triggered a police investigation.

Ultimately, it was social services' belated concerns about her siblings' safety and her parents' failure to comply with arrangements agreed with social services that got the Worthington case into the family court in 2014 in front of the senior High Court judge, Mr Justice Peter Jackson. He brought his fastidious eye to the evidence and delivered a damning inventory of police failures. Though there had been a duty to investigate and a trail of clues, including blood at the home, the ambulance and the hospital, the police had not preserved the evidence or checked the parents' phones and computer; interviews with the parents and other witnesses had not been properly conducted or cross-checked.

The public interest

A coroner's inquest had thrown no light on the cause of death: it lasted a meagre seven minutes, heard no evidence and declared her death 'unexplained'.

The Poppi Worthington story only became known because, unusually, judgments were made public. Family court proceedings are not secret but they are strictly confidential to protect the privacy of the children. The family courts are increasingly under pressure to respond to public interest.[50] They draw evidence widely and deeply; they are not just concerned with criminal acts but also contexts, pressures and patterns – anything that bears upon a child's life. The evidence is governed by 'balance of probability' rather than the criminal standard 'beyond reasonable doubt'.

The judge took an unusual and important decision: the father and the police wanted the opportunity to seek alternative experts, and the judge agreed to a rehearing of medical evidence in public before releasing his judgment.[51]

In December 2015 I joined a small coterie of northern reporters in Liverpool family court to hear a revelatory interrogation of the disputed medical evidence and hypotheses about what had happened to Poppi Worthington.

The ghost of Cleveland

As in Cleveland in 1987, the Cumbria police had spurned suspicions of sexual abuse and refused to investigate. By now, however, the court had the benefit of the *Purple Book* and the settled view of around 30 professional organisations. Once again, the Worthington case rehearsed the old Cleveland debate.

All the experts agreed that there was anal injury, dilatation and bleeding, but they disagreed about the cause and the significance. The old McCann research was invoked by some of the police experts, among them Britain's 'most eminent pathologist' Dr Nathaniel Cary[52] and Dr Victoria Aziz, who had conducted many autopsies for the Metropolitan Police.[53]

Dr Cary introduced a novel hypothesis: the bleeding could have been caused by viral infection. He was forced to abandon that when no infection was found. Yet he was unyielding, 'I strongly disagree with any suggestion that there has been penile penetration,' he insisted. Dr Cary and Dr Aziz were adamant – citing the old American studies claiming that anal dilatation was of no significance.[54]

Mr Justice Peter Jackson's judgment published on 19 January 2016 did not agree.[55] He accepted many of the observations of the first pathologist, Dr Armour. He found that the father had 'perpetrated penetrative assault'. The father had described Poppi as going rigid and clenching her teeth on the morning she died. If so, commented the judge, 'sadly this would have been in the context of an assault'. But the judge was careful not to infer cause of death from the sexual assault. The injuries taken together were significant.

'Careful assessment of the meticulous pathological and paediatric evidence has clearly established that the injuries were the result of trauma from outside the body,' concluded the judge, by the father 'either using his penis or some other unidentified object'. This was not a case 'where a child has collapsed without any abnormal signs. The evidence is not at the frontiers of science. Poppi was bleeding, there must have been a source for the bleeding, and there is evidence that explains it.'[56] The ghost of Cleveland shadowed the medical dispute and the refusal to investigate – though the mainstream coverage did not make that connection: historical memory had become very short.

Refusing to answer 252 times

The case also triggered another debate about the relationship between civil and criminal proceedings and standards of proof, and outcomes in children's cases.[57]

Law lecturer Hannah Quirk claimed that the judge's decision to publish his judgment 'forms part of a recent trend in which – rightly or wrongly – criminal proceedings have not been possible and other agencies have taken it upon themselves to pronounce on a person's culpability'.[58]

Family law barrister Lucy Reed replied in her legal blog, *Pink Tape*, that in the Poppi Worthington case 'the police were palpably failing to build any case at all'. The family courts determine facts, she explained, and apply the law to those facts. The typical problem confronted by family courts was a recording of 'no further action' by the police, 'without proper investigation, an interminably long and ponderous investigation … or a dropped prosecution'. Rarely was there a prosecution or a conviction that proceeded within the family court timescale: 'children cannot wait for the slow disaster that is the prosecution of such offences'.[59]

Lucy Reed's pessimism was confirmed by the 2015 report on sexual abuse investigations by Her Majesty's Inspectorate of Constabulary (HMIC). Despite law reform and endless inquiries, there remained 'mismatch between stated priorities and practices on the ground'. The HMIC's bleak inventory recorded 'at all stages of the child's experience', and (particularly salient to the Worthington case) noted that often leads were not followed up and 'simple activities' to gather forensic action were not undertaken.[60]

All of this was aired again at the second inquest into Poppi Worthington's death in 2017. The Cumbria coroner David Roberts heard all the expert witnesses and the evidence of her mother and father. Paul Worthington had gone into hiding and now appeared behind a screen shielding him from public view. Unlike the mother, the father had not been under scrutiny, his parenting behaviour was not considered and 'was never assessed'.[61] If he was not notorious before, he became so when he exercised his right to silence: he refused to answer questions 252 times.[62]

Once again, he was found culpable by the coroner: 'Only Paul Worthington can provide an account of what happened,' he concluded, but Worthington's various accounts could not be relied upon. He accepted that during her last night alive she suffered bruising and tears caused by anal penetration. The coroner described her sleeping environment with her father that night as unsafe, and concluded that she had been deprived of oxygen while asleep and died. The cause of death was asphyxia.[63]

Predatory men

While the family court and coroner tried to establish the cause of death, the context was analysed in a serious case review by an expert in family violence and abuse, justice and gender, Clare Hyde.[64]

Just as the family court, the coroner and the IPCC spotlighted the police failures, so the serious case review focused on health and welfare practitioners' failure to address the vulnerabilities and needs of a woman with a history of childhood abuse and exploitation, and exposure to men from whom she might not be able to protect herself or her children – a common theme in contemporary serious case reviews.

Perpetrators were a lacuna in the Cleveland Inquiry and its legacy. It did not consult any experts on sex offenders; it did not address their research on perpetrators' exploitation of women and children's vulnerabilities. This was not only an opportunity squandered, but it also contributed to a historic failure in the statutory services to focus on a key feature of child sexual abuse: the people who do it.

Specialist independent reviewer Clare Hyde provided a summary of the mother's life: a tale of neglect, violence, abuse and exploitation, loss and poverty. Her own mother had been brought up in the care system, and she became the second generation in her family to endure violence, abuse and the care system; her first child, born when she was 16, became the third generation to become a looked-after child in this family.

Poppi Worthington's mother was believed to have been groomed for sexual exploitation as a teenager, yet over the years her frequent contact with the statutory services never attracted 'any tailored therapeutic intervention in terms of her own experience of sexual and other abuse and or the trauma of her child being placed in care'.[65] She met Poppi's father when she was 23 and he was nearly twice her age. He had an abusive history and he already had two children with whom he had no contact whatsoever. The age gap and his behaviour did not attract professionals' curiosity.

After the loss of her first child, she had six more. In fact, she presented, remarkably, as resilient, coping and competent. But the Hyde Report stressed that her youth and many pregnancies should have alerted health and welfare practitioners to her history of abuse and loss. Her 'unresolved significant and traumatic life events were indicators at the very least that her parenting capacity and ability to protect herself and her children from harm could be compromised.'

She was at risk of further exploitation or abuse, cautioned the review; indeed, 'her relationship with any male could be a source of potential risk'. This was a stark reminder of the problem 'with no name' that had not been addressed in the Cleveland Report: the correlation between masculinity and sexual abuse, and vulnerable women's entrapment by abusive men. In this case (as in the Cleveland cases) medical evidence was primary but the police would not follow its logic. The evidence demanded an explanation by Paul Worthington: he was the last person to see Poppi alive, but the police would not entertain him as a suspect.

Between Cleveland and Cumbria, medical evidence had been marginalised, gender and the problem of perpetrators erased, doctors discouraged, social workers disempowered and safeguarding processes endlessly revised to little effect.

This was the bleak bequest to Poppi Worthington.

9

Tremendous conservatism

Social work

No one was prepared for the counter-revolution in 1987. 'We anticipated a backlash, but thought we had more time,' wrote feminist academics and activists Mary MacLeod and Esther Saraga – they had organised a practitioners' conference on sexual abuse in the spring of 1987; then Cleveland combusted.[1]

Professionals throughout the UK expected the Butler-Sloss Report to grasp the issues that beset them: difficulties with joint investigations; how to manage children with medical and behavioural signs who could not or would not speak; how to work with a non-abusing parent; what to do if a mother supported a father figure against whom there were strong suspicions; how to assess the risk of leaving a child at home versus removing them to safety. And how to develop expertise.[2]

A senior practitioner told me:

> 'No one in the field was naïve. There was denial, there were resource restraints, and perpetrators of sexual abuse were known to act in the knowledge that someone, a wife, an older child, a friend in authority, and even the victim herself, would have their back. We also knew how serious and complex this was and how raising awareness would only take us so far.'[3]

What was not appreciated was how effectively the armies of conservatism would muster and how the Establishment, whether knowingly or not, would use the shortcomings of the Cleveland Inquiry to suppress facts that needed to be known. The effect was that conservative and pessimistic government guidance would be interpreted as sensible and reassuring, and that it would influence practice beyond the millennium.

Thirty years later, reading the files in the National Archives, it dawned on me how easy it was: the symbiosis of determined bad faith, ignorance and carelessness quelled the great movements of victim-centred and perpetrator-focused practice in the 1980s. This book is written in the context of an apparent re-re-discovery of sexual oppression in the 2000s – which could be similarly endangered.

The Cleveland Report endorsed a suspicion of proactive child protection and prevention that infused policies and protocols. By recoiling from medical evidence, by giving an uncritical platform to Ralph Underwager and claiming, perversely, that only on 'rare occasions' do children 'choose not to tell' the inquiry's mistrust of proactive child protection dumbed policy.

Many practitioners held on to hope and tried to perform their statutory duty, but one of the witnesses who had been wounded by the inquiry, the Great Ormond Street Children's Hospital psychiatrist Arnon Bentovim, believed that the baleful hegemony of the report extinguished the great optimism of the 1980s and what could be called a 'heroic age' of awareness: 'a tremendous conservatism' followed, he told me. Children met their nemesis, 'a negative culture' that even 'cast doubt on whether the extensive prevalence of sexual abuse was a real or mythical finding'.[4]

Bentovim was right: in the aftermath of the Cleveland Inquiry, the new enlightenment was assailed, expertise squandered and resources squeezed as the government clamped the means by which children might be better seen and heard, and safeguarded; the echoing voices of adult survivors of sexual abuse were often disparaged as 'false memories';[5] police and medical responses to sexual offences against children began to disintegrate, leaving the burden on local authority children's services and the law.

Intervene!

This was at odds with frameworks for managing child abuse that had been steered by the impact of inquiries into child deaths: the fate of Tyra Henry, Kimberley Carlile and Jasmine Beckford commanded national attention and reflected negatively on social workers: they had not been sufficiently interventionist in 'dangerous' families.[6] The message was unequivocal: use the authority of the law, and intervene!

New guidelines for assessment of risk, *Protecting Children: A Guide for Social Workers Undertaking a Comprehensive Assessment*, known as the *Orange Book*, and the Children Act 1989 radically affected both the structure and practice of local authorities.[7] Thus, social workers were presented with procedural, professional and ideological contradictions: they were to identify 'dangerous families' yet they were to protect those not deemed dangerous from the scrutiny of the state.[8] The effect was to displace sexual abuse.

By the time of the Second Reading of the Children Act in Parliament in 1988 the political priorities were explicit: the very, very Conservative MP for Edgbaston, Dame Jill Knight, welcomed 'the emphasis on keeping families together. ... It is a comfort that the lessons of Cleveland have been learnt. ... No longer will it be possible for children to be torn from the family home and kept away for weeks as happened under the truly disgraceful regime of Dr Marietta Higgs.'[9]

Stuart Bell MP was keen to defend the traditional authority of parents and 'perhaps more accurately those of fathers', commented Professor Nigel Parton, and to restore 'balance between the family and the role of the local authority'.[10] Other Labour MPs stressed deprivation and disadvantage; while feminist MPs argued for universal services for children and families, and tried to introduce inequality and power into the debate.[11]

There was little mention of the specific risks and harm of sexual abuse. A remarkable feature of the debate, in many ways thoughtful and unusually bipartisan, was how ignorant Parliament was of the facts about sexual abuse. MPs were insightful about the reform of legal processes, yet there was little understanding of what the Cleveland crisis had been about.

After the Children Act became law in 1989 the courts became the theatre for decision-making. This required social workers to have a steady eye on evidential requirements, and child protection became more forensic at the same time as the Children Act required them to work in partnership with parents. It did, however, encourage reaching out to a non-abusing parent or relative to secure some safe space for the child within the nuclear or extended family.

Manchester: 'played by the Cleveland book'

A hospital's worries about a four-year-old girl's behaviour initiated the Manchester case in 1989. Social services and the police knew the girl's extended family well – several cousins were in local authority care and two of her siblings had died. The mother was a convicted sex offender and was now living with another sex offender. The girl and her sister needed protection, but from whom?[12]

The children were made wards of court and went to foster homes, where the sisters seemed compliant and content. During journeys to and from access visits to their parents, however, they regaled their escorts with highly structured, weird, scary narratives, but amid all their talk, carers noticed 'an unusual fear of talking about life in their family'. A senior CID officer, Chief Inspector Norman Wyper, was appointed to head up an investigation. 'All we knew was that they were very frightened,' he told me. 'We stopped wondering *what* it was because we knew we would never get an answer.' But without more evidence there would be no more resources, and without resources, more evidence was unlikely.[13]

Despite the Cleveland Report's cautions, the police and the official solicitor strongly urged removal of the children as the only way to get evidence. Homes were raided, children were taken into care and medical examinations found chronic penetration. A father was arrested and charged, and after his denial he was released; formal interviews yielded little or nothing.[14] The investigators did something desperate – another raid to rescue more children who had been identified, in the hope that they would deliver more evidence. Now that all the cousins were safe, the original children seemed to feel released; they began to identify people, places and awful practices. But it was too late. The children were now safe, but so were the suspects. 'We have accepted a version of investigation that would be derisory in any other criminal context,' the team manager told me at the time. The case was 'played by the Cleveland book', said the manager, but 'the book' assumed partnership with a protective parent. Hostile parents, including sex offenders, were beyond the book and so, too, were multiple perpetrators and networks.

The defence tried to discredit the children; it was said that horror videos or 'zealot' professionals had generated the evidence. Mr Justice Hollings criticised the investigation – the Cleveland guidelines had been breached, he said – but he acknowledged that in complex cases more than the prescribed two interviews might be needed. He concluded, however, that 'There was probable abuse of a satanic nature in bogus ritual circumstances.'[15] The Manchester case duly vaporised into legends about videos and zealous interviewers.

The message

Professionals barely had time to adjust to the Children Act before the Government published *Messages from Research* in 1995.[16] The message was that the pendulum had swung too far toward risk assessment and investigation. The Department of Health and Social Security advocated refocusing towards greater investment in *family support*, away from an approach to child protection that had been dominated 'by a forensic approach',[17] and social workers that had lost their way. This plea converged with a widespread belief that Thatcherism had laid waste to poor families' support systems. But Nigel Parton argued that the researchers failed 'to fully appreciate the significance of risk'.[18] Not least the risk of sexual abuse.

A clue to the politics underlying *Messages from Research* could be found in *Parental Perspectives in the Cases of Suspected Child Abuse*, published in 1995 and written by Hedy Cleaver and Pam Freeman, who lamented that the 'legacy of investigations' – broken marriages, children in care – so 'violating to families' were 'high prices to pay for a bruise'.[19]

The flood of sexual abuse referrals that began in the 1980s had compounded the crisis of a childcare system that was unlikely to attract new resources. Indeed, the problem of resources in Cleveland 'was seen as an effect rather than a cause of the crisis'.[20]

The *Orange Book* did not address sexual abuse. It produced a one-size-fits-all template for assessment that, to some professionals, seemed designed to miss the point. The new framework did not rectify the Cleveland Inquiry's failure to address risk and perpetrator behaviours and, I suggest, contributed to what child protection specialist Martin Calder has described as a 'perpetrator friendly' approach in contrast to a 'perpetrator challenging framework'.[21]

Sexual abuse became a problem without a name. Every generation of social workers had to face the shock and fright of sexual abuse afresh. My discussions for this book with many highly qualified professionals in their 40s, left the impression that they were only aware of the *myths* of Cleveland, and scarcely knew how to confront the problem of sexual abuse.

Ironically, the government had created a problem that everyone regretted: a *forensic* approach, infected by ancient adult suspicion of children. The *Memorandum of Good Practice*, a protocol for interviewing children published in 1992, exemplified the problem.[22] The attitude 'owed little to the collective wisdom of child-centred professionals and more to the application of judge-made rules and inflexible principles of evidence', warned the barrister David L. Spicer, at that time chair of the British Association for the Study and Prevention of Child Abuse and Neglect. 'Among the expectations when child welfare legislation was revised were reaffirmation of the paramountcy of the welfare of the child,' and a more consensual, child-centred approach and avoidance of the courts.[23]

But despite the intention of the Children Act, many professionals regarded children's proceedings, particularly in private law (between divorcing parents) as being more adversarial, and Spicer warned that the 'paramountcy principle', originally intended to assert children's interests, would not prevail. The Children Act envisaged 'a more inquisitorial role' for the courts, rather than 'acting as umpires between the contending parties', but Spicer commented that 'proceedings are far more adversarial'.

For Spicer, one of the UK's most committed legal advocates for children, this exposed workers 'to the scandal of scarce resources being used to service expensive and inappropriate decision-making mechanisms'.[24]

4.3 million children below the poverty line

By the mid-1990s the shuddering evidence of the scale of childhood adversity was laid bare by a National Commission of Inquiry into the Prevention of Child Abuse, in *Childhood Matters* – at least 1 million children were being harmed every year and of these an estimated 100,000 suffered 'a harmful sexual experience'.[25] This was in the context of alarming child poverty: a third of children – that is, 4.3 million – were in households living below the poverty line in the UK, where income inequality rose faster than in any other industrialised society.[26]

Childhood Matters fell into a cauldron of contradictory pressures: an emerging populism that was targeting children who were causing trouble, rather than children with troubles, managerialism in public service, feminist campaigns for universal childcare and against sexual violence, political pressure to reduce child protection registrations, political pressure to enhance vigilant responses to risk, and worry about the 'neglect of neglect'.[27]

Certainly, the flood of sexual abuse referrals had compounded the childcare system's crises at a point when its resources were already stretched, shrinking and unlikely to be ameliorated by a government hostile to the public sector and the welfare professions. Many social services managers gave a qualified welcome to refocusing. Some sighed with relief: it might mean more support for poor families and children for whom harm was 'born of need rather than abuse'.[28]

Others worried that it was rationing and a cover for cuts, and that parents' needs might supplant those of the child – and some gave up on sexual abuse. Martin Calder flagged the persistent decline in the numbers of children subject to protection plans and the failure to address perpetrators. Social work training on sexual abuse and risk assessment by local authorities waned.[29] The very notion of 'risk assessment', so central in the late 1980s and early 1990s, had almost disappeared.

The *Framework of Assessment for Social Workers*, known as the *Lilac Book*,[30] which replaced the *Orange Book* in 2000, required social workers to look at clients' 'strengths' as well as 'vulnerabilities'. For sure, it proposed a welcome holistic and ecological approach; it encouraged evidence-based interventions in the context of diverse cultures and communities, and a contemporary understanding of family structures. There was a clear intention to avoid families being pushed, as a matter of course, through a child protection funnel in order to receive resources.

But the *Lilac Book* contained no specific chapter on sexual abuse. Prioritising *need* rather than *risk* would, of course, be appropriate for vulnerable families living in poverty or with mental ill health, a senior guardian told me, 'but it could *never* on its own be appropriate for sexual abuse or violence: for that there could no other *criteria* than serious risk.'

The post-Cleveland approach was reinforced much later by the Munro Report, which advocated an emphasis on working with the *strengths* of vulnerable families. Munro, too, did not address sexual abuse – the most inaccessible problem for professionals and non-abusive family members.[31] Martin Calder echoed the critique expressed by other child professionals to whom I have spoken, who complained that yet again sexual abuse and violence in families had not been confronted, that the assessment of risk had not been equally prioritised within the Munro template even though it is fundamental to protecting children from sexual abuse within families.

Disappearances

Professionals told me that their local authorities had actually banned the word *risk* because it is correlated with 'negative' and alienated families.[32] They reckoned that local authority risk assessments rarely addressed sexual abuse in families – despite case notes recording suspicious sexualised episodes, children's remarks or complaints. Others described children being referred not to child protection but to the Children and Adolescent Mental Health Service that was already overburdened – and was not mandated to investigate. Calder was pessimistic: 'We are no clearer about perpetrators in the family than we were in the 1980s ... and Cleveland.'[33]

Professor June Thoburn reported in 2019 that after many reorganisations – and, it might be said, refocusings – child protection interventions had actually grown: this was the result of *falling* funding by central government and *rising* numbers of children in need of services.[34] Between 2010 and 2020, revenues available to local government – responsible for children's services – had been scythed by almost 40 per cent. Cuts in spending per child during this time were around 50 per cent in London's poorest boroughs.[35]

The effect of the swerve away from sexual abuse is eerily palpable in its presence and then absence in rising child protection plans: eye-watering research by Kairika Karsna and Liz Kelly, published by the Centre of Expertise on Child Sexual Abuse in 2021, showed that in 1992–3 the sexual abuse category matched neglect: around 21 per cent of those on the Child Protection Register. A decade later it had sunk, and remained low thereafter. By 2018–19 the sexual abuse category was a meagre 4 per cent.[36] In some local authorities it disappeared altogether. Clearly, sexual abuse had not disappeared in real life. It had become obscured. Furthermore, the flight from *sexual* abuse had contributed nothing to the prevention of *physical* abuse tragedies. The agonising deaths of Victoria Climbié and Peter Connelly shocked the UK public, because of the extent of their injuries and the cruelty which they had experienced, and the recycled trope of professional incompetence.[37] Former social services director Ray Jones chronicled how, yet again, welfare workers were strategically scapegoated.[38]

But things were not always what they seemed. For example, in 2009 Stephen Barker, the stepfather of Peter Connelly, known as Baby P, was convicted with his brother and Baby P's mother of causing or allowing the death of a child. Two years later he was convicted of the anal rape of a two-year-old girl, Peter's sister, on the basis of her testimony.[39]

This little girl confounded myths about children's credibility,[40] and the Cleveland Report's ignorance about the conditions in which, when – and more likely if – a young child might tell her story: she did indeed 'choose' to tell, but *only* after she had been rescued, only when she was safe, out of her family and in the warm world of foster carers. It is unlikely that any family assessment – beguiled by the 'needs' and 'strengths' discourse enshrined in the new lore of family services – would have contemplated risks of sexual abuse and violence. These categories were not on the agenda.

Would her 'disclosures' have been enunciated before she was rescued? Would they have been noticed or interpreted? Would her testimony have been registered had she not been lifted out of her family and had prosecutors not already investigated the killers in her family? Would her alleged abuser have warranted investigation if he had been a respectable family man – rather than a criminal – living in Cleveland in 1987?

Social work had been neutralised. The other vital parts of the professional triumvirate in child protection, the police and medical assessment, we will see, were also unprepared and disengaged.

10

Off the hook

While commentary on Cleveland focused on individual social workers and paediatricians, a cordon sanitaire was wrapped round the police and the criminal justice system. But the Cleveland Report had thrown down an unnoticed gauntlet to the corporate culture of the police: it urged that they needed to consider their organisational capacity to cooperate with other agencies and to confront sexual abuse. That brief, brisk comment muted the inquiry's opinion of the constabulary's arrogance and ignorance. And it was reiterated by police inspectorates for the next 30 years.

Correspondence in the National Archives confirms that it was believed at the highest level that Cleveland Police had been let off the hook. The documents show that in 1988 Tony Newton's successor as Minister for Health, David Mellor, strayed slightly from the official script in a wrangle with Home Office Minister John Patten. Mellor reminded him that the inquiry seemed to have let Cleveland Police off lightly: 'I think the criticism of the police in the Butler-Sloss report was of less significance than those of the doctors and social workers involved,' wrote Mellor. 'I nevertheless think they were significant enough for a proper public response. You will be aware of the criticism levelled at us that we are being less than even-handed in tackling the RHA [Regional Health Authority] and the County Council whilst ignoring the police.'[1]

This was no mere tiff; it went to the crux of the conflict – the constabulary's closed corporate mind that relied on masculine intuition and the defensive shield of operational autonomy.

The Home Office was immovable and it invoked the Cleveland Report on its side. Patten replied to Mellor on 7 December: he acknowledged that the *Working Together* guidelines made no distinction between contexts of abuse, within or without the family, but he insisted that 'it could equally well be argued that the procedures now in operation in Cleveland are entirely in line with the conclusions of the Butler-Sloss Report'.[2]

He was right. On page 251, the Cleveland Report said that the police would be freed up from joint working in extra-familial cases: they would 'normally be investigated and prosecuted by the police without the involvement of other agencies'. Patten outwitted Mellor by reminding him that 'both of our departments have commended the Butler-Sloss report ... we did not indicate that we disagreed in any way. ... It is not immediately apparent to us that the Butler-Sloss report was wrong.'[3]

We would learn how very wrong it was.

Mellor had been relying on an SSI inspection, in the hope of making a reassuring public statement that the situation was getting better in Cleveland. What he learned was that it was, and it wasn't.

Documents in the National Archives show that the status quo in the police *before* the Cleveland crisis remained the status quo *afterwards*: in October 1988, the SSI's highly regarded chief inspector, William Utting, told the Minister of Health that following an inspection the SSI rated the social workers as mostly experienced and acting appropriately. But joint working remained a dream: it happened in only 9 per cent of cases, and even then it was not so much joint as police-dominated, he added.[4] Insofar as the police investigated extra-familial cases, they would merely notify social services 'in due course', by which time opportunities for recognising risk to children 'had been lost', he warned.[5]

Utting was worried enough to write a challenging memo to Mellor on 30 November 1988, reiterating that *all* agencies were required to protect children from harm, whatever the context and 'whoever is the alleged perpetrator'. The situation, Utting warned, 'raised some very difficult issues which will require further national guidance'.[6] It was not forthcoming. The demarcation dispute remained unresolved – with disastrous consequences.

Once again, the obstacle was the Home Office. Throughout the 1980s experts had been urging the government to enhance children's opportunities to participate in criminal proceedings and help them survive the hazardous encounter with the accused. During the Cleveland Inquiry, experts had great hopes that the Criminal Justice Bill going through Parliament would at last establish children's right to be heard in a criminal trial, but it was not to be: there was a 'disappointed outcry' at the Bill's 'timid' reforms.[7] The Home Secretary was obliged to appoint a new committee to review arrangements, the Pigot Committee. Where the Home Office had been reluctant and Butler-Sloss restrictive, the Pigot Report in 1989 proposed ways to release children's testimony.[8] It was nearly three decades before Pigot was fully implemented.[9]

It was the pessimism of Butler-Sloss's report, not the optimism of the Pigot Report, that drove new official guidance. In 1992 the Home Office published the *Memorandum of Good Practice*, the guide to interviewing children: it followed the Cleveland Report's recommendation that children should be interviewed without aids, only once and for under an hour. Anatomically complete dolls, designed to help very young children show what might have happened to them, were banished – some witnesses had told the Cleveland Inquiry that children might be aroused by them.[10]

With little of her usual gracious gravitas, Elizabeth Butler-Sloss had mocked these 'appallingly misnamed' dolls in a speech to lawyers: 'May I tell you that the Women's Institute of Somerset have been knitting them! [Laughter] If nothing else, we really ought to keep those particularly hideous dolls away from most children.'[11] However, research published in 1989 had found that although children noticed the dolls in their play, they generally weren't cued by them. Nevertheless, the dolls were doomed.

The *Memorandum* was hailed as a great aid for both children and the courts, but it was neither. It was the result of a gruelling drafting process: experts found to their chagrin that their concerns had been ignored or minimised, yet their names were published in the *Memorandum* as if it had their endorsement. One of them was Professor Graham Davies, one of the UK's premier researchers into children's reliability as witnesses, who told me that the suspicion that children are particularly suggestible 'lies in the origins of the *Memorandum*'.[12]

Eighteen minutes to tell their story

The *Memorandum* prescribed one interview early in an investigation, for no more than an hour and by both a police officer and a social worker, using no prompts or leading questions; the child's evidence, video-recorded in a special suite, should be spontaneous. It was designed as if disclosure were not difficult, an event not a process, and as if it concerned events unencumbered by the real lives and loyalties of children in adversity.

Follow-up research found that the police dominated the process – in only 2 per cent of interviews was there parity between the police and social workers. On average, children took 18 minutes to tell their substantive stories. Later research confirmed that too much depended on the child's one chance to tell his or her story: 'The videotaped interview was often the first time the child had spoken in detail about the offence. It was typically a rambling, incoherent account.' This was hardly surprising. Cases were not being built, and sometimes interviewers were unaware of the case details, with 'no clear idea of the nature of the child's allegations'.[13]

Islington

Liz Davies, an Islington social worker, noticed a lot of children, young teenagers, hanging around her new neighbourhood office in Holloway in the mornings, often before the office opened. Neighbours reported vans picking them up in the evenings and the children returning early in the morning looking exhausted. Davies and local police began gathering intelligence and put together a dossier of sexual exploitation in children's homes. The case exemplified exploitation – and the indifference to it – that was exposed two decades later.

They asked for resources to mount a joint investigation. They were refused and told to stop. They didn't – and accumulated evidence on 11 children's homes. Still nothing happened – until award-winning journalist Eileen Fairweather began a series of stories in London's *Evening Standard* from 1992, and reported that around 30 members of staff had been 'allowed to quietly resign after serious allegations, including child pornography, drugs, buggery, child abduction and dishonesty'.[14] Racism and homophobia had been mobilised as defensive barricades against accusation. This was sensationalism and gutter journalism, complained Margaret Hodge, council leader, later a Labour MP and – controversially – Minister for Children.[15] Fairweather's coverage demanded a response, and an inquiry reported in 1995;[16] this report was not published, although a redacted version became available many years later. It affirmed the whistle-blowers. Yet when BBC Radio 4's *Today* team investigated, Hodge disparaged one of the victims, Demetrious Panton, and complained to the BBC's director general. In 2003 she was forced to apologise.[17] Twenty-five years after the *Evening Standard*'s exposé, Islington Council acknowledged that 'the Town Hall was culpable for the children's homes scandal' and apologised for the 'darkest chapter in the council's history'.[18]

The journalist Christian Wolmar describes the conducive context of endemic abuse in the UK's children's homes generally: two thirds of the staff were women in the 1960s, thereafter homes metamorphosed into masculinised and often militaristic institutions targeted by men who sexually exploited children.[19] A queasy ambivalence about sexual abuse among the professional elite allowed the Paedophile Information Exchange (PIE) to operate as 'a fifth column ... right at the core of social work education'[20] – via the charismatic social work impresario Peter Righton, a founder member of PIE.

Police had raided his home after child pornography posted from the Netherlands was intercepted, and found an enormous cache of material, including correspondence with public figures and diaries identifying the many children he had assaulted – graded with the obsessional detail of an addict. But he was prosecuted only on a minor charge. An outraged police constable invited the head of Worcestershire's specialist child protection unit, Peter McKelvie, to delve into this enormous archive. McKelvie and social services director David Tombs asked the DHSS – in vain – to fund a joint investigation. Tombs complained that the Cleveland Report's legacy left 'social services nationwide to carry out their work with one hand tied behind their backs' because they could not access police suspicions. When he warned the DHSS about suspects with links to the Establishment, he was told – prophetically – that he was 'probably wasting his time' because there were 'too many of them over there', in Whitehall and Westminster.[21]

Not serious crime, not serious cops

By the end of the decade specialist police officers were very worried. The expert Police Research Group, whose members had been engaged in complex and sometimes controversial sexual abuse cases across the country, concluded that the police were so overwhelmed that 'offenders remain unconvicted and unchecked'.[22] There was 'no obvious strategic thinking' about child abuse by senior managers; in fact, there was 'considerable ambivalence if not reluctance'. Sexual crime was not regarded as 'serious crime' and child protection officers were not regarded as 'serious cops'. The Cleveland Report's family/non-family split remained sovereign, and so 'stranger abuse' referrals went to the CID or Vice Squad without engaging child protection systems, only to disappear into 'No further action'.

These specialists were 'unanimous' in their critique of management indifference, made worse by the transfusion of private sector performance targets into public service. The criminal justice system, they said, needed to get with child protection.

Did it? In 2002 the *Memorandum* was succeeded by *Achieving Best Evidence*. It contained no guidance on work with sexual abuse or traumatised children. It consolidated the dominance of the police – most interviews had no social work presence, most were unplanned and often the tone 'almost resembled that of an interrogation'.[23] Far from freeing up children's narratives, only 1 per cent reached the benchmark of good practice for the 'easy' cases. No hope, then, for the trepidatious or traumatised child.

A question of attitude

One of the most important legal developments was initiated by the Labour government's feminist law officers who led the most radical reform in a generation, the Sexual Offences Act 2003.

Now consent could not be assumed; it had to be sought and given. Children could not consent: under no circumstance could adults claim that a child had consented to the penetration of their bottoms, vaginas or mouths – that was rape. The act also specified grooming and abuse of trust.[24]

This was of the greatest importance. There could be no confusion – there could be no consent. But the impact was imperceptible. In 2005 a London Metropolitan University team led by Professor Liz Kelly revealed just how grim the prospects of prosecution and conviction were. Kelly's team studied the largest ever dataset in the UK on rape and sexual assault: between 1985 and 2005 more rapes were reported year on year, but victims entered a culture of scepticism: the proportion of victims who achieved justice was the lowest ever – just 6 per cent.[25] Only 14 per cent of reported cases went to trial, and acquittals were twice as high in cases involving children. The 'justice gap' grew and grew – according to Professors Jennifer Temkin and Barbara Krahe, driven more by 'perception and prejudice' than often-claimed evidential difficulties.[26]

In London, the Metropolitan Police strategic adviser, Professor Betsy Stanko, an internationally recognised expert on gendered crime, did what no one had done before: she entered the heart of the beast – police records.

Of the 677 rapes reported in April and May 2005, a third were simply 'not-crimed', that is, not recorded.[27] For the first time, Stanko traced the suspects and their records: many suspects in 'not-crimed' reports had previous records of violent offences and sexual attacks. No one had ever correlated the victims' stories with the records of the accused until now: a third of suspects whose victims were under 18 were not investigated, and they too had histories of violent offending.

So, as long as men targeted girls, women who had been drinking or who were acquainted with the man, or those who had mental health problems, the police would be unlikely to interview the suspect, or investigate – there would be nothing 'on the books'. The overwhelming majority of rapes reported to the Metropolitan Police – 87 per cent – attracted a preoccupation with the virtues or vulnerabilities of the victim rather than the propensities of the perpetrators.

Stanko's analysis circled the desks of police managers in the Met and the Home Office, and was quietly filed away. Yet her research was 'dynamite', commented Liz Kelly; it was based on 'unadulterated data' to which researchers had previously had no access. The synergy of scepticism and sexism in police culture, said Kelly, had created a context of 'virtual impunity'.[28]

Real victims

Despite official discouragement, Stanko returned to the police files regularly for ten years, accumulating a unique cache of data about victims, suspects and police practice. Yet a decade after Stanko's first review, stereotypes of 'real' victims and 'real rape' still saturated the system and outcomes for victims actually 'declined noticeably': England and Wales had one of the lowest rape conviction rates in Europe.[29] Half of all sex offences recorded by the police were against children. A meagre 6 per cent resulted in a charge.[30]

When child sexual abuse was first specified in statutory duties in the 1980s, although reported levels were low, the conviction rate was 24 per cent. A decade later it had dropped to 12 per cent. In 2005 it was 6 per cent, and then settled at 7 per cent. Following a rush of historic child abuse scandals after 2010, sexual offences recorded by the police tripled.[31] But between 2016 and 2021 prosecutions and convictions roughly halved.

The system was antipathetic: the Cleveland Report had conveyed both ignorant optimism about children's 'choice' to tell and pessimism, not to say paranoia, about the processes of telling and hearing; the problem of perpetrators was an empty space. What children themselves had to say about the criminal justice system was grievous: Joyce Plotnikoff and Richard Woolfson, veteran researchers into the courts and children's experience of the system, interviewed young people taking part in trials in the 2000s. They found that apart from being allowed to give evidence via video link, 'in almost all other respects, the process let these young people down'.[32]

Plotnikoff and Woolfson, together with lawyer Penny Cooper, founded the Advocates Gateway in 2012 to promote the highest ethical standards in the treatment of vulnerable witnesses; together with many practitioners, they campaigned for intermediaries to support children through the forbidding process, for implementation of 'special measures': aids to communication – frowned upon by the Cleveland Report – including picture boards, drawing, electronic devices; they also trained advocates in the use of language when questioning witnesses – even the semantics of seemingly simple challenges in cross-examination could demand complex reasoning and could be experienced as incomprehensible.[33]

After spending more than 20 years as researchers and advocates for children in the courts, Plotnikoff and Woolfson, the quiet pioneers, reviewed the state of the system before they retired: no one knew more about the pace of change and the quality of justice for children. They consulted almost 300 policymakers and practitioners, reviewed policy documents and data, and finally reported that the number of children having their day in court suffered a 'dramatic fall' for which no reason has been identified.[34] In their professional farewell they could not avoid this pitiless conclusion: 'the gap between best and poor practice has never been wider'. It was heartfelt.

By 2020 the justice inspectorates, too, had acknowledged the special obstacles encountered by victims – a third of them children – who were ill-served by funding cuts and political practices in public services and the police that minimised the numbers and the response: 'intelligence-gathering is not meeting the demands of the rise in recorded rape' and the former 'performance regimes have acted as an encouragement to keep the number of recordable crimes down to an irreducible minimum'.[35]

If justice for children demands that they are heard and enabled to participate in the justice system, everything is against them. In 2015 Her Majesty's Inspectorate of Constabulary had been candid: the police are at risk of failing another generation of children.[36] By then another generation had already been failed.

11

A new sexual abuse crisis

A decade after the DHSS had been warned that the legacy of the Cleveland Report left the authorities 'with one hand tied behind our backs' the impact of the report's bifurcation of family–non family, of structural impediments and incompetent 'intelligence' was gruesomely exposed in a case that commanded national attention: the killing of ten-year-old best friends Holly Wells and Jessica Chapman in the Cambridgeshire village of Soham in 2003.

Murder in Soham

School caretaker Ian Huntley was the last person to see them alive. No one in Cambridgeshire knew that he was a danger to girls until a woman watching a television report on the huge hunt for the girls recognised him. She informed Cambridgeshire Constabulary that he had previously been charged with rape in Humberside.

The Soham tragedy provoked two inquiries:[1] Sir Richard Bichard's inquiry condemned the hapless police response to Huntley – in the 1990s he had attacked several girls, often runaways, but they were not regarded as children, and because Huntley was not a family member they were not recognised as child sexual abuse cases. Bichard was unforgiving about police intelligence systems: Humberside's arrangements were 'worthless' and the Home Office had failed to organise a national intelligence-sharing system.[2] Sir Christopher Kelly's serious case review considered the response to runaways in Humberside neighbourhoods that were among the most deprived in England: it was again noted that Huntley's assaults on girls going back to

1995 had not received social services' attention because he was not a family member. These girls dripped into services starved of resources and skilled staff, only to drain away.[3] Poor girls were rich pickings for predatory men because they weren't 'recognised as children'.

Sex, race and class

The Soham chronicle dramatised the consequences of the Cleveland Report's family and non-family demarcation, an abstraction that framed administration but not real life that was aggravated by parallel political processes:

- The reorientation – by both Conservative and Labour governments – of the welfare state away from *social* problems and *social* solutions towards targeted antisocial children and their 'problem' families.
- The reinterpretation of victims: girls in trouble *were* trouble – their pregnancies, boyfriends, truanting and their tracksuits, parodied in the TV comedy series *Little Britain* character Vicky Pollard. They became objects of class contempt.
- When services lost sight of male domination, they lost their ability to 'see' sexual abuse.[4]

This was the political context of the next sexual abuse crisis: thousands of girls exploited *outside* the family by networks of men; the girls were treated with disrespect not only by their exploiters but also by statutory services in towns and cities all over the country, from Rotherham and Rochdale, to Telford and Oxford.

Their ordeals had only been recognised by specialist community sexual health services, sponsored by the Labour government in the 1990s to target teenage pregnancies. Child sexual abuse was not on the political agenda, but sexual abuse was what these community workers perceived.

Between the mid-1990s and mid-2000s, in Rochdale in Greater Manchester, Sara Rowbotham, a youth sexual health specialist, referred more than 180 sexual exploitation cases to the police and social services, where they fell into a void.

Rowbotham later told MPs that the children were treated with 'absolute disrespect. … They were discriminated against. They were treated appallingly by protective services.'[5] A Greater Manchester review concluded that the girls had not been treated as victims and that the men weren't viewed as sex offenders, 'just men of all ages from one ethnicity taking advantage of kids…'. This was 'a depressingly familiar picture … in many other towns and cities across the country'.[6]

In the Yorkshire town of Rotherham in 2000, a Home Office-funded researcher on street prostitution, Adele Gladman, arrived for her first day at work with Risky Business, a sexual health outreach project working with vulnerable girls and women. The office was empty. Shocked staff arrived later: they had been visiting a pregnant girl in hospital. Her fate was a savage warning to hundreds of other abused girls: she had been taken to a car park by her 'boyfriend'/pimp who belonged to a network of men of Pakistani heritage who targeted vulnerable girls. She was stripped, beaten and raped. She was left bleeding and miscarried. Yet, she was not interviewed by the police, and the foetus (and therefore DNA) was not retained by investigators. It was as if she was just 'white trash' making her own choices: bad ones.

The police also regarded Risky Business not as a resource but as 'a nuisance'.[7] So, too, was Adele Gladman when in 2002 she presented a seminar on her prodigious research into hundreds of victims and the pimps' modus operandi to Rotherham's police, politicians and local authority officers. It was not welcomed, and did not inspire action – only malice.[8] Gladman's office was burgled, her computer hacked and her Home Office research data stripped out. It was assumed that everything had been lost. But it wasn't – she had been warned and had taken precautions.[9]

Between 2002 and 2007 South Yorkshire Police Drugs Strategy Unit researcher Angie Heal had discovered links between men distributing crack cocaine and trafficking in girls. This was 'really, really serious crime', she said, and the police should have felt a moral, if not a legal, duty to act.[10] They didn't. In 2006 Heal presented a report on violence, guns, sexual exploitation, prostitution and drugs. The official response changed from disinterest to dislike; in 2007 her Drugs Strategy Unit was disbanded, followed by the closure of Risky Business.[11]

Heal had reported that people of Pakistani heritage in Rotherham were as alive to the perpetrators' violence as their victims – Pakistani girls were also being raped and exploited. Schools and children's services had alerted the police and council that Asian drivers were collecting girls at children's homes and the school gates. This was all in vain. The excuse offered by South Yorkshire Police was that sexual exploitation did not feature in national policing targets.[12]

A serious case review into Oxfordshire, where an estimated 370 girls between 11 and 15 years old had been sexually exploited between 1998 and 2015, noted 'a professional mind-set which could not grasp that the victims' ability to say "no" – or even to speak at all about their experiences – had been totally eroded'.[13] These girls sometimes roused adults' worry, sometimes they broke practitioners' hearts, but they rarely attracted a strategy by the police or social services.

A campaign of rape against children

From bad to good

There were pioneering exceptions to this bleak chronicle: Derbyshire Police investigators had reason to feel proud after convictions in three trials of scores of offences against vulnerable girls in 2010. It began with serendipity, a chance arrest in 2008 of men in a car in Staffordshire with girls who were missing from a 'care home' in neighbouring Derbyshire. The men were released and their car was put under surveillance. A proactive investigation, Operation Retriever, led by Detective Superintendent Debbie Platt, identified Asian men cruising the streets, offering White girls a ride in a posh car and vodka.[14]

On 24 April 2009 two tearful teenagers stumbled out of a Derby flat that police were watching and called 999 to report they had been raped. They also identified other girls being abused; one victim led to another – and the total reached nearly 30. Operation Retriever worked proactively with victims, finding forensic evidence and plentiful corroboration. The experience led the city to a new, collegial approach to protection and prevention, and to community awareness-raising.[15]

Detective Superintendent Platt chose her words carefully: what they had uncovered seemed to be 'a campaign of rape against children'.[16]

From no problem to 700 victims

Northumbria Police didn't think there was a problem of organised sexual exploitation on Tyneside until a young woman's disclosures to a social worker in 2014 triggered what became a model multi-agency investigation. Operation Sanctuary was organised at the highest strategic level of the police, Gold Command, also involving social services and scores of local agencies, the CPS and the courts.

The victim was terrified. The perpetrators were terrifying. Before this, perpetrators had not been investigated, and the victims had been pressured or punished. This encouraged 'arrogant persistence' among the men, while the girls learned that 'nothing would be done' against perpetrators.[17]

Police officers told me that they contacted hotels and leisure 'hot spots', venues, food outlets and taxi drivers in the city of Newcastle and Tyneside generally, and together the agencies crafted novel, flexible approaches to hard-to-reach girls. They worked with the Black and Asian communities, particularly women's organisations, and learned that it was not only White girls who were at risk.[18]

Any and all services used by young people were flooded with publicity about sexual safety. It was resource-intensive, it was expensive – and it worked.

A serious case review into Operation Sanctuary by barrister David Spicer offered unprecedented praise: 'it is difficult to overstate the positive impact' on the city.[19] Together, the police and social services identified scores of perpetrators and about 700 victims across the county. The CPS mounted a series of successful criminal trials, all in front of the same judge. Seventeen men and one woman were convicted.[20]

These cases were unusual: they were a direct challenge to the Cleveland Report: the standout operations were jointly organised between police and social services, trespassing across the frontiers of family/non-family; they were not deterred by the victims who 'choose to not tell'; agencies brought empathy, tenacity and security to victims; they galvanised community knowledge, built cases and mobilised professional resources to match the power of the perpetrators. Although these operations were costly and exhausting, when they succeeded their communities were positively, albeit sometimes briefly, enlightened and proud.

David Spicer cautioned that Operation Sanctuary had revealed the limits and fallacies of the post-Cleveland system. And he was uniquely placed to know – his career had spanned the entire era. He had been Nottinghamshire's Chief Children's Legal Officer during and after the Cleveland Inquiry, he had been involved in the largest inquiry into extended family abuse at the time and he had conducted several serious case reviews. Newcastle was his last. Spicer's final recommendation in his serious case review was adamant: 'assume it is happening'. That was precisely what the Cleveland professionals had been *accused* of doing.

A new crime wave?

By the early 2000s feminist practitioners, scholars, rape crisis centres, specialist services in the voluntary sector, campaigning mothers and daughters, from the South-West to the North-East, had gathered intelligence on vast numbers of exploited girls and the men who were harming them. Some men operated alone, usually White, and others, some also White, operated in networks and often shared the same language and culture, typically men of Pakistani, Turkish, Kurdish, Afghani and Somali heritage. They ran taxi companies and food takeaways, they could access and provide mobility to girls, and sometimes they were engaged in other criminal activities, drugs and guns. As Heal had found in Yorkshire, the police seemed to be – inexplicably – uninterested.[21]

When some women running services to support the girls shared their information on perpetrators, they were sabotaged – the response to them revealed another flank of disrespect: they, too, were not regarded as *knowers* and their collective data and intelligence was not valued as real *knowledge*. Barnardo's ran several specialist services for girls, and by 2010 had published two reports on sexual exploitation. But the story of widespread sexual exploitation was not treated as a real story.[22] And victims were rarely valued as witnesses by the criminal justice system. It was only after a new chief prosecutor in the North-West, Nazir Afzal, read a report by *The Times* reporter Andrew Norfolk that he reversed the CPS decision not to prosecute, and in 2011 charged ten men in the Rotherham jurisdiction.[23] Cases were finally reaching the courts and the national media. But by then the women who had raised the alarm had all been forced out of their jobs.

Unusually, once this became national news, the Cleveland Report was *not* invoked as a caution. Here was an alluring alternative to the usual lexicon of 'false accusations', 'mass hysteria' and 'witch-hunts': here was a purportedly new crime wave by new folk devils.[24] It was proposed that *Muslim* men raping *White* girls and 'Asian grooming gangs' were being shielded by political correctness. The new template found form in Andrew Norfolk's report in *The Times*, 'Revealed: conspiracy of silence on UK sex gangs', on 5 January 2011. *The Times* mounted a campaign against 'Muslim grooming gangs' and 'political correctness' that supposedly placed ethnic and religious minorities 'beyond criticism'.[25] Norfolk's reports attracted accolades and awards for exposing a new crime threat.[26] *The Times* columnist David Aaronovitch, usually a child sexual abuse sceptic, proclaimed without hesitation: 'let's be honest, there's a clear link with Islam…'[27] What, though? Men, misogyny, religion generally?

Male power and disrespect of children

This narrative met a torrent of criticism by prosecutor Nazir Afzal, criminologists and specialists in child prostitution: Afzal argued that the key factor was not Islam, it was the men's control of the night-time economy and the fact that 'they are men … this is about male power'.[28] Whistle-blower Sara Rowbotham told the Parliamentary Home Affairs Select Committee in 2014: 'I seriously believe that protective services didn't not respond because it was an issue of ethnicity. That seriously was not the case.' Rather, she said, it was disrespect for the girls.[29]

Oxford linguistics professor Deborah Cameron noticed that the 'Muslims' ascription was 'more an ethnic label than a reference to any active religious observance'. By contrast, the White girls 'were never, to my knowledge, referred to as "Christians"'.[30] Barnardo's sexual exploitation expert Wendy Shepherd cautioned that perpetrators always used their community resources and solidarities: 'In the North and Midlands it may have been British Asians, in Devon it was White men, in Bath and Bristol Afro-Caribbeans, in London, all ethnicities – Iraqis, Kurds, Afghans, Somalis...' And they always capitalised on shared cultures, local businesses and venues.[31]

Professor Aisha Gill warned that the racialised crime threat eclipsed the patriarchal norms that sustain sexual violence across all cultures.[32] The Muslim Women's Network challenged the myth that these men 'only abuse outside of their own community, driven by hatred and contempt for White females'. This 'ignores the reality that sexual predators, regardless of their ethno-cultural or religious background, will target the most vulnerable and the most accessible children and young people'.[33]

Rotherham activist Zlakha Ahmed, founder of the Apna Haq resource centre for Black women, reported that Asian girls' needs were not met by services: of the hundreds of girls identified, 'about 100 were Pakistani, but only one contacted the authorities and there were no convictions'.[34]

Systemic failure to address child sexual abuse was being reframed, argued media expert Katie Elliott, as failure to confront the 'twisted dogma of multi-culturalism'.[35] So the problem was traduced as Muslim men and pinko political correctness. However, the alleged special impunity of Muslim men was not supported by the government's own figures. Black people have been many times more likely to be stopped and searched than White people for decades.[36]

In fact, Rotherham police showed no reluctance to arrest Pakistani men. In September 2015, after frequent demonstrations in the town by White far right groups headlining child abuse, and following the murder of an elderly Muslim man, a counter-demonstration was organised by anti-fascists. They were attacked by the far right Britain First, and after night raids by the police 12 Pakistani men were charged, all of whom were subsequently acquitted.[37]

The state's response: sexual abuse decriminalised

'Muslim gangs' raping White girls become a proxy for another national argument about race and religion and the state of the nation.[38] This seemed to be the argument the government itself wanted to have: England's children's commissioner's first report on mass sexual exploitation in 2012 provoked choleric protest in the office of Education Secretary of State Michael Gove: 'it is difficult to overstate the contempt the government has for the methodology and analysis'.[39]

Why? Apparently, the children's commissioner had not delivered on Muslim men and White girls or 'political correctness'; instead she had addressed the statutory services' abject responses to child sexual exploitation generally: only 6 per cent of safeguarding boards met government requirements; an alarming 16,500 children were estimated to be at risk.[40]

In 2014, Professor Alexis Jay's inquiry into Rotherham, the most notorious case, delivered a scorching critique of the statutory services' indolence, pessimism and sexism. Senior officers in the police and children's services had minimised the scale by simply cutting the numbers categorised as sexual exploitation. Jay calculated that there had been at least 1,400 known victims in Rotherham alone between 1997 and 2013, and a further unknown number of children at risk. Jay heard critics muttering that the figures were excessive. Not so, she said; she had checked *all* reports of victims of sexual exploitation to Rotherham agencies to arrive at her numbers. Even after she completed her study, the authorities could still not quantify the problem – a sign, she said, of their attitude. Jay was unforgiving about Rotherham's professional and political leaders: after specialist seminars in the early 2000s describing the phenomenon to them, 'nobody could say "we didn't know"'.[41]

Meanwhile, nationwide, sexual abuse within the family had vanished; it was 'unseen and unheard' and perpetrators were freed up to live with, contact or harass their victims. An Ofsted report published in 2020, *The Multi-Agency Response to Child Sexual Abuse in the Family*, could hardly have been more condemnatory: local or national strategies were lacking, social workers had lost confidence, case decision-making was led by the police, collegial challenge was absent, there was little engagement with health professionals, there was a failure to recognise 'signs and symptoms' of abuse and a lack of support for victims during investigations.[42]

This could have been written in the 1980s.

Child sexual abuse prosecutions in England and Wales more than halved between 2017 and 2021, from 6,394 to 3,025, and convictions dropped by 45 per cent, from 4,751 to 2,595. Cases took nearly two years to get to court.[43] So, nearly 30 years after the Cleveland and Pigot reports, institutional culture had assimilated little about the strategies of perpetrators or their victims' troubles, survival strategies and skills. Betsy Stanko concluded that rape and the sexual assault of children and vulnerable women had been 'effectively decriminalised'.[44]

This was the context of a perfect storm of a scandal that thundered into the English Establishment following the deaths of 'national treasures' in politics and show business: Liberal Party politician Sir Cyril Smith in 2010 and TV personality Sir Jimmy Savile in 2011. Only then were these 'knights of the realm' fully exposed as serial sexual predators who had targeted children in plain sight for decades.

Talk of their horrible behaviour had circled the highest echelons for years: Prime Minister Margaret Thatcher had commended both of these men for their knighthoods, despite Cabinet Office concerns about their sexual proclivities. They had been welcomed at Buckingham Palace, knelt on the red silk 'knighting stool' while they were tapped on the shoulder with George VI's 'knighting sword'.

Soon this crisis converged with other epiphanies: the Establishment and civil libertarian milieux were accused of sheltering VIPs in the Paedophile Information Exchange (PIE) in the 1980s; and evidence of historic abuse in North Wales children's homes was resurrected and recognised.[45] All these men used their social power and influence, class, culture, milieux and workplaces to access, abuse and control vulnerable boys and girls.

Jim 'fixed it'

On 3 October 2012 ITV broadcast a documentary, *Exposure*, in which several women described sexual abuse by Jimmy Savile, star talent at the BBC for decades. That was shocking enough, but worse, the BBC itself had had the story first and suppressed it – a *Newsnight* documentary by two of the BBC's most experienced journalists, Meirion Jones and Liz MacKean, had been blocked at the eleventh hour in 2011. It was made clear to Jones and MacKean that they had no future with the Corporation. They didn't go quietly, and the debacle over the suppression of the story provoked 'the biggest scandal in its history' to that date.[46]

Savile had always bragged about flocks of girls, with boasts, denials and threats at the same time, a feint that, according to his biographer Dan Davies, evidently protected him.[47] Celebrity gave him extraordinary access to hospitals, schools and prisons, including Broadmoor Hospital, a high-security psychiatric hospital, where he offered to help the government in their dispute with the powerful Prison Officers' Association by passing on information.[48] After his death the Metropolitan Police launched Operation Yewtree: within weeks Yewtree reported hundreds of alleged victims, the youngest an eight-year-old boy.[49]

An independent inquiry into the BBC's culture by Dame Janet Smith in 2012 found that Savile abused people of both sexes on BBC premises in London, Manchester and Leeds, in his own home and his campervan, from the 1960s onwards. Savile was protected by the revered status of 'the Talent' – the 'deference or even adulation' accorded to celebrity – and the 'macho' environment of light entertainment at the BBC.[50] What surprised her was that there had been few complaints, and none that yielded disciplinary action.

Labour MP Tom Watson upped the political ante in October 2012 when he rose to his feet in a crowded House of Commons and asked for an investigation into a suspected paedophile network 'linked to Parliament and Number Ten'.[51] In November 2012 the storm gathered force: Cyril Smith's successor, Rochdale's Labour MP Simon Danczuk, outed him in Parliament and demanded an independent inquiry.[52] For more than 40 years police officers, victims, journalists – and notably community radicals and their intrepid 1970s community publication, *Rochdale Alternative Paper* – had tried to call Smith to account (see Chapter 2).[53]

Now the PIE was tossed back into the political arena, and in 2014 Thatcher's former Home Secretary Leon Brittan was blown into the storm.[54] In 1983 Brittan had been given a dossier naming names by Tory MP Geoffrey Dickens, who urged him to ban PIE. There were long-standing rumours – unsubstantiated – that the Home Office had funded PIE. A lost and belatedly rediscovered note discovered in a Home Office file showed that Dickens had indeed sent Brittan a dossier and met him to discuss it.[55]

It was certainly the case that PIE had friends and members in high places. One of them was diplomat Sir Peter Hayman, a deputy director of MI6. When Hayman left a bundle of child pornography on a bus in 1978, it was handed to the police and the address guided them to his flat, where they found a large cache of child pornography and correspondence between several Establishment figures. This led to the arrest and trial of other offenders – but not Hayman. In 1980 Margaret Thatcher banned officials from naming him publicly as a PIE member.[56]

PIE treasurer Charles Napier, half-brother of John Whittingdale, a Conservative MP, had left the country to work for the British Council in Cairo, which, he boasted, was full of boys, '98 per cent of them available'.[57] Napier was undisturbed until he was arrested 20 years later, when Establishment culture was under scrutiny as never before.[58] The writer Francis Wheen, who had been assaulted by Napier at his public school, outed him in 2005, but it was only after Watson's speech that he was fully investigated. In 2014 Wheen gave evidence against him in court: Napier was jailed.[59]

MPs across the political spectrum were impatient: in 2014 a high-level cross-party parliamentary team, known as the 'Group of Seven', put pressure on the government to set up the public inquiry. Their interventions were spiced by old television footage, previously hardly noticed but now going viral: in a 1995 BBC documentary about the parliamentary Whip's Office, Tory chief whip Tim Fortescue described a 'black book' or 'dirt book' on politicians' misdemeanours:

> Anyone with any sense, who was in trouble, would come to the whips and tell them the truth, and say now, I'm in a jam, can you help? It might be debt, it might be … a scandal involving small boys, or any kind of scandal … they'd come and ask if we could help and

if we could, we did … we would store up brownie points … if we could get a chap out of trouble then, he will do as we ask forever more.[60]

The excuse that times and crimes had changed, that what was acceptable then would not be tolerated now, was refuted by an impeccable source: one of Margaret Thatcher's lieutenants and a colleague of Leon Brittan, Norman Tebbit. Asked whether there had been 'a big cover-up', he replied, 'there may well have been'. He wasn't talking about conspiracy; there was no need, it was systemic: 'it was almost unconscious', he said. At the time, 'I think most people would have thought that the Establishment, the system, was to be protected … it was more important to protect the system than to delve too far.'[61]

A tsunami of historic abuse allegations hit constabularies – with thousands of people contacting a police service that was already deemed scarcely competent to deal with already soaring reports of *current* sexual offences.[62]

Operation Midland, an inquiry into Brittan and several other public figures that got underway in 2014, proved calamitous for the reputation of the police: its investigation was inexperienced, incompetent and extravagant; it ignored independent specialists' cautions about the reliability of its prize witness, a hoaxer called Carl Beech; he had been promoted assiduously by the Exaro online news site. Operation Midland failed to follow basic police practice – check leads, allegations, events and timelines; it failed to find corroboration for outlandish claims, including murder. This mess obscured the successes of the other historic abuse investigations: the police Operation Hydrant historic abuse hub identified about 7,000 suspects. Many had died, but of 11,346 allegations, 4,024 resulted in convictions – 35 per cent led to guilty verdicts – much higher than the current conviction rate of 7 per cent.[63]

But for some commentators, the gush of allegations about VIPs – usually deemed credible, sometimes questionable, muddled or mad – was altogether too much, and they called up old shibboleths to service their scepticism:

in Cleveland, alongside real abusers completely innocent people were deprived of their children on the basis of a faulty diagnosis of a paediatrician and a social worker. Not long afterwards there was panic on Orkney and in cities such as Rochdale and Nottingham ... the unattractive (because complicating) truth is that sometimes people do lie about being abused. When it all collapsed, as it had to ... what was left was the continuous problem of the zealous imposing new histories on the impressionable.[64]

The hysteria, the prurience, the general shrieking that surrounds discussions of sexual conduct.[65]

[The diagnostic test in Cleveland] ... proved, as fail-safe diagnoses always will, deeply flawed.[66]

The so-called satanic abuse cases of Cleveland and Orkney ... [children] were actually manipulated by professionals with a doctrinal attachment to lurid and fashionable theories.[67]

[The persistence of allegations] into the twenty-first century repeats the questions that I thought I had answered at the end of the twentieth! This is, first: how is it that 'victims' can tell stories of gruesome experiences that they never had? Secondly: how is it that adults, many of them sensible, educated people, believe these stories? These two questions are also raised by the cases of so-called 'historic abuse'.[68]

The Cleveland Inquiry never said that the diagnosis was 'faulty' or 'deeply flawed'. Children's 'lies' were not the issue in Cleveland. These habitual recitals exemplified Jenny Kitzinger's critique of so much child abuse coverage in the aftermath of Cleveland: writers and readers were relieved of the effort of thinking and conclusions were reached 'with the minimum of analysis'.[69] The myth was never far from the sceptics' keyboards.

12

National inquiries, national identities

At the beginning of the 21st century child sexual abuse was recognised as an atrocity that roused an unprecedented global wave of accounting for children. There were national inquiries from Iceland to Poland and South Africa, crossing jurisdictional borders into war zones, international armed forces and aid agencies, not least United Nations peacekeepers.[1] Any place with children could be a place where children had been and would be raped. These inquiries enabled private grief and shame to become matters of public concern.[2]

The Republic of Ireland and Australia are considered here as a prelude to – and ultimately a model for – the UK's catharsis because they sponsored two of the widest and deepest excavations of children's sexual oppression inscribed in national institutions and identities.

Ireland and the 'enemy within'

The Republic of Ireland is the only state in the world where sexual crimes against children, specifically by Christian priests, felled a government.

In November 1994 Taoiseach Albert Reynolds resigned because his Attorney General, Harry Whelehan, had failed to extradite a prolific offender, Father Brendan Smyth.[3] It was a dangerous conjuncture: Reynolds had been a tenacious and creative proponent of a political solution to the Northern Ireland armed conflict. Now the peace process lost one of the architects of a settlement at the very moment when it was closer than it had ever been.

Yet the significance of the Smyth case could not be overstated: it was a watershed, it put 'a face to the dark, faceless knowledge that has clung to Irish childhood for generations', wrote *Irish Times* journalist Fintan O'Toole. The Catholic Church ran the schools where 'the risk of being molested was taken for granted'.[4] For generations the Church had protected abusive priests – rather than their victims – under the shield of canon law. In the 1980s several constitutional referendums secured the Vatican's sovereignty over the country's sexual life, but they also had another effect, spinning bodies, abuse and the pain of children and women into vision. Finally, a year after Reynolds fell on his sword, in 1995, with great reluctance, the Catholic Church agreed to submit to the law of the land.[5] By the end of the decade, an RTE television series, *States of Fear*, by the investigative journalist Mary Raftery, documented the cruelty of Church-run 'industrial schools',[6] dubbed the 'Irish gulag'.[7] The series caused a maelstrom of shock, and in May 1999 the government offered a 'long-overdue apology' to the victims of childhood abuse 'for our collective failure to intervene, to detect their pain, to come to their rescue'.

In 2000 the government launched the Commission to Inquire into Child Abuse, known as the Ryan Commission,[8] which promoted a decade of national self-discovery. Its five-volume report described childhoods from hell. It 'wasn't child abuse', commented the writer Pauline Conroy, 'it was torture and hatred'.[9] The commission had created secure, private spaces in which people might talk about being kicked, scalded, punched and raped. Many of the survivors had lost their parents, and then their identity, lamented the report; they didn't know who they were.

In 2011, provoked by yet another report into past and current sexual abuse by priests,[10] Taoiseach Enda Kenny did the unthinkable: he condemned the Vatican. In an exceptional speech in Dáil Éireann (Ireland's parliament) on 20 July he said that the report unearthed 'the dysfunction, disconnection, elitism, the narcissism that dominate the culture of the Vatican to this day'. The Church had refused to honour the promise to abide by the secular law of the state, and now, 'For the first time in this country, a report into child sexual abuse exposes an attempt by the Holy See to frustrate an inquiry in a sovereign, democratic republic.' Incredibly, Ireland closed its embassy at the Holy See.

However, the state was also implicated, he said: the public care of children had been franchised out to the Church and bankrolled by the state. These institutions' deeds had constituted 'arguably the gravest and most systemic human rights violations in the history of this State'.[11] Indeed, they were also the history of the state.

No one would have imagined in 1994 that inquiries into the sexual oppression of children would ignite a cultural and constitutional revolution.

Australia condemns the cardinal

Around the time that Hollywood's Academy Awards ceremony in 2016 honoured the film *Spotlight* about the *Boston Globe*'s exposure of sexual abuse and cover-up in the Catholic Church, Cardinal George Pell was sitting in Rome's Hotel Quirinale giving evidence about his knowledge of child sexual abuse in the Church to Australia's Royal Commission into Institutional Responses to Child Sexual Abuse sitting in Sydney.[12]

This was a poignant moment for journalist Joanne McCarthy: her classic regional reportage – for which she was rewarded with Australia's highest award for journalism – exemplified the necessary synergy between survivors, practitioners, police and journalists that translated 'private' heartache into public and politically radical narratives. That movement prompted Australia's premier Julia Gillard to create the Royal Commission into Institutional Responses to Child Sexual Abuse in 2012, and now the commission straddled two time zones to talk to Cardinal Pell.

Reckoned to be the third highest-ranking official in the Vatican, Cardinal Pell declined to leave Rome. The commission insisted that the cardinal answer to it somewhere, somehow. We'll come to you, said the commission; we'll talk virtually or in person, but you *will* talk to us. Across a video link for several days, Cardinal Pell was forced to address allegations spanning half a century.[13] In 2017 he became the highest-ranking priest in the world to be charged with child sexual abuse. He was convicted. After a year in prison, however, he was acquitted on a technicality.[14]

McCarthy's investigations had begun in 2006 with a priest convicted of sex offences who still had access to children. She had called him, listened to his denial and when he asked if she was 'going to write something?', she replied, 'Of course.' He told her, 'I hope you have a good lawyer.' This was the first of many such conversations, beginning with sharp intakes of breath, silences and 'I'll get back to you…'. She worked with survivors and a police whistle-blower. 'I just kept going', she told me, and people kept calling her, 'women sobbing, businessmen sobbing…'. Their stories changed her: 'my starting point was the Catholic Church, now it is men – the whole thing is about men, the institutions set up by men, all about male power'.

One night in 2012 she woke in the small hours: one of her contacts had killed himself. He left a note: 'too much pain'. That was it: in grief she was inspired to demand a royal commission. Her paper launched a campaign, and in November 2013 Australia's prime minister Julia Gillard announced a Royal Commission into Institutional Responses to Child Sexual Abuse that would be allocated abundant resources and a wide mandate to reach everywhere. Like the Ryan Commission, it delved into the heart and soul of Australian society and state.

Every public hearing was followed by more people calling with something to say. Cardinal Pell 'became a lightning conductor', an Inquiry insider told me. 'People told the commissioners "You know, I was going to take this to my grave and then I saw that fella…" Pell was so inflammatory.'[15]

It consulted more than a million documents and commissioned surveys and copious research by psychologists, historians, theologians, sociologists and scientists. It also adapted the Irish commission's model of private as well as public hearings that allowed thousands of people with little or no entrée to the 'public sphere' to become participants, to access the means of translating private suffering into social knowledge.[16] Criminologist Michael Salter describes it as a case study of public inquiries as 'transitional space', a place to 'bridge the gap between private suffering and public understanding', a mechanism for the 'co-construction of knowledge between survivors, commissioners and experts'. Its importance should not be underestimated.[17]

In a seemingly dry phrase, the commission's final report concluded that the country's trusted institutions had '*contributed* to the abuse of children'. This went beyond indifference or incompetence to *culpability* for 'a national tragedy'.[18] When it announced its recommendations in 2017, the commission was adamant – despite unyielding opposition by the Church – in its affirmation of a *mandatory* duty to respond to suspected abuse. People in any institutions, not only the Catholic Church, who do not act but 'knows or suspects ... or should have suspected' sexual abuse should face criminal charges.[19]

It transcended the formal discourse of commissions of inquiry whose legitimacy derived from the authority of the authors by giving the last word to the survivors: its final act was to present a memorial to the National Library, a book containing a 'Message to Australia' from more than 1,000 witnesses. One of them said, 'In 1978 a little boy started crying ... he still is.'[20] Thus was a man's personal sorrow memorialised as both social knowledge and public protest.

Back to the future in England

An independent panel of inquiry was announced by UK Home Secretary Theresa May in 2014 to assess how the various institutions had managed their duty of care to children. But the government had not learned the lessons of these two national catharses, and instead of calming the storm, it was cursed by a new tempest: instinctively the government had grabbed a grandee to lead it, Elizabeth Butler-Sloss. She was in her 80s, she was healthy and a safe pair of hands. But the survivors' movements that had campaigned for the Inquiry didn't want safe; they wanted the best, a seeker-after-truth to investigate the Establishment. But Butler-Sloss embodied the Establishment. Furthermore, the very *raison d'être* of the Independent Inquiry into Child Sexual Abuse (IICSA) was, in effect, a rebuke to her Cleveland Report: the survivors' movements that had campaigned for an *empowered* inquiry were the generation that had been sacrificed by the blind eye the Cleveland Inquiry had turned towards the institutions warehousing children – not all of the Cleveland children were living at home with their families; some were in care or in residential schools. Unlike the Irish and Australian commissions, the Cleveland Inquiry could be seen as a classic case of what the legal scholar Angela Hegarty describes vividly 'such processes ... give legal cover to governments ... while constructing an official version or "memory" that denies the original abuse'.[21] That was anathema to the survivors' movements. The government, however, did not appear to understand who they were dealing with, their stamina, or what they wanted. They weren't children; these victims were adults. Some had talked to the police, some to therapists; some spoke through their behaviour, bad sometimes; some were very unwell; some self-soothed through drink or drugs; others were heroic, ran support services, became champions of other victims, well-informed advocates and investigators, exemplified by Nigel O'Mara; some were cussed; some were strategic and made alliances. Their secret weapons were legal aid, access to lawyers and to knowledge and the Freedom of Information Act. Social media transformed their means of communication – across the UK, around the world, with each other, with reporters and politicians. Above all, they would not shut up.

Apparently, the government had no historical memory of the Cleveland events, but it should have known that Butler-Sloss was compromised: she would be investigating her own brother Sir Michael Havers, Margaret Thatcher's Attorney General, who had been accused of a cover-up in the 1980s. He had defended the decision not to prosecute Peter Hayman, had warned Conservative MP Geoffrey Dickens not to name him in Parliament as a member of the Paedophile Information Exchange (PIE); and when the spy Geoffrey Prime was convicted of several counts of espionage and sex offences against children, Havers had supported the suppression of Prime's membership of PIE, to spare the security services' embarrassment.[22]

Butler-Sloss would have to investigate abuse in the Church of England. However, she had already been criticised for her review of Chichester Cathedral and was now accused of misrepresenting a major witness, Phil Johnson, who had been abused while he was a choir boy and was chair of Minister and Clergy Sexual Abuse Survivors, a major participant in the pressure for an inquiry. Butler-Sloss claimed that *he* had chosen not to name Bishop Peter

Ball in her Chichester report. 'Oh no', said Johnson, who released an audio recording of a conversation between them, confirming that it was *she* who had wanted Ball's name kept out.[23] On 14 July, less than a week after her appointment, Butler-Sloss had to quit.

In September 2014 the government reached for another grandee, this time someone with nothing about sexual abuse on her CV: Fiona Woolf was a corporate lawyer. But after admitting that she sometimes dined with her neighbour Leon Brittan – a person of interest to the inquiry – she, too, was doomed. She resigned in October, to the chagrin of the Establishment's defenders who regarded her as the victim of a 'kangaroo court' and 'our weird current public culture'.[24]

So the Home Office looked far away for someone who would not be compromised by Establishment connections. In February 2015 it appointed Lowell Goddard, a New Zealand lawyer, about whom it knew little.[25] The Home Office also agreed to give the inquiry significantly more power to compel sworn testimony and examine classified information. During her tenure she was accused of bullying and racist remarks, and after being confronted by her panel of expert colleagues, she, too, quit.[26]

The inquiry was collapsing and the Establishment didn't know how to save it. The corridors of Westminster bristled with complaint; in the House of Lords I recall peers grumbling, 'you can't have survivors dictating...'. *Telegraph* journalist Charles Moore whined that 'our Establishment is running scared', that it should never have caved in: the inquiry (of which he did not approve) needed members of the Establishment to run it, because they know how to run things and they know the people who run things.[27]

But the Establishment didn't know how to run this. Into the breach walked Alexis Jay, a member of its expert panel, a Scot, a social work academic and Scottish government adviser. She was eminent but absolutely not Establishment. If she didn't step up, would the Inquiry survive?[28]

Staff were exasperated by the mess, by the clunkiness of the Home Office infrastructure, worried that the inquiry would be hobbled by a dependence on the Home Office – of course the Home Office was implicated – and by the severe reputational damage of an allegation of sexual harassment within the inquiry itself.[29] Some survivors' groups withdrew their support in despair. But it endured.

In October 2017, after the omnishambles, the lights went up on the inquiry's first public hearings and began into its profoundly radical remit: the sexual abuse of children in institutions that had persisted despite – or perhaps because of – everything.

After the Cleveland Inquiry, the lid of Pandora's box had been slammed on a generation of children: some didn't make it, but some who did got organised – they had questions, they wanted answers and they wanted recognition and redress. They wanted from IICSA everything, in short, that had not been addressed in the Cleveland Report in 1988.

The UK Establishment's manoeuvres and muddle confirmed what the Irish and Australian inquiries had revealed: that child sexual abuse is embedded in the very stones of the state and national institutions and identity.

To make its brief manageable, the inquiry selected a dozen modules, ranging from VIPs and Westminster, to local government, churches, schools and children's homes. The cases that follow are a small selection that exemplify institutional corruption and dereliction in churches, political parties, policing and national and local government.

Rochdale: a lesson not learned

On the morning of 12 October 2017, a slim man in his early 70s, with white hair and wearing a casual cotton jacket, ambled into a long, low-ceilinged room, a rather blank space that could have been a hospital waiting room. That was the setting for IICSA's public hearings. This was a historic day. The man was David Bartlett, who with his friend John Walker had co-edited the *Rochdale Alternative Paper* (*RAP*), a community paper that 38 years earlier had done what no national newspaper had dared to do: expose the cruelties and corruptions of Cyril Smith.

The space filled with lawyers and their bundles of papers, and finally the panel: Alexis Jay, its chairperson, Ivor Frank, a barrister who had himself been brought up in care, Sir Malcolm Evans, professor of international law, and Drusilla Sharpling, a barrister and, since 2009, HM Inspector of Constabulary.

Avid reporters were familiar with the name but not the man. They watched Bartlett on the live stream on a large screen. He explained to the inquiry that in the 1970s he was a sociology lecturer, and together with fellow-lecturer Walker he had set up *RAP* in the spirit of the community journalism movement – to give a voice to 'people who didn't normally have a voice in public'. *RAP* was published from their homes. It cost 3p and its mission was 'to upset the Establishment and challenge the powerful', he explained. 'I'm still proud of that,' he added.[30]

When Cyril Smith stood as the Liberal Party parliamentary candidate, he projected himself as 'Smith the man' – and *RAP*'s riposte was a two-page spread: 'The strange case of Smith the man.' It focused on two themes: Smith's paid advocacy for Turner & Newall, an asbestos conglomerate that suppressed information about asbestos as a cause of cancer, and the sexual abuse of boys.

Although they were 'amateurs', this was bravura reportage. Bartlett expected Smith to be litigious, and encouraged his victims whose evidence appeared in the spread to sign affidavits, to protect themselves and the paper. He had interviewed staff in boys' hostels, controlled by Smith, officials from probation to education, police who had investigated Smith, and journalists in the national media, from the *Telegraph* to the *Sun*, and notably *Private Eye*.

A Lancashire Police file had been submitted to the Director of Public Prosecutions (DPP) advancing a strong case for prosecution. But within days the DPP told the police and Smith himself that there would be 'no further action'. *RAP* invited Smith to comment. He didn't respond. Bartlett told the inquiry that *RAP* asked the head of the DPP, Sir Norman Skelhorn, about that Lancashire Police file. The DPP said it could not 'confirm or deny receiving it', so *RAP* wrote to Skelhorn at his club, the Athenaeum. Someone then telephoned Bartlett 'claiming to be Sir Norman on holiday and from a coin-box saying he could remember nothing about such a case'.

Bartlett said that he had consulted journalists in the national media about Cyril Smith. They had information on him but, as a *Daily Mirror* reporter told him, they were all afraid of a libel threat and so they were 'waiting for him to die'. Only *Private Eye*'s investigative reporter Paul Foot dared to run *RAP*'s story.[31]

'We were very careful with everything we wrote', Bartlett told the inquiry, 'because both John and I stood – and our wives stood – to lose our homes if we were wrong'. He believed that the boys, whose stories they were telling, were worth it: they 'should not have been left with the indelible mark of their experiences at the hands of Smith', he said.

The exposé didn't make any difference: in the 1979 General Election Smith was sent to Parliament with an increased majority. 'That was depressing', commented Bartlett, looking back. Maybe it was no surprise to the town – the story had been circulating 'in most tap rooms of the town for a very long time', he said, and now that it was in print, people just 'shrugged their shoulders'. Shoulders went on being shrugged for the next three decades.

That was all Bartlett had to say. Throughout his testimony reporters exchanged fascinated glances with each other across their mobile phones and laptops; they had witnessed a 'quiet hero'. 'What a star!' beamed one of the television reporters.

The inquiry learned that Smith's political profile seemed to create both more scrutiny *and* more immunity. It was told that Smith was under the eye of MI5 – his name was 'not news' to police officers working in the 1970s and 1980s in London's West End, particularly around the Piccadilly 'meat rack' where men picked up boys. Talk of Smith and 'rent boys' was widespread; several officers told the inquiry, but when one of them recommended Smith's arrest the operation was closed down. They were told this was 'far too political and they were to stop', they said. In fact, in the 1980s, said Holmes, officers were warned that any surveillance operation that caught VIPs would be shut down.[32]

Untruthful denial

Bartlett's evidence about the DPP episode, the coin-box telephone call and the ambiguous denials led the inquiry to gentlemen's clubs, state secrets and Downing Street. The CPS, the successor to the DPP, was asked by the Inquiry to explain the mystery of the missing Lancashire Police file. The answer was supplied by MI5: yes, the police file on Smith *did* exist, MI5 had been told about it by Skelhorn's successor, Sir Thomas Hetherington, and the DPP had 'untruthfully' denied it.[33]

There was another conundrum: Lancashire Police had delivered the file to the DPP on Friday 13 March 1970, receipt was acknowledged on Monday 16 March and on 19 March the DPP replied: 'No further action'. Laura Hoyano QC, representing Smith's victims, asked the DPP why the whole thing took only three days. The DPP was unable to explain. Witnesses described Smith's obsessive fretting about the police investigation. He had told the police that he could not seek selection as a parliamentary candidate unless and until he was cleared. Yet 'before the police file had even been submitted to the DPP' he stood anyway, said Hoyano, and was duly selected, which 'had serious consequences for the case in later years'.[34]

At a later IICSA hearing in March 2019, former Liberal Party leader David Steel astonished everyone when he explained that following the *RAP* report and the *Private Eye* follow-up, Steel went to Rochdale to 'check out' Smith. Smith 'accepted the story was correct', Steel told the inquiry. 'Obviously, I disapproved but as far as I was concerned it was past history.' But might not Smith 'still be offending against children', he was asked. 'I have to admit, that never occurred to me and I am not sure it would occur to me even today.' Steel went on: 'I must say I am a bit concerned about the unqualified way in which you cannot libel the dead. The dead have got relatives and friends, and I think it is rather scandalous the way some of the things have been said about people who are not around to answer.' Steel said he had always regarded the reports in the *RAP* and *Private Eye* as 'scurrilous' and 'tittle tattle'.[35]

The verdict of IICSA was unyielding: 'Lord Steel should have provided leadership. Instead, he abdicated his responsibility. He looked at Cyril Smith not through the lens of child protection but through the lens of political expediency.'[36]

Steel had been wrong. Smith's activities were not past history; he was arrested again in 1981 and was released following intervention from the security services. Lancashire Police were worried they would be blamed for a cover-up. 'That is precisely what did in fact happen', concluded the inquiry.[37]

Smith had been involved in Knowl View School, a special residential school for children with behavioural problems, since the 1960s. There had been allegations by the boys that he had sexually abused children there, that the boys – some as young as 11, some in care – were known to be exploited by men using nearby Smith Street toilets, a notorious 'cottage', and that a known sex offender was allowed to frequent the school where he abused children. It was estimated that a quarter of the boys at the school had been sexually abused. Yet the inquiry heard that Smith 'maintained an inexorable rise in political life' and received royal honours, 'even though those involved in facilitating his rise knew of the police investigations'.[38]

Why would the Liberal Party want such a candidate as Cyril Smith? And why did Margaret Thatcher want him to have a knighthood? The Public Honours Scrutiny Committee had considered everything: the 1970 police investigation, the DPP's response, the *RAP* report and the *Private Eye* follow-up, all of which was passed on to Margaret Thatcher. Little did Bartlett and Walker know that Sir Robin Butler, head of the Civil Service, would put their paper in front of the prime minister.

Scared shitless

Meanwhile, Hoyano told the inquiry, children languished in squalid conditions in the boys' hostels controlled by Smith, 'lonely and lost', while Smith was protected by 'corporate lassitude'.[39]

One of the men who had told his story to Bartlett in 1979 now appeared as IICSA witness 'A4'.[40]

He had gone to live at Cambridge House, one of Smith's hostels for working boys. Within a couple of days Smith took him into a room, told him to take his trousers off and began touching him: 'I was 15 years old, I was scared shitless.' A4 met Bartlett at a youth club he ran, told him what Smith was up to and became one of the boys who signed an affidavit. The police contacted him about Cyril Smith in the 1990s and he told his story again. Nothing happened. When A4 heard that Simon Danczuk was writing a book, he contacted him. He received no reply. IICSA was his last chance. 'I think you'll find I've not changed anything, I'm still saying the same thing,' he said. 'I'm happy to confirm that,' replied Counsel to the Inquiry Brian Altman QC. Before A4 left the room, Jay faced him. 'I'd like to thank you very much on behalf of the panel. We are very grateful for your contribution to the inquiry,' she said. He replied, unforgettably, 'Right. Thank you. Thank you very much. Thank you very much for listening.' Like the other witnesses, this man had offered a pared-down, modest, yet stinging disclosure with courteous indignation.[41]

Hoyano reminded the inquiry that two witnesses had been too unwell to give evidence in person:

> such was the determination of two others to testify that they overcame formidable obstacles: one who is facing back surgery refused to take, against my advice, his regular dose of morphine because he was afraid that it would affect the clarity of his recall and his account; another had not been downstairs in his own home for 18 months, but insisted on being stretchered down a narrow staircase by ambulance crews to his GP's surgery so that he could access Wi-Fi in order to testify. We are grateful.[42]

Wrapping up the case for Rochdale Council on 27 October 2017, Steven Ford QC suggested: 'The death of Cyril Smith in September 2010 marked the beginning of a period of greater public awareness about childhood sexual abuse and the damage that it can cause.' *Beginning*? Had he listened to Bartlett and witness A4? Had he forgotten the Cleveland controversy 30 years earlier?

By the end of the 1980s, the Cleveland chill effect and the backlash, I suggest, had serious impact on Rochdale's readiness to investigate and intervene. This followed the 'damning' verdict on workers in the Middleton case by Mr Justice Brown in the High Court on 7 March 1991. The IICSA panel had been 'perplexed' by the appointment of psychologist Dr Valerie Mellor to assess pupils' safety at Knowl View. She was not an education expert, but she had been an important critic of interviews carried out in the case involving several households in Middleton, known as the Rochdale case.[43] Appointing Mellor may have been 'a defensive reaction, in other words, one by which no one could criticise Rochdale if it brought on board the very expert whose opinion had been used to devastating effect in the Middleton case'. Mellor had decided not to interview the Knowl View pupils. The Inquiry panel disagreed – she should have talked to the children. Ultimately, 'complacency if not complicity' prevailed at Knowl View, and although exploitation of the boys in adjacent Smith Street toilets was widely known, 'no one in authority regarded this as an urgent child protection issue'.[44]

Following his disastrous evidence to the inquiry, Lord Steel faced calls for his expulsion from the Liberal Democrats and chose to resign and also retire from the House of Lords.[45] The verdict of IICSA was unyielding: 'Lord Steel should have provided leadership. Instead, he abdicated his responsibility. He looked at Cyril Smith not through the lens of child protection but through the lens of political expediency.'[46]

The behaviour of Rochdale officials left the inquiry 'incredulous': sexual abuse of children in care 'was treated as if it was normal'.[47] Despite robust police investigations, Smith used his prominence and standing in Rochdale 'to exert influence on others locally – in particular to put pressure on them to keep quiet'.

After the Cleveland Report and the Middleton case, senior staff told the inquiry there was 'pressure not to over-react'; managers were encouraged 'to keep a low profile', and Rochdale was transformed 'from being an interventionist authority to one that made it very difficult to get children into care'. The inquiry's report on Smith was scathing: his knighthood had been promoted in 1988 when 'it is clear that there were some frank discussions at the highest political level about the rumours in circulation about him, with no obvious concern for alleged victims'.[48]

Nottinghamshire: 'so many lives could have been saved'

In Nottinghamshire, police chiefs had been estranged from the county's social services during and after the Broxtowe case (see Chapter 6) and the backlash then precipitated deeper rifts, chaos and loss of professional confidence. In the space of 18 months 18 children had been killed by their carers – a normal rate of one or two children a year had flown to one or two a month by 1993.[49] Things were going terribly wrong.

In 1989 staff at the county's notorious Beechwood children's home 'were in a state of desperation' and pleaded for urgent attention to the 'horrifying' and 'atrocious' conditions there. In 1985, for example, there had been 400 incidents of children absconding. Yet, during nearly 40 years of Beechwood's existence, noted the inquiry, there had been 'only two recorded instances of an institutional response to allegations of sexual abuse made against staff'. The place was managed by 'autocracy and intimidation', and elected councillors, who were technically responsible for the children's well-being, were 'next to useless'.[50] Staff running the children's homes were usually untrained, often men from a military background, and managers tended to treat allegations not as a category of child protection but as personnel and employment matters.

This was the background to a remarkable mea culpa in the IICSA Nottinghamshire hearings: Director of Social Services David White had signed off a report on a 14-year-old girl from Beechwood that said she had 'many sexual relationships' with a 'number of boys', she was 'a willing participant or the instigator' and 'at no time' had it been 'against her will'. Streetwise children were 'not receptive to guidance or instruction'. The report did not analyse the question of 'consent', the power differential power between children and adults, between boys and girls. White was deeply chastened: 'I am shocked and appalled at what I have read.' He was 'flabbergasted' by the failure to recognise the crisis in the children's homes and the sheer scale of sexual abuse as 'a systemic problem'.[51]

One of the significant events in any public inquiry is the moment when the powerful are offered the opportunity to take responsibility and they take it. This was one of those moments.

When the IICSA was created, Nottinghamshire Police Commissioner Paddy Tipping invited the inquiry to probe the history of Nottinghamshire Police. The inquiry heard that there had been 'a long-standing reluctance to work jointly with the local authority in investigations'. After post-Savile reviews of all constabularies, Her Majesty's Inspectorate of Constabulary declared Nottinghamshire to still be 'unsatisfactory'; a second inspection was not reassured.[52]

Why had it all gone so wrong in a county where the professionals in the Broxtowe case had been commended by the prime minister? The work of the social services team in the Broxtowe case had been 'fabulous', he told the inquiry.[53]

So why were its lessons squandered? Why were children in families regarded as 'victims' while those in children's homes were 'trouble'? And why was policing so 'unsatisfactory'? The IICSA report did not have an answer: between the 1960s and the 2000s, it concluded, 'Despite decades of evidence and many reviews showing what needed to change', neither the city nor county councils 'learned from their mistakes'.[54] It could have added that they didn't learn from their successes either.

Nottinghamshire had featured strongly in the work of Survivors UK, the first service to support boys and men living with sexual abuse and prostitution. It had been launched by gay men in 1986, but they noticed – as did women's rape crisis services – that a significant number of adult men were talking about childhood abuse. One of its founders, Nigel O'Mara (see Chapter 8), recalled that 20 per cent of their clients came from around the East Midlands – Nottinghamshire and Leicestershire – and many of them had been in children's homes.[55]

O'Mara became a core participant in the inquiry's *Accountability and Reparations Investigation Report*. After the scandal over Jimmy Savile broke, he tells me, he recalled those young men. As he talks, O'Mara catches his breath, he can't speak for a moment or two, and tears drip down his pale, tired face. It is 30 years after those events and still this veteran of helplines and support services is wracked. He goes on:

> 'If someone was under 18 and running away, I'd have to advise them not to go to the police because they'd just be sent back – that's a horrible thing to have to do. I couldn't conceive of sending someone back to their abuser. They wouldn't get justice, they wouldn't get support. It was catch-22. There was no form of support anywhere. All we could do was talk.'

Rape and abuse, of himself and of hundreds of young men with similar life stories, he explained, 'affected me all of my life. It changes the way you feel about the world. If this had been taken seriously then, in the 1980s and in the Cleveland Inquiry, so many lives would have been saved.'[56]

The Church of England

For the first time the scale of the Establishment's protection of bishops and clergy was laid bare, from the testimony of Archbishop of Canterbury George Carey to his successor, Justin Welby.[57] IICSA demanded that these VIPs explain themselves. Welby was asked what he had learned from the victims who had given evidence. He paused, and said, 'I have learned again to be ashamed of the Church. ... I don't know how to express it adequately, how appalled I am and how ashamed I am of what the Church did to those survivors.'

He warned that those who harmed children should better have a millstone round their neck and be thrown into the sea 'than face the judgement that God will give them'. When Welby gave evidence on 21 March 2018 he accepted that the Church of England had 'colluded and concealed' the offences of Bishop Peter Ball.[58] This was an extraordinary admission about the Church – the soul of the Establishment, whose bishops are recommended by the Crown Nominations Commission, via the prime minister, and who sit on the government's side in House of Lords, close to the throne.

For 400 years in England, sedition and sexual abuse were the only crimes that led Anglican bishops to be detained at Her – or His – Majesty's pleasure. In 1688 King James II locked up seven bishops in the Tower of London for declining to proclaim his Declaration for the Liberty of Conscience. It was a fate that befell no English bishop until 2015, when Bishop Peter Ball was finally imprisoned for sexual abuse and misconduct in public office.[59]

James II's audacity had been his undoing – he had provoked a constitutional crisis and he was forced to flee by the Glorious Revolution of 1688. There was no constitutional crisis after Ball's conviction and imprisonment: no heads rolled; no one was exiled.

It was too late for one of Ball's most tenacious accusers, Neil Todd, a vulnerable teenager who aspired to be a priest. In 2012 he killed himself, 20 years after he had first reported Bishop Ball's harassment, ritualistic sexual rapacity and violence, and pleaded for Ball to be stopped. 'The story of Peter Ball is the story of the Establishment at work in modern times,' barrister William Chapman QC told the inquiry in July 2018. It could also be described as a case study of the Cleveland effect: the Church was not the family; the police had no obligation to engage social services, and in the cruel absence of pastoral care by the Church, 'victims and survivors' – in contrast to the accused – were castaways, 'dismissed or disbelieved' and even 'stigmatized' by those in authority.[60]

In the 1960s Ball had improvised a creed that required abject sexual surrender as spiritual observance. Although the early 1990s was a time of dramatic discoveries about religious cults and ritual abuse in popular culture, Ball's system was disaggregated into individual acts, rather than a regime that bent the victims' faith to his credo and his power. Ball was hailed by the Church as a great persuader, a recruiter to the faith and a model of saintly proselytising possessed of 'winning ways' with boys. By the 1980s he was Bishop of Lewes, and senior clergymen were already alive to 'Ball's boys' and sexual sadism as 'part of the austere regime of devotion and religious teachings'.[61] The Church's hostility to homosexuality left the boys trapped, with no safe place to confide.

In 1991 Ball was promoted to be Bishop of Gloucester with the support of Thatcher's successor, John Major; his ordination was attended by the Prince of Wales.[62]

In December 1992 one of the 'Bishop's boys', Neil Todd, tried to alert the Church, to no avail. When Ball's housekeeper and gardener, Mr and Mrs Moss, were about to go away on holiday, Todd told them he was terrified, so they took him away with them. They visited Lambeth Palace to alert the archbishop. Nothing was done. They told another bishop, and another. Nothing was done. After all efforts to engage the Church had failed, Todd's parents went to the police, and then there was an investigation. Lambeth Palace, by now well aware of the scandal hurtling towards it, fortified its defences. Archbishop Carey refused to take action against Ball – he didn't like being told what to do, he told the inquiry in 2018. He issued a public statement proclaiming instead Ball's 'outstanding pastoral work', and reassured him: 'be encouraged and do not lose heart'.[63]

After a chorus of letters followed from 'the great and the good', including the Prince of Wales, the archbishop and a judge, the DPP was persuaded to merely issue a caution: Ball had to resign. 'Almost as soon as the ink was dry upon Peter Ball's resignation,' he began a campaign for Archbishop Carey to exonerate him and restore him to ministry. 'This campaign continued, with frequent letters and conversations with senior staff at Lambeth Palace, for over 17 years', commented the inquiry report. The archbishop had a notion that there had been no abuse because Ball's acts did not involve penetration. It was as if the 'new enlightenment' had never happened.

Ball was provided with a home on the Prince of Wales's estate in Cornwall. The prince's intervention was condemned by the inquiry as 'misguided' and open to misinterpretation as an expression of support. Ball did indeed feel supported, and began a 20-year campaign to restore his religious role and reputation; this only ended when he was finally imprisoned in 2015. None of his advocates gave a thought to his victims, said the inquiry report.

An independent review of the Ball case by Dame Moira Gibb, published in 2017, condemned the Church's cruel disregard for victims, criticised its misinterpretation of abuse as homosexuality and accused the Church of collusion.[64] These conclusions were shared by the IICSA report. It noted with savage ambiguity that when the Establishment – judges, politicians and the heir to the throne – rallied round Ball, 'they did so in the belief that their opinions of the character of Peter Ball mattered' and would carry weight.[65] They were right; they did.

The Church of Rome

During the Cleveland controversy sexual abuse was chronic and common at England's premier Catholic private boarding school, Ampleforth College, housed in a grand mansion in a Yorkshire valley of fields, woods and lakes. In 1987 one of the school's prolific predators, Father Gregory Carroll, confided to a superior that he had been inappropriately involved with a pupil. Only one, he lied. It was not reported to the police.[66]

Although Ampleforth was half an hour or so away from Middlesbrough, it was its pupils' misfortune not to have access to the paediatricians who had examined boys at the nearby residential school, Saltergill. No one thought to get help from doctors, social workers or the police. Ampleforth's proximity to the sexual abuse storm in Cleveland was not insignificant: vigilant professionals were within reach and Childline was only a telephone call away. While many pupils were being harmed, few told anyone.

IICSA held hearings on sexual abuse and sadism going back decades in celebrated Catholic schools – Ampleforth, Downside School in Somerset and St Benedict's School in Ealing, West London.

David Greenwood, a lawyer representing survivors of clergy abuse, explained that predatory priests – there were many – were typically spirited away to the Church's many boltholes. It wasn't until the early 2000s that Ampleforth invited psychological assessments of several abusive priests about whom, solicitor David Greenwood reminded the inquiry, there was a 'large amount of smoke around a fire of hard evidence'.[67] The inquiry learned that when the psychologists insisted that these men be reported to the statutory authorities, the Abbot of Ampleforth refused. The psychologists reported them anyway, and thus began a bitter conflict with the Church. Non-cooperation and threats were the Church's modus operandi. 'To challenge the church in any way was literally to invite eternal damnation,' commented Richard Scorer, an expert on religious abuse. To confront it 'requires a special kind of courage'.[68] The priests were ultimately prosecuted and jailed. A notorious, charismatic St Benedict's priest, Father Laurence Soper, a man of independent wealth, fled the country in 2011. In exile he was able to rely on his huge Vatican bank account. The Vatican did not respond to Metropolitan Police requests in 2015 for information, and only in 2018, after bank withdrawals were reported to Interpol, was Soper arrested, tried at the Old Bailey and sentenced to 18 years in prison.[69]

During the inquiry's public hearings on the Birmingham diocese, the largest in England, the panel was stunned by a sudden intervention: Father Gerard Doyle made contact after watching the IICSA live stream in December 2018 about Father Samuel Penney – Penney had raped children since the 1960s. Suddenly Doyle remembered a telephone call from the Vicar General,

Monsignor Daniel Leonard, in the early 1990s: Leonard had told him to hasten to Penney, hand over hundreds of pounds and warn him to get out of the country because he was about to be arrested. 'It was in some ways like receiving a phone call from God.' Doyle told the inquiry.[70]

The inquiry also investigated the case of Father John Tolkien, another career offender. His father was J.R.R. Tolkien, the celebrated author of *The Lord of the Rings* trilogy and *The Hobbit*, iconic children's English fiction. Although the Church hierarchy had known about his sexually abusive behaviour for 35 years, it was only in 2001 that the police finally investigated him. The CPS decided that it was 'not in the public interest' to charge him. IICSA was adamant: 'the Church was aware of the risk Father Tolkien posed to children and yet the Archdiocese took little or no steps to protect children'.[71]

The Catholic Church was supposed to change all that after 2012 when the Nolan Report on clergy abuse proposed the formation of the Catholic Office for the Protection of Children and Vulnerable Adults. Did it? A former diocesan head of safeguarding, Jane Dziadulewicz, reported that 'many times' the bishops 'had not read those policies or did not agree with them'. Reform was sabotaged. There were 'more weaknesses than strengths' after Nolan, commented IICSA's final report. 'The default position was to take no action or to move the priest to another parish.'[72]

The report's quiet, prosaic language masked what the inquiry really thought of the Church: it was horrified – 'The consequence of these failings cannot be overstated.'[73] If the inquiry had revealed anything it was the systems and structures of great resistance – the Church would not police itself. It needed *external* oversight, as it would not change the habits of a millennium; state regulators, external inquiries, clerical visitations, reports by 'the great and the good' had all failed, Scorer told the inquiry. Offending monks were still protected by the Church, said his colleague, Greenwood, because the perceived 'duty is to the brothers, not to the children'. After representing so many victims, Greenwood had no doubt: 'They're dangerous, these monks.' All over the world the Catholic Church remained impervious: monarchical, yet so thoroughly devolved that nobody accepted responsibility for anything. The problem was not 'a few rotten apples, but a rotten system', said Greenwood. 'What else do you call that?' he said: 'conspiracy'.[74]

Westminster

Ironically, the scandal that provoked the creation of IICSA was the subject of its most hesitant report: the Westminster Report which was published in February 2020.[75] There had been a long, long wait – six years – since Tom Watson's demand that the government act on allegations about Parliament.

We have seen how Watson's speech in 2014 to the House of Commons was followed by rumour, reckless reporting and incompetent investigation.[76] IICSA was determined that it not be tainted by the Carl Beech–Exaro debacle, an extravagant investigation instigated by a hoaxer who had been relied upon, contrary to independent expert advice, but I would argue that it had no need to be quite so restrained.

Hearings for 'Allegations of Child Sexual Abuse Linked to Westminster' were held between 2018 and 2019. IICSA considered whether there was evidence of tolerance, conspiracy, cover-up or interference, and whether governmental political and law enforcement institutions were aware and had taken appropriate steps to safeguard children. The inquiry heard from senior MPs, party whips, members of the House of Lords, the former leader of the Liberal Party, civil servants, journalists, police officers and survivors.

The inquiry's report into the Westminster investigation concluded that there was no evidence of 'an organized network' or of individuals connected via a 'coordinated, organized group'; no 'cover-up' or 'suppression of information' about 'such a ring' by MI5, GCHQ, the security services or the police.

But there was the powerful network, the PIE, that reached high places: the diplomat Sir Peter Hayman, a knight of the social work Establishment, Peter Righton, who was Watson's target, and Cyril Smith. They had capacious influence and support systems. Despite the prosecutions of several members of PIE, Home Secretary Leon Brittan decided in 1983 not to ban the group for the time being.[77]

IICSA found it 'extraordinary that such an organization' could have attracted support 'for such a long period of time'. Yet it also concluded that 'we have seen no evidence that establishment figures were aware of the activities of Righton...'. However, there was evidence – there was plenty of talk in the 1980s, and 'establishment figures' had been alerted by senior social workers Peter McKelvie and Liz Davies in the 1990s.

IICSA could have said that we would never know the answers, that nothing much could be inferred from the absence of evidence because there had been so little effort to seek it. Home Secretaries had been assured by the police that 'we don't investigate' several Westminster 'cottages ... frequented by celebrities and MPs' – an approach, said IICSA, 'demonstrating deference towards, or at least reluctance to investigate, those in power...'.[78]

What is deference if not a protection racket?

The Westminster Report described these themes:

- Deference towards politicians and others of importance, and different treatment accorded to wealthy people versus poorer people 'who had no access to networks of influence'.
- Senior officers thwarted investigations – any investigation into 'rent boys' that identified prominent people would be stalled.
- Almost every institution failed to put the needs and safety of children first.
- The police paid little regard to the welfare of sexually exploited children.
- Political parties were more concerned about political fallout and reputation than children's safety.
- In some cases, the honours system prioritised reputation and discretion, with little or no regard for victims of those nominated.

These were examples 'of a political culture that values its reputation far higher than the fate of the children involved'. IICSA found no evidence of an 'organized paedophile network in which people of prominence conspired to pass children amongst themselves', but there was 'ample evidence that individual perpetrators of child sexual abuse have been linked to Westminster', it said, and Westminster institutions failed to recognise it, turned a blind eye, 'actively shielding and protecting child sexual abusers and covering up allegations'.[79]

The cause was not corruption or bribery, but rather a 'blind eye', the 'old boy network' and a 'culture of deference' – it was just the way things were. However, I suggest that 'deference' and 'old boy network' are terms that lose their sting when they are stripped from their context and their purpose: deference was, and is, organised and enacted through force, economic and cultural coercion, ritual and ideology; it was and is, administered by private and public institutions' hierarchies and cadres, to safeguard established power. In this case, deference means nothing if not a protection racket to menace the powerless and provide cover for those wielding power.

Deference circulated between men with connections and reputations; it was a resource for the powerful whose weaponised social capital far exceeded the submission of the subaltern. The inquiry heard how powerful men organised: they deflected or disbelieved reports of abuse;[80] they whispered words in ears – that phrase, 'I'll have a word...' – confident that justice would be prevented before it could ever be perverted.

Furthermore, deference was not natural or inevitable; it was achieved. It was never settled or hegemonic; the term cannot account for the historical record of resistance: children and women did not merely *defer*. The 'conducive context' of sexual oppression creates the experience of surrender, the shaming defeat and dishonouring of the victim, and the pleasures of mastery among the perpetrators and their allies. There have always been vulnerable people who, somehow, overcame their dread and, emboldened by their outrage, took their protest to whoever might listen.

What is deference and the old boy network if not collusion and corruption and a promise of immunity? Impunity incubates pessimism about politics and the means of making a difference; it does not come from confusion about what is, or is not, abuse: it is collusion in the impeachment of victims and survivors. What is impunity if not an admission that cynicism and collusion saturate society? What is it if not a description of the limits of democracy and the sovereignty of sexism that sponsors sexual crime?

Thus far, the inquiry had been resourceful, productive, robust and challenging. By comparison, the Westminster Report seemed more cautious than the evidence before it warranted. A comparison with the Cleveland Report is instructive: with double negatives, scapegoating and evasions, the Cleveland Report in effect helped to sink the new enlightenment about sexual crimes against children. IICSA, by contrast, confronted the Establishment.

By the anxious repetition of what the inquiry was *not* saying, however, it dissipated the impact of what it *was* emphatically saying: that no institution or political party is equipped to properly safeguard children, and that historically, the sexual abuse of children had not been 'considered at all'. Perhaps that should have been the beginning, not the end, of its analysis.

13

What is to be done?

A confession: I have been writing about sexual violence for decades, and I've often felt uncomfortable at being positioned among 'believers' in contrast to 'sceptics' – those who claim to bring 'reasonable doubt' to the child abuse debate. My encounter with Cleveland as a journalist began with curiosity and not belief. Nothing prepared me for the controversy: neither 'belief' nor 'doubt' described my standpoint. Nor did it derive from my personal experience or my own biography as a White, working-class woman of a certain age, whose people were Christians and communists, who hails from a small border town, a landscape of railways, factories, public service and council estates, and who feels blessed to belong to a generation that has been habituated to challenge everything. So I resist this standpoint alone as my point of entry into these debates – though, that said, every woman knows about sexual intrusion and oppression, in herself, in her family, among her friends.

And I refute the sceptical standpoint as a way of thinking. Scepticism brings only ice and alienation to conversations about sexual abuse that are already studded with rhetorical violence. Scepticism is a way of not thinking. It claims objectivity, but it is the antithesis. Roland Summit's analysis of the McMartin daycare case commentaries, an inventory of inaccuracy, comments that sceptics enjoy the luxury of commenting on events 'in retrospect' and from 'a distance that passes for objectivity'.[1] Professor David Pilgrim condemns scepticism as 'knowing cynicism'.[2] Professor David Garland argues that scepticism is typically emptied of empirical work, it is 'not detached realism', or even 'just-the-facts empiricism', but an exercise in debunking: sometimes 'amoral scepticism is all that there is'.[3]

We are familiar with it: we hear it from governments, from scholars who refuse to let reality disturb their theoretical conceits, from some psychoanalytic, postmodern and queer theorists for whom child abuse is unknowable,[4] and we hear it every time sexual violence is on the political agenda.

Scepticism is another way of furiously not-knowing and not caring, a brittle complacency and an impossible demand for validation. The philosopher Stanley Cavell proposes that pain poses a particular problem for the sceptic 'precisely because of its commonness and its recognizability, it is something knowable about the other if anything is', but unlike laughter, he adds, 'with pain there is a moral demand to respond to its expression'.[5] That's where the sceptic baulks and doesn't listen or learn.

Professor Dori Laub, psychoanalyst and co-founder of the Holocaust Survivors Film Project housed at Yale University, writes of the listener as 'party to the creation of knowledge de novo ... a participant'. It is hard work. Laub describes Holocaust survivors' silence as a way 'to protect themselves from the fear of being listened to – and listening to themselves...'. Silence serves simultaneously as a place of sanctuary and of defeat. The listener needs to 'know all this, and more', warns Laub.[6]

Herein lies the gauntlet thrown down by what the Harvard psychiatrist Judith Lewis Herman terms 'the dialectic of trauma' that has exercised child sexual abuse debates, and most of all the child victims themselves, forever: 'The conflict between the will to deny horrible events and the will to proclaim them aloud is the central dialectic of psychological trauma.'[7] The dialectic is altogether too much for sceptics: it is a damnable refusal to yield to their insatiable demands for *certainty*. The demand for more and more proof, suggests Cavell, reaches the disabling discovery that 'the cure for suspicion cannot come from within suspicion'. What kind of task, he asks, 'is it to study social suffering?' It is to make ourselves available to others, not as a gesture of surrender, but of curiosity and recognition. Scepticism, concludes Cavell, is by contrast, 'a wish for the other's non-existence'.[8]

The hush, the noise of the unsaid, is the soundscape of child sexual abuse. The Cleveland Inquiry could have contemplated children's silence as Laub's 'sanctuary and defeat'; it could have elaborated the implications of physical symptoms that announced the unspeakable – everyday rape and buggery – the recognition of which demands action to stop it. But it was steered furtively by a government mandate that was less interested in 'arrangements for children who have been abused' – including the needs of those who had not, or could not, deliver a culprit – than by the protests of some parents, among them suspected perpetrators, by refusing to confront police mutiny and resource crises that the government itself had created.

The inquiry was initiated by the Establishment's 'amoral scepticism' and by the regime in which the Establishment lives: patriarchy. Its enemy, feminism, which helped to pioneer the new enlightenment, emancipated my own thinking, and was certainly in the government's sights during the Cleveland crisis: Elizabeth Butler-Sloss said as much when she described what motivated the inquiry and her own appointment in her Gresham College interview in 2003.[9]

It was the great misfortune of the new enlightenment to be blighted by the hegemony of Thatcherism and Reaganism in the 1980s and then New Democrats and New Labour in the 1990s: a new global sexual settlement was inaugurated, neo-liberal-neo-patriarchy, a new articulation of male domination. Inequalities increased year on year; child protection systems were overwhelmed, disoriented and diminished; perpetrators enjoyed impunity; 'new imperialism', war zones and mass migration incubated rape, pillage and the plunder of bodies, specifically women and children, not as collateral damage but as strategies of subordination.[10]

After the emergence of the liberating World Wide Web at the end of the 1980s, platforms for child sexual exploitation and pornography proliferated. Childhood itself has been transformed by this technology, argues Beeban Kidron, filmmaker and independent peer in the House of Lords. Children are both viewers and participants: Internet Watch Foundation reported in 2023 that images of children under the age of 11 being coached to perform sexual acts – usually at home – soared by over 1,000 per cent following COVID lockdowns beginning in 2019.[11]

Wicked

First, we have to learn from the past, about how that historic opportunity became a historic defeat. When the government launched an inquisition in 1987 into half a dozen Cleveland professionals who had acted in good faith, it absolved itself from responsibility for everything.

The Cleveland Report recycled an ignorant theory: that if children being interviewed don't tell it is because they have nothing to say. It is worth repeating the report's fallacy: 'There may be rare occasions when a child does not choose to tell...' And so the report framed the architecture of child protection on an untruth. In fact, not-telling was not *rare*. When in 2020 I reminded a specialist government adviser of that comment on page 207 of the report, the response was shock, 'oh ... oh ... good grief. Good grief! That's wicked. That's wicked!'[12]

That wickedness was compounded by the report's injunction to professionals against trying to facilitate children's testimony. Inevitably, post-Cleveland protocols regulated the conditions in which they might speak and restrained what they might want or need to say, and where, when and to whom they might say it, or show it.

The inquiry's interpretation of its brief ('arrangements for children who have been abused') did not address what children were up against: fright, shame, perpetrators and power.

The files in the National Archives disclose something of who knew what and when, and the government's intentions. The files are unequivocal: state intervention on the side of children was to be minimised; doctors who had suspected rape or buggery were correct in 'at least 80 per cent of the cases' – but this was to be suppressed. The numbers were decisive: they signalled new opportunities for the detection of undiscovered crimes against children, for moral and material recognition and redress, and for the elevation of 'common knowledge'. But the Treasury and the Department of Health and Social Security regarded the numbers as 'dangerous', so significant that they had to be censored.[13] What was that if not a cover-up?

The children did not attract official curiosity, they were not followed up, they were rendered objects of speculation that was marshalled against protective intervention – and so they were 'instrumentalised' to spearhead political retreat.

Ah, some people might reply, do the numbers really matter? Wasn't the Cleveland Inquiry about the response, the procedures and the political and professional conflict? Yes. But by the time the government ordered the inquiry, the conflict was being resolved and the government could have encouraged everyone to calm down; it could have decided to assess the exponential rise in referrals everywhere, dispatch Her Majesty's Inspectorate of Constabulary to check out – and sort out – Cleveland Police; it could have expedited reform of outdated procedures and commissioned research into this re-revealed phenomenon.

Although the medical signs at the heart of the controversy were not themselves the cause of the crisis, they certainly disturbed 'common sense' about the meaning of sexual acts and about silence as a survival strategy. The Cleveland Inquiry elected not to think about all that, and it didn't help professionals and the public think about it either. The Cleveland Inquiry didn't answer the key questions: were the children abused, what do we know about sexual abuse and what can we do to stop it?

Untruths and half-truths

Public untruths matter: we all know that presidents and princes deceive, just as motorists, drinkers, artful dodgers, parents and poker players do; we expect ministers to manipulate and mislead us, although it is inscribed in their ministerial code that they must not, and we believe that they should not. People do not want to be conned. Deceit matters.

If we didn't know it then we know it now: the damage to democracy of lying, faking and concealing (in the context of Donald Trump's presidency in the US and Boris Johnson's premiership in the UK) is well understood.

The Cleveland story is a classic case of secrets, half-truths and untruths; it is about facts and figures that were known and made to not matter, covered up, to mislead Parliament and the public about the possibility that the children had been raped and buggered, that health and welfare workers had identified terrible assaults and that perpetrators may have been let off.

The impact on public opinion was to encourage the myth that the doctors and social workers had got it wrong, that adults (men) had been wrongly accused and 'innocent families' had been assailed. The effect on 'common knowledge' was to staunch the creation of 'an educated public'.[14] The impact on the careers and reputations of professionals deemed competent and caring was ruinous. The experience of a generation of specialists and survivors was lost to us. The effect on policy and policing was to freeze the investigation and prosecution of sexual crimes against children: anyone interested in raping children could do so with impunity; professional recognition of child sexual abuse as serious social harm was virtually erased.

After Cleveland, child sexual abuse in families was excised from social work training, policing and from political priorities. Inexorably, it fell under the radar and stayed there. Concern about the family as a 'conducive context' faded, and arrangements for children living under sexual siege in their homes were going 'unseen and unheard'.[15] Agencies responsible for safeguarding were intellectually asset-stripped, hollowed out, left hopeless.

When Tony Newton presented the Cleveland Report to Parliament on 6 July 1988 he announced that the events in Cleveland must never happen again.[16] Public confidence must be restored! But public confidence was never the problem. On the contrary, despite Stuart Bell's impact on the region's media and on ministers, the only attempt to canvass public opinion came from the public themselves: Cleveland Against Child Abuse was a campaign formed out of 'increasing exasperation that nobody asked them what they want'. It conducted a house-to-house survey, organised education events and a mass meeting that called for Dr Higgs's return to Middlesbrough General.[17] The campaign reached beyond Middlesbrough to Tyneside and the formation of another community movement, People Against Child Sexual Abuse. But so great became the NRHA's seeming panic that when a community health council planned a discussion of sexual abuse, it was met by the authority's warning: don't.[18] Meanwhile, the purported popularity of Stuart Bell (rather than his party) was a chimera: in the 1980s he had refused to hold weekly surgeries – the vaunted tradition of Britain's constituency electoral system

– and ultimately he was accused in the national press of being 'Britain's laziest MP'.[19]

The mantra circulating among policymakers and managers after the inquiry was 'we don't want another Cleveland'. Now we must say 'never again' to the concealment and the cynicism. There must be a public reckoning with the real Cleveland crisis – that strange inquiry, its culpably flawed report, the government's misleading response, the determination to penalise those closest to the Cleveland cases, the banishment of Drs Higgs and Wyatt from child abuse – a field in which they had shown themselves to be remarkably veracious – the suppression of the medical findings and the betrayal of the Cleveland children.

The government must deliver an apology.

A place for truth to dwell

There is a belief that truth will out, that telling the truth in the context of mystification and myth is radical, and yes, it is. But here I take my cue from Hannah Arendt's review *Lying in Politics: Reflection on the Pentagon Papers* and Sir Richard Scott's inquiry into the illegal sale of arms to Iraq and the practice of governance, and the elusive history of the UK's constitution.[20]

Arendt and Scott were concerned with 'national security', war and peace. Here, we are concerned with the national security of children. Arendt insists that 'Facts need testimony to be remembered and trustworthy witnesses to be established in order to find a secure dwelling place in the domain of human affairs.'[21] The Scott Inquiry was commissioned in 1992 about events that synchronised with the Cleveland crisis in 1987–8.[22] It exhaustively dredged ministers' duties and the irreducible importance of truth-telling to democracy. The inquiry delved into semantic war games over the meaning of truths, half-truths, secrets and lies, and their implications for democracy. Scott relied upon *Questions of Procedure for Ministers (QPM)*, a code of behaviour received by every minister, a 'constitutional convention' that established that politicians and public servants should withhold information only when disclosure would not be in the public interest, and they should not deceive or knowingly mislead.[23] Most important was paragraph 27:

<u>Accountability</u>
Ministers are accountable to Parliament, in the sense that they have a duty to explain in Parliament the exercise of their powers and duties and to give an account to Parliament of what is done by them in their capacity as Ministers or by their Departments. This includes the duty to give Parliament, including its Select Committees, and the public as full information as possible about the policies, decisions and actions of the Government, and not to deceive or mislead Parliament and the public.[24]

Note: 'as full information as possible' ... and not 'mislead Parliament and public'. Sir Richard Scott used this template to interpret whether ministers had honoured their obligation to account to Parliament.[25] The head of the civil service in 1988 was Sir Robin Butler. In his evidence to the Scott inquiry he followed *QPM* almost word for word. However, he added, the 'convenience of secrecy' was a 'matter of being in the interests of good government'.[26] The judge did not agree: ministers had been 'determinedly' and 'designedly' – and inexcusably – misleading, Scott concluded. The suppression of information was constitutionally improper; it thwarted the national conversation; it produced 'debate without knowledge'.[27]

This seems to me to be a precise description of what I call the Cleveland cover-up.

This constitutional sacrament was recited in an unprecedented parliamentary censure of former Prime Minister Johnson, for deceiving parliament and the public about partying in No 10 during the pandemic.[28] It was 35 years to the month after MPs debated the Cleveland Report when they were misled and trooped into 'debate without knowledge'.

The wish of Witness D31

The Cleveland Inquiry took place in the Victorian grandeur of Middlesbrough Town Hall, with the more or less continuous presence of the media. The IICSA was housed in the recycled, dull air of an identikit block; the ambience often seeming focused, industrious, but without drama, and only the intermittent presence of the media. The evidence about the Cleveland children remains classified in the National Archives; all the IICSA documents and evidence are available online.

The IICSA became an arena in which personal stories that had waited decades could be heard at last, in safety, and in public. For all its limits, it created the conditions in which private suffering became public narratives and political knowledge. Unlike the Cleveland Inquiry, the IICSA, was concerned with whether and how the institutions had failed to respond to sexual abuse. It started with the protest of survivors and whistle-blowers who worked with journalists, lawyers and politicians, and networked through unmediated social media.

There was a kind of ease: little or no courtroom drama, no 'Perry Mason' moments, except for rare occasions of hubris – former Liberal Party leader David Steel, Prince Charles and Archbishop Carey. Unlike the Cleveland Inquiry, survivors – *adults* – and their allies were the prime witnesses. While virtually nothing had been aired about the 121 children who were the subjects of the Cleveland Inquiry, a great deal was learned at the IICSA hearings about what survivors lived through, what they needed and what they wanted. The IICSA elicited the participation of people from every social class, from the aristocracy and archbishops, to politicians and managers, to people at the edge of society.

But there was a lacuna in the IICSA: arrangements to deal with abuse in families – the theme of the Cleveland Inquiry – was not its theme, and yet it is typically the prelude to many of the participants' experiences of institutional harm and the authorities' failure to address it: 48 per cent of the witnesses who confided in the IICSA's confidential Truth Project described abuse in their families.[29]

A remarkable feature of the testimony given in the subsequent IICSA hearings is the motivation of the survivors: noticeable by its absence is vengeful, noisy, retributive rage. The survivors are rather reticent but their request is radical: that the offence be acknowledged and denounced, and above all stopped.

That was the great wish of witness D31. She had been multiply abused and assaulted in Nottinghamshire children's homes.

She felt unable to speak her statement out loud in the public hearing, but she agreed that some of it be read to the inquiry on her behalf. She was then asked if she had anything to add. 'Yes,' she said. 'It doesn't matter if you say sorry because it isn't enough. It doesn't matter whether you're given compensation. It's not enough. Changes need to be done and you need to get them done as soon as, so it don't happen to any more.' Her testimony is recorded for posterity in the IICSA transcripts for 5 October 2018.[30]

Witness D31 is the same age as Minnie, whose story begins this book. Minnie shared with us the commotion of her own experience, memorialised in her body; her gratitude to her saviours; and her memories of the pitiless repetition within her family and her society, that the 'baddies' weren't in her family, they were the professionals who tried to get her out, to rescue her. The response to the Cleveland case, and the failure to follow up the children, ensured that they would not be heard, *they* would never be *we*, they would become the disappeared.

Since then, the rise and rise of victims' readiness to report abuse to the authorities has been answered by the decline and fall of the institutions' capacity to reciprocate. Witness D31's greatest wish, 'that it don't happen to any more', was doomed to be unrequited: by 2021 the proportion of reported sexual offences against children that were prosecuted was the lowest on record, and sexual abuse had almost disappeared from child protection systems.[31]

New strategies

But there is light and hope: the system collapse and the impact of IICSA's Truth Project is palpable in two historic interventions in the UK: the Welsh government's *National Action Plan: Preventing and Responding to Child Sexual Abuse*, published in 2019, and the Home Office's *Tackling Child Sexual Abuse Strategy* in 2021.[32] These initiatives signalled a new mood in government departments, or at least in Westminster a need to be seen to be saying something, if not doing anything.[33]

The Home Office declared: 'This strategy is the first of its kind in setting out the government's vision for preventing, tackling and responding to child sexual abuse in all its forms ... and provides a robust framework for government to drive action across all agencies, all sectors and society as a whole...'.

These strategies were notable because they enlisted *everyone*. And they could – should – have been written 40 years earlier in the 1980s, when clinicians, social workers, scholars, the women's movement, community activists, children's charities, parents and children themselves were engaged in the new international enlightenment.

The Welsh Government's *National Action Plan* began with a seemingly modest yet radical, reasonable and doable first priority: to get society talking about child sexual abuse, to break the taboo so powerfully exploited by perpetrators and to 'help people understand that the ways in which we can talk – or don't talk – about child sexual abuse is an important part of changing attitudes and preventing abuse'.[34]

The centre of its attention was children's experience, and more generally men's sexual violence; it scheduled awareness campaigns to challenge attitudes among both children and adults, the creation of an evidence base and a phased programme of action in all the contexts where there are children.

By contrast, in UK Home Secretary Priti Patel's foreword to *Tackling Child Sexual Abuse Strategy* in January 2021, she proclaimed: 'The UK has a proud record as the global leader in tackling child sexual abuse.' Keeping children safe 'is one of the State's most fundamental roles. And, as Home Secretary, it is a responsibility that I take extremely seriously.'[35] At last, it might be said.

The UK did indeed become a global leader after it was forced to accept an amendment to data protection and trade legislation, moved in the House of Lords by filmmaker Beeban Kidron, requiring all websites and apps to abide by a code obliging them to have due regard to children's needs – the first of its kind.[36]

But implementation was beset by 'twists, turns and delays', wrote John Carr, Secretary for the UK Children's Charities' Coalition on Internet Safety. Implementation of the Children's Code and the age verification duty was resisted by the Office of the Information Commissioner, until pressure by Carr and the coalition forced a U-turn and the commissioner agreed to assess whether sites were being accessed by significant numbers of children.[37]

In the *Tackling Child Sexual Abuse Strategy*'s 90 pages two comments stand out; they may appear bland but they are profound:

> Professionals working with children have a responsibility to raise concerns and identify children who are at-risk of, or experiencing, sexual abuse. However, this can be difficult. In 2015, the Children's Commissioner reported that just one in eight children who are sexually abused are identified by professionals. There is concern that professionals do not have a good enough understanding of the signs of child sexual abuse and lack the confidence and skills to talk about it.
>
> It is not the responsibility of a child to stop sexual abuse and it is never a child's fault if they are targeted.[38]

The Cleveland Report, I suggest, left children with the responsibility to stop abuse, and undermined professional understanding and confidence. The new *Strategy* did not explain *how* this had happened, or how, finally, to lift responsibility from children, re-educate and re-empower professionals and mitigate their burdens of risk, uncertainty and blame. It did not indicate how the police and criminal justice systems – currently in crisis – might be reconfigured, or how to end impunity. It seemed un-touched by IICSA and much of Patel's introduction to the *Strategy* repeated her government's obsession with racialised reports of sexual exploitation and 'grooming gangs', despite research published by the Home Office itself that debunked these reports.[39] Her priority was the familiar, tired 'law and order' discourse: to 'relentlessly pursue' offenders, impose stronger sentences and 'to ensure there are no safe spaces online for offenders to abuse and exploit children'. Yet it offered no strategy for perpetrators' *safest space*, the home, nor the sexist cultures that generate sexual abuse. That, of course, would confront the king of the castle, his privacy, his liberties and his entitlements.

So more punishment and more incarceration at a time when research on what works and doesn't work with different types of perpetrators shows that on its own the prison deterrent does not seem to deter. We have begun to discover what does – and doesn't – work.[40] And we have learned that among some men who have a sexual interest in children there is unease. Men are not born that way, desire is *developed* in culture and they have to overcome resistance – more than half of calls to the helpline Stop it Now! come from troubled actual or potential abusers about what they have done or are about to do.[41] Survivors' needs, painfully exposed by the IICSA's witnesses, are barely touched.[42]

That said, the *Strategy* provided useful insights and research, much of it from the exemplary Centre of Expertise on Child Sexual Abuse. In May 2023 Home Secretary Suella Braverman 'accepted the need to act on all but one' of the IICSA panel's (unexpectedly modest and muted) recommendations.[43] 'Accepted the need', however, did not mean actual action. The capacious network of change makers – survivors, experts and children's organisations who had made the inquiry happen – was outraged. 'We are deeply disappointed', said IICSA chair Alexis Jay.[44] That was the polite version. 'It's absolutely disgraceful, a shambles', said a senior change maker. Unlike the Home Office, the UK's former police lead on child sexual abuse came to believe that alternatives to law enforcement were needed: the scale of child sexual abuse demanded more than prosecution, 'we have reached saturation point.'[45]

The Home Office evidently had not listened to or learned from exemplary strategies in Ireland and Australia, for example.[46] Nor did it acknowledge the crises crunching the justice and mental health systems,[47] or the egregious state of the police. Weeks earlier Dame Louise Casey's savage review of the Met announced 'a finding of institutional racism, sexism and homophobia'.[48] Its neglect of child safeguarding had already attracted the most severe criticism 'of any force, on any subject ever',[49] and Casey found that it 'has not listened and it has not learned', nor had it suffered any consequences.[50] More than three decades after the Cleveland crisis, neither had the government.

New world order

Yet with characteristic 'British exceptionalism' Patel boasted that the UK would continue its 'role as the world leader in tackling child sexual abuse', and – ironically, in the context of Brexit – promised to 'strengthen the international response and protect children overseas by driving common global standards and enhancing safeguarding and law enforcement systems in key at-risk countries'.[51]

This seemed oblivious to the new conjuncture: European Union Home Affairs Commissioner Ylva Johansson declared child sexual abuse her number one priority.[52] In 2017 the World Health Organization, for the first time, issued guidelines to health providers on child sexual abuse.[53] The United Nations' Special Rapporteur on the Sale and Sexual Exploitation of Children, Mama Fatima Singhateh, drew attention to the 'drive by' sale of children in some countries, the impact of COVID-19, children being sold by traffickers inside vehicles; children being sold through social media and messaging applications; decreased humanitarian aid in refugee camps leading to children being sold for food and basic supplies.[54] In the UK, the National Society for the Prevention of Cruelty to Children reported that in the COVID-19 context there had been a record number of calls by adults concerned about abuse and neglect within families – during lockdown when there were fewer opportunities to share experiences with anyone outside the home.[55]

The United Nations' Special Rapporteur Maud de Boer-Buquicchio warned that sexual abuse 'is a reality in all parts of the world', and everywhere the information technology revolution, reproductive technology, armed conflict, natural disasters, mass migration and human trafficking expand the contexts in which children are abused.[56]

All of this is unprecedented: this is a new world. The efficacy of national procedures in isolation is long gone. The civil libertarian resistance to state intrusion in private life lost credibility long ago. Everything about our bodies, our homes, our streets and rivers, the very air we breathe, is monitored and regulated.

Shoshana Zuboff has mapped the epoch of 'surveillance capitalism' that has disrupted the very notion of privacy, freedom and autonomy.[57] A child trafficked in Asia may appear on a pornography site watched online anywhere, organised by businesses targeting impoverished and frightened families and children.

Above all, this moment demands that we confront the cause: the sexism that sponsors men's sexual entitlement to the bodies of children and women. To those who carp that this implies a miserable paranoia and an anti-man thing, it should be remembered that there is a child, somewhere in everyone's radius, who is being raped or assaulted; there are women and men doing their best to survive well; there are men fantasising, contemplating, planning and buying the means to take virtual or actual command of a child's body; and there are men wishing they didn't.

This lamentable history should remind us that there are no guarantees that our 'common knowledge' of sexual abuse will find a place to dwell. A historic opportunity beckons a cultural revolution against child abuse, an empathic welfare state and criminal justice system, resilient civil society and 'an educated public' as alert to child abuse as to terrorism and the environmental crisis. The anthropologist Veena Das reminds us that 'the choke and sting of experience only becomes real' when it is told and heard; the story is allowed to break through the 'taken-for-granted meanings of things as they are' and to change 'utterly the commonplace'.[58]

We know that sexual abuse is commonplace, it flourishes. It co-exists with surging awareness, alarm and resistance, *and* with cynical complacency. This is a 21st-century paradigm, the environment that demands a response to IICSA witness D31's ardent wish: 'changes need to be done and you need to get them done as soon as, so it don't happen to any more.'[59] We know enough to know what is to be done – all we need to do is do it.

Epilogue

The reporter is always a positioned interlocutor – never neutral, never nowhere – and those of us who tell this story are also shadowed by an ethical ache, because we have access to bits of the fragmented archive, we know things about some of these children's circumstances that they don't know themselves; childhood ailments and symptoms, what was done to their bodies, suspected rapes, the motives for protective interventions.

Do we have the right to seek out these individuals? Do we track down Cleveland children and 'doorstep' them? This question is troubling. We mostly decide that we should not, in all conscience, intrude, even when stories appear in the mass media that utterly contradict what we know to be in the records.

'Are there a few of us, like me?'

Again we meet Minnie, a sprite, small and wiry, her hands eternally busy. She always seems to be thinking, thinking, working things out. She is, remarkably, the *first and only* Cleveland child to go public with her childhood experiences before and after delving into her records. Fewer than a handful of the Cleveland children have appeared in the media accusing the paediatricians and other professionals of doing them ill – apparently before they had access to their records.

When Minnie asked that haunting question in 2017, 'Are there a few of us, like me?', she had received only lies from the national narrative. Although much of her childhood had been organised and monitored and recorded by the 'public parent' and statutory services, there seemed to be no public place that held who she was then, and could give answers to her questions.

Thirty years after she met Dr Higgs at Middlesbrough General, her own children were around the same age as she was then, but they are adored, thriving and safe. She knows that when she was a child she was in jeopardy. When she was 40 years old she decided to find out why she became a Cleveland child and why her 'saviours' were so smeared. She told me that she contacted the local paper, the *Middlesbrough Gazette*:

> 'I explained to a member of staff, "I'm looking for the child protection scandal", and she said, "Oh the mad doctors" and gave me the telephone number for the local library. The library lady said there was a book by Stuart Bell. I said I don't want to read that, full of lies. She said she'd look for *your* book.'

Her mother had joined Stuart Bell's campaign against the doctors and social workers. He, of course, was a hero to protesting parents, press and politicians, and wrote up his campaign against the doctors in his book, *When Salem Came to the Boro: The True Story of the Cleveland Child Abuse Case*, in 1988. I wrote the first edition of *Unofficial Secrets* about the case in 1988, too.[1] But nothing in any book, and nothing in any library, could give her what she needed: access to her story, to peace of mind and justice.

In her semi-detached house in Yorkshire, there are dogs in and out of the kitchen and chickens in the garden. Everywhere there are photographs of her children and her husband, testaments to love in heart-shaped frames.

She can still be devastated by that faraway child who was saved, she told me, by Dr Higgs:

> 'Oh, the tears I've wept for that little girl. I used to try to take my own life, it was stupidity, I'd tie things to my neck and hope I'd die. I once put super-glue on my lips. But I'm so far removed from that person now, that little girl, I can talk about her as if she was someone I used to know.'

The day she married, 'I shook all of that off.' She loved her married name. She formed a new family with her husband, a craftsman, and their children; she works hard, earns a living and loves the life she has made for herself with her loved ones.

Her husband tells me he always knew his wife had troubles:

> 'I knew something … but I didn't want to probe. I picked up things, I found out bits and bobs as we've gone on. I never like to pry; things have come out when she's ready. In the early days when we were intimate, sometimes she'd shudder … whoa! You don't ask. I'm always here for her, but only when she's ready.
>
> Over the years things have changed. We've just grown closer together. I hate to see her upset. I'd do anything to make her smile. It's been very hard; she's a moody bugger sometimes. But I love her to bits. I just do. I just love her more and more – and because of what she's been through.'

She could not, would not, rest; she wanted answers. In 2017, together they researched: they found newspaper reports on the internet, they read about angry Cleveland children denouncing Dr Higgs, and then they found Tim Tate's 1997 documentary for Yorkshire Television, *Cleveland: Unspeakable Truths*. All ambiguity vanished.

'Watching that documentary, I was gobsmacked', said her husband. 'We were thinking who can we get in touch with? We tried all sorts.' Minnie told me that she contacted the local paper to set the record straight:

> 'They didn't want to know. I said you printed all the other stuff, but you won't print what I say was the truth. They weren't interested. I told them I'd got evidence now! They said, "It isn't something we would be interested in publishing." That just fuelled the fire. I knew as soon as they said it that I was on to something … all the rubbish I'd read. … That's why I contacted you.'

'I talk back to the voices'

A man in his forties goes shopping for cigarettes; he is small, chunky, the palest white, and he is talking to himself. No, not to himself, to the voices, he tells me: 'I have voices that tell me to hurt people. I could be walking along and voices tell me to punch someone; I mutter to myself, I talk back to the voices. I swear at them.' He is Mark, Minnie's brother.

No one would know, looking at him in the street, edging away from him, that with reckless courage when he was a child in 1986 he indicted the most powerful person in his universe, his stepfather.

He was at a special school, and his stepfather's extreme sadism 'got brought to light when I drew a picture' that alarmed his teacher. Another teacher noticed scars across his back. He said that they had been caused by his stepfather whipping him with a belt buckle. The head teacher called his parents in for an explanation. The boy told the police what his stepfather was doing to him. For years, he tells me, his stepfather 'would tie my hands behind my back and he'd...'. The man treated him as if he was a dog. Everything changed after a visit to his aunt's house:

> 'I was so hungry that I nicked the cat biscuits. My auntie caught me and asked what I was doing. I said I was hungry. She asked me why. I said I wasn't getting fed. She asked me what was going on at home and then she turned round and said, "he's not going back there tonight". That's when it all started coming out.'

In fact, his mother had seen it, she admitted to me: 'One night I came home and he was on all fours, and...' Out of respect for this man's dignity, I won't repeat what she said. He sways back and forth as he tells his story. His mother has come to stay in his neat, smoke-filled, ground-floor flat with its tended garden – she is a frequent visitor – but he doesn't want her to hear his story and nor does she, so she slaps her hands over her ears while he talks, or she goes out or into another room, but not for long. 'Mam can't deal with it,' he confides. 'Mam was trying to win us back,' he explains. She is back in the room and intervenes, 'It was going to be the end of my marriage.' The stepfather tried – and succeeded – in getting their mother back. 'He asked us to go back to him and the abuse started again,' says Mark, during home visits, when 'Mam was out, working. It started all over again.' No one was prosecuted and he wasn't protected.

In the mid-1990s Mark was imprisoned, and at the end of the decade he decided to take legal action against his stepfather: he believed that the man's abuse contributed to his own offending behaviour. He went to the police and told his story again. The case reached Teesside Crown Court in 2003. He asked his younger sister to give evidence, but she was reluctant – she was married, she had a baby and she didn't want this in her life again. However, without much enthusiasm, she agreed and told the court what she had witnessed. Under cross-examination she was accused of money-grabbing: 'As soon as the barrister brought up money, I said I earn my own living, I don't need the money, and I don't need this.'

The case failed; the stepfather was found not guilty. The Cleveland connection was raised to negative effect – hadn't this all been considered and discarded a decade ago? Minnie's brother tried a year or so later to bring a private prosecution. That failed too. 'My sister and I had horrific childhoods. I wanted justice for me and my sister,' he says. They didn't get it. The stepfather died in 2010.

Minnie's brother is disabled by mental illness: he harms himself, cuts his arms and fends off malign voices. 'I'm fucked up in the head, it's affected my entire adult life.'[2]

The brother and sister are exemplars of Cleveland children: he had talked and talked, there was medical evidence and there were witnesses. His sister had medical signs, but her survival strategy was silence.

The last word

Finally, we return to Minnie. She describes the wild commotion of her own experience, memorialised in her body, and the triumphal repetition, in her family and her society, that the 'baddies' weren't in her family; they were the people who got her out: 'To everybody Dr Higgs was a bad person, a bad person, a bad person.' But Minnie is ardent – Dr Higgs saved her.

There is no analogy or metaphor adequate to represent the cruelty of the people who caused Minnie harm: the man who raped her, the mother who colluded and those who stole her story and stopped everyone – including Minnie herself – learning from it.

'Now', she says, 'I've got a burning fire in me, it won't go out. Even now people say "you shouldn't be poking around". "I was abused and I've just got on with it". Well, for 30 years I got on with it. We've all been getting on with it. I'm sick of getting on with it. I'm sick of it.' Her fire roars.

She began this book with her anguished question, 'Are there a few of us, like me?'

The answer is yes, in Cleveland and everywhere. We know they are here, there, everywhere, but the brother and sister who begin and end this book appeared only as coded ciphers on pieces of paper that flitted in and out of the Cleveland Inquiry's attention as the pages were turned.

The anthropologist Veena Das reminds us that 'The choke and sting of experience only becomes real' when it is told and heard, the story is allowed to break through the 'taken-for-granted meanings of things as they are' and to change 'utterly the commonplace'.[3] That is this book's challenge and invitation.

Timeline

1970s

1970   Politician Cyril Smith, later Liberal MP for Rochdale, investigated by police for abusing boys; police recommend prosecution; Director of Public Prosecutions decides not to prosecute.

1977   Henry Kempe, co-author of the 1962 watershed paper on the 'Battered Child Syndrome', addressing the International Conference for Child Abuse and Neglect in London, urges that child sexual abuse be recognised as significant child maltreatment.[1]

1978   Police search London flat of diplomat Sir Peter Hayman and find a large cache of pornography and correspondence on violent sexual fantasies involving children.

1979   In the US, David Finkelhor's first national survey, *Sexually Victimised Children*, published.[2] The *Rochdale Alternative Paper* publishes allegations of Cyril Smith's abuse of boys.

1980s

1980   Geoffrey Dickens sends dossier to Home Secretary Leon Brittan about Hayman and others.

1982   Patricia Mrazek and Henry Kempe publish pioneering anthology, *Sexually Abused Children and their Families*.

        Twelve million people in the UK watch TV documentary *A Complaint of Rape* by Roger Graef and Charles Stewart.

1983   Tyneside Rape Crisis Centre and Northumbria Police set up Women Police Doctors Group to examine rape victims.

The Metropolitan Police in London review methods of interviewing children and recommends joint interviews between police and social workers.

Senior officials resist a knighthood for Jimmy Savile.

1984 Canada's influential *Badgley Report on Sexual Offences Against Children* is published.[3]

1985 The Republic of Ireland sets up a National Sexual Assault Treatment Unit in Dublin.

Cleveland Area Review Committee designs new systems. Police managers reject joint investigations.

Eleven sex rings are investigated in Leeds in the north of England; ten men are convicted and jailed for under three years.

In the US, the psychologist Richard Gardner proposes 'parental alienation syndrome'.

1986 David Finkelhor publishes *A Sourcebook on Child Sexual Abuse.*[4]

Christopher Hobbs and Jane Wynne's pioneering paper 'Buggery in childhood' is published in *The Lancet.*

The UK Department of Health and Social Services publishes *Working Together* guidelines on child abuse.

Childline, a telephone helpline for children, is launched.

North Wales social worker Alison Taylor reports sexual abuse of children in care to police.

Northern region paediatricians' leader Bob Nelson warns of huge escalation of child sexual abuse referrals.

Northern Regional Health Authority decides child sexual abuse is not a priority.

1987

Jan Dr Marietta Higgs becomes consultant paediatrician at Middlesbrough General Hospital.

Feb   Dr Higgs identifies RAD.

March   Some parents dispute medical signs.

May   The total sexual abuse cases almost doubles. Police officers told not to investigate Dr Higgs's referrals.

June   Hospital sexual abuse cases peak, at 110. Police break off relations with social services. Social services insist on responding to referrals and set up a specialist Child Resource Centre. Paediatricians are asked by management to reduce the number of sexual abuse admissions. They refuse.

         Social services director Mike Bishop proposes a second-opinion panel.

         MP Stuart Bell in Parliament accuses child protection consultant Sue Richardson and Marietta Higgs of having 'colluded and conspired' to keep the police out of sexual abuse investigations.[5] Police surgeon Dr Alistair Irvine challenges the medical evidence of anal abuse. Cleveland Police management criticises social services consultant Sue Richardson. Hospital staff sign letter supporting the paediatricians.

         Margaret Thatcher is re-elected prime minister.

July   Stuart Bell writes to Health Minister Tony Newton, alleging that Cleveland Social Services are empire-building.[6]

         NRHA sends report to Newton.

         The prime minister is asked in Parliament to allocate more resources to child abuse. She replies, 'No.'[8]

         DHSS decides to hold local judicial inquiry into Cleveland.

Aug   The police concede joint investigations.

Sept   Elizabeth Butler-Sloss is appointed to chair the inquiry.

1988

Jan   The inquiry hears final submissions.

May   The Political Honours Scrutiny Committee tells Margaret Thatcher that, despite 'some hesitation', Cyril Smith's history should not render him 'unsuitable' for a knighthood.

July   Ministers discuss the *Cleveland Report*. Treasury acknowledges that 'at least' 80 per cent of the medical findings are correct, but that this will not be made public.[7]

Oct   NRHA tells the Minister of Health that around 70 to 75 per cent of diagnoses were correct.

    SSI Chief Inspector William Utting tells the Minister of Health that, in Cleveland, joint working happens in only 9 per cent of cases, is police-dominated and opportunities for recognising risk outside the home are lost.

Dec   Dr Wyatt is banned from child abuse work. Dr Higgs is not allowed to return to Middlesbrough.

    There is no follow up on the 121 Cleveland children.

1989

Feb   A letter by 11 Cleveland paediatricians in *The Guardian* says 90 per cent of the diagnoses were correct.[9]

    Three hundred people attend a public meeting in Middlesbrough and launch CAUSE, a community campaign against child abuse.

    In the US, a team led by paediatrician John McCann says that anal dilatation is so common among non-abused children that it may be considered normal.[10] Wynne and Hobbs publish new research showing that RAD is rare and indicative of anal abuse.[11]

    Ten adults are convicted in the Broxtowe case.

    Dr Higgs appeals against 'constructive dismissal' by NRHA.

Nov   The Children Act is passed in Parliament.

1990s

1990   Jimmy Savile receives a knighthood.

1991   Leicestershire children's homes manager Frank Beck receives five life sentences for sexually abusing children. Leicester NW Labour MP Greville Janner is reported to the police for abuse. He is not prosecuted. The *Independent on Sunday* publishes an investigation into sexual abuse in North Wales children's homes.[12]

1992   In the US, the psychologist Anna Salter exposes 'distortion and inaccuracy' by Cleveland witness and defence expert Ralph Underwager, an expert witness in the Cleveland Inquiry.[13]

Peter Righton is fined for importing child pornography. Eileen Fairweather, with social work whistle-blower Liz Davies, breaks long-running story of child exploitation in Islington residential care.[14]

US False Memory Syndrome Foundation is launched.

UK *Memorandum of Good Practice* guidelines are published on joint interviewing children.

1993   Dutch paedophilia journal *Paidika* publishes interview with Underwager.[15]

Around 20 per cent of children on the UK Child Protection Register are in the sexual abuse category, the same proportion as neglect.

1994   Police Superintendent Gordon Anglesea wins libel case against press for 1991 *Independent on Sunday* exposure of sexual abuse in North Wales children's homes.[16] 'False memory' successfully invoked for the first time in English court against abuse survivor Fiona Reay.[17]

1995   Government publishes *Messages from Research*.

NSPCC report *Childhood Matters* estimates that one million children endure harm every year, and 100,000 suffer sexual abuse.

In a BBC documentary by Michael Cockerell, Tory Chief Whip Tim Fortescue describes using sexual abuse scandals to control MPs.[18]

1996　*Jillings Report* into sexual abuse in North Wales children's homes, commissioned in 1994, not published.

1997　Sir William Utting's report on residential children's homes, *People Like Us*, draws attention to 'serious and systematic abuse'.[19]

2000s

2000　The Waterhouse Report, *Lost in Care*, vindicates whistle-blower Alison Taylor and condemns widespread sexual abuse and violence in public and private children's homes.[20]

Government publishes *Framework for Assessment for Social Workers*.

The Republic of Ireland launches the Commission to Inquire into Child Abuse.

2002　New guidelines, *Achieving Best Evidence*, are published.

Adele Gladman reports to Rotherham police, social services and politicians that hundreds of girls are being raped and exploited by networks of men of Pakistani heritage.

2003　Mothers tell Labour MP Ann Cryer about sexual exploitation by Asian men.

In the Cambridgeshire village of Soham, Holly Wells and Jessica Chapman are sexually abused and killed.

2004　Historic response to Huntley condemned by Richard Bichard and Sir Christopher Kelly.[21]

2005　Professor Liz Kelly's team at London Metropolitan University reports that the proportion of victims of rape and sexual assault who achieve justice sinks to its lowest ever: 6 per cent.[22]

2006　Angie Heal reports links between sexual exploitation, trafficking in drugs and guns around Rotherham.[23]

2007   Heal's research unit in the South Yorkshire Police is disbanded.

Betsy Stanko publishes research on the Metropolitan Police's records of sexual offences.[24]

Peter Connelly, known as Baby P, is killed by his parents and stepfather.

2008   National roll-out of the Witness Intermediary Scheme to support vulnerable witnesses, including children.

2009   Stepfather Stephen Barker is convicted of raping Peter Connelly's sister when she was two years old; she is four when she gives evidence in court, the youngest ever witness.

2010s

2010   Sir Cyril Smith dies.

Thirteen-month-old Poppi Worthington dies.

2011   Pathologist concludes that Poppi Worthington died following anal abuse/sexual trauma. The police refuse to investigate.

The Times journalist Andrew Norfolk reports on the sexual exploitation of girls by men of Pakistani heritage in Yorkshire.[25]

Crown Prosecutor Nazir Afzal initiates the criminal prosecution of men accused of sexual exploitation in Rochdale.

Sir Jimmy Savile dies.

2012   The BBC abandons a documentary on Savile. ITV broadcasts *Exposure*. Reports reveal Savile's extraordinary influence in the BBC, hospitals and Broadmoor Prison, and tolerance and complicity at the highest levels.[26]

Office of the Children's Commissioner publishes *Research into Gang-Associated Sexual Exploitation and Sexual Violence*.[27]

Labour MP Tom Watson demands an investigation into suspected paedophile network 'linked to Parliament and No 10'.[28]

Australian Prime Minister Julia Gillard launches Royal Commission into Institutional Responses to Child Sexual Abuse.

2013 A redacted version of the *Jillings Report* is published.[29]

2014 Alexis Jay's *Independent Inquiry into Child Sexual Exploitation in Rotherham* is published.[30] The justice inspectorates conclude that, despite rising child rape referrals, *Achieving Best Evidence* in child sexual abuse cases is failing.[31]

Northumbria Police and social services launch Operation Sanctuary into the sexual exploitation of girls, accompanied by massive public awareness campaigns in Newcastle.

Rochdale whistle-blower Sara Rowbotham tells MPs that it was not ethnicity but disrespect for girls that led to protective services' indifference to sexual exploitation.[32]

Welsh government launches child sexual exploitation National Action Plan.[33]

Former Home Secretary Leon Brittan is accused of rape.

Following pressure by survivors' movements, the Independent Inquiry into Child Sexual Abuse is launched.

Lord Justice Peter Jackson allows public rehearing of medical evidence in the Poppi Worthington case.[34]

2015 *The Physical Signs of Child Sexual Abuse* is published by the American Academy of Pediatrics and the UK's royal colleges of paediatrics, physicians and forensic medicine.[35]

2016 Jackson concludes that Poppi Worthington died following abuse.[36]

2017 During the second inquest into the death of Poppi Worthington, her father refuses to answer questions 252 times. The coroner accepts evidence of abuse and concludes that she died of asphyxia.[37]

Islington Council apologises to survivors of abuse in its care homes.[38]

The Home Office launches the Centre of Expertise on Child Sexual Abuse.

2018   IICSA hearings proceed into Nottinghamshire children's homes.

2019   Child Protection records show the decline to only 4 per cent in the sexual abuse category.

Carl Beech is jailed for perverting of the course of justice.

Welsh Government launches child sexual abuse *National Action Plan*.

2020s

2020   Ofsted multi-agency report on child sexual abuse is published.[39]

IICSA report on Westminster accuses political institutions of 'actively shielding and protecting child sexual abusers'.

The Scottish Child Abuse Inquiry hears of violence and abuse by Nazareth House nuns.

2021   Operation Hydrant – the police investigation hub for historic abuse – published its annual report.[40]

Home Office publishes *Tackling Child Sexual Abuse Strategy*.[41]

2022   International expert John Carr and the UK Children's Charities Coalition on Internet Safety persuade the UK's information commissioner to implement a legal duty upon internet companies to prevent children's access to pornography sites.

2023   Baroness Jay criticises government's response to its reports into child sex abuse.

Sinéad O'Connor dies.

Notes

Prologue

1 Her nickname in childhood.
2 The accusation, 'unfounded' suspicions and allegations were recycled for decades: A. Pain (2008) '20 years on from the Cleveland child sex abuse scandal', *Teesside Gazette*, 8 July, available at: https://www.gazettelive.co.uk/news/local-news/20-years-cleveland-child-sex-3729871.
3 A complex hub of symptoms including weight loss, delayed mobility, physical, mental and social skills, excessive distress or sleepiness, caused by physical or social deficits: poverty, lack of bonding, neglect and abuse. It requires a complex differential diagnosis.
4 The medical evidence included Reflex Anal Dilatation (RAD), a sign suggesting chronic anal penetration, which although well established in forensic pathology, had been identified in children by paediatricians in Leeds, and their radical research had been published in Britain's oldest medical journal, *The Lancet*, in 1986: C.J. Hobbs and J.M. Wynne (1986) 'Buggery in childhood – a common syndrome of child abuse', *The Lancet*, October, 4/2(8510): 792–6, available at: https://www.researchgate.net/publication/20727236_Buggery_in_childhood_-_a_common_syndrome_of_child_abuse. It described RAD as the dynamic opening of the anus after minimal buttocks traction, with relaxation of the external and internal sphincter muscles. 'We have not seen this in normal children', wrote Hobbs and Wynne.
5 Confidential inventories provided to the inquiry by health and social services, police and lawyers, summarising the histories, sources and context of referrals, medical signs, disclosures by relatives, disclosures by children, if any, responses by agencies, if any, and outcomes.
6 Interview with the author, 2018.
7 A court order made before a final hearing when all the evidence is presented to a judge.
8 Hobbs and Wynne, 'Buggery in childhood'.

Introduction

1 M. Nava (1988) 'Cleveland and the press: outrage and anxiety in the reporting of child sexual abuse', *Feminist Review*, January, available at: https://journals.sagepub.com/doi/abs/10.1057/fr.1988.9?journalCode=fera.

2   R. Barker (2015) 'Sir Stuart Bell: Labour MP who defended constituents over the Cleveland child sex abuse scandal', *The Independent*, 15 October, available at: https://www.independent.co.uk/news/obituaries/sir-stuart-bell-labour-mp-who-defended-constituents-over-the-cleveland-child-abuse-scandal-8212414.html.

3   Stuart Bell, House of Commons 29 June 1987, available at: https://api.parliament.uk/historic-hansard/commons/1987/jun/29/children-in-care.

4   T. Newton: 'It is extremely important that if there appears to be a case of child abuse it should be carefully and sensitively investigated. If the current investigations confirm suggestions that there have been significant failings in achieving this in Cleveland, the Government will be ready to institute an inquiry.' 29 June 1987, available at: https://api.parliament.uk/historic-hansard/commons/1987/jun/29/children-in-care#S6CV0118P0_19870629_HOC_189.

5   See https://api.parliament.uk/historic-hansard/commons/1987/jul/09/child-abuse-cleveland.

6   B. Campbell (1988) *Unofficial Secrets*, London: Virago.

7   Treasury official R.B. Saunders to Chief Secretary John Major, 'Confidential Butler-Sloss Report', 5 July 1988.

8   This 1986 consultation document became in 1988 *Working Together to Safeguard Children: A Guide to Inter-Agency Working to Safeguard and Promote the Welfare of Children*.

9   Dr Bob Nelson, letter to Liam Donaldson and to paediatricians across the Northern region, 27 May 1987.

10 *Preventing and Responding to Child Abuse: National Action Plan* (2019), available at: https://gov.wales/preventing-and-responding-child-sexual-abuse-national-action-plan.

11 Home Office (2021) *Tackling Child Sexual Abuse Strategy*, 22 January, available at: https://www.gov.uk/government/publications/tackling-child-sexual-abuse-strategy.

12 R. Branche (2020) *Papa, qu'as-tu fait en Algerie?*, Paris: Editions La Decouverte; R. Branche (2020) 'Papa, what did you do in Algeria?', *The Conversation*, 2 September, available at: https://theconversation.com/profiles/raphaelle-branche-1149406/articles; see A. Shatz (2021) 'Dynamo current, feet, fists, salt', *London Review of Books*, 43(4), available at: https://www.lrb.co.uk/the-paper/v43/n04/adam-shatz/dynamo-current-feet-fists-salt.

13 J.L. Herman (2005) 'Justice from the victim's perspective', *Violence Against Women*, 11(5): 571–602, available at: https://dash.harvard.edu/bitstream/handle/1/34961943/Justice%20from%20the%20Victim.pdf?sequence=4&is.

Chapter 1

1   B. Campbell (1988) *Unofficial Secrets*, London: Virago.

2   NRHA (1988) *Action Taken Following the Report of the Judicial Inquiry into Child Abuse in Cleveland*, 28 October.

3   Tim Tate (1997) *Cleveland: Unspeakable Truths*, Channel 4/Yorkshire TV, available at: https://www.youtube.com/watch?v=Q0oTaxZaBvc&t=16s.
4   NRHA, *Action Taken Following the Report*.
5   S. Heppell, Head of Policy, Department of Health and Social Services, correspondence, 1 November 1988.
6   S. Heppell, Head of Policy.
7   NRHA press release, 'Dr Wyatt', December 1988.
8   S. Begley (2020) 'Trump said more Covid-19 testing "creates more cases." We did the math', 20 July, available at: https://www.statnews.com/2020/07/20/trump-said-more-covid19-testing-creates-more-cases-we-did-the-math/.
9   O. Gay (1995) *Questions of Procedure for Ministers*, Research Paper 96/53, House of Commons Library, London, 19 April, paragraph 27: 'Each Minister is responsible to Parliament for the conduct of his or her Department, and for the actions carried out by the Department in pursuit of Government policies or in the discharge of responsibilities laid upon him or her as a Minister. Ministers are accountable to Parliament, in the sense that they have a duty to explain in Parliament the exercise of their powers and duties and to give an account to Parliament of what is done by them in their capacity as Ministers or by their Departments. This includes the duty to give Parliament, including its Select Committees, and the public as full information as possible about the policies, decisions and actions of the Government, and not to deceive or mislead Parliament and the public.'
10 Interview with the author, 2018.
11 Tim Tate, interview with the author, 2016. Bell's pressure on Yorkshire TV shook Sue Richardson's employer in Scotland, National Children's Homes, where she managed a specialist service for adult sexual abuse survivors: she was forced to quit, to the chagrin of women's organisations in the city, for participating in Tim Tate's film. See S. Nelson (1997) 'Breaking the silence', *The Herald*, 26 May, available at: https://www.heraldscotland.com/news/12324829.breaking-the-silence/.
12 In June and July the DoH was alerting the Minister to rising referrals, workloads and costs.
13 https://hansard.parliament.uk/Commons/1987-06-29/debates/11297a75-64f0-4a4b-88fa-c2a6c875ee3f/ChildrenInCare.
14 https://hansard.parliament.uk/Commons/1987-06-29/debates/11297a75-64f0-4a4b-88fa-c2a6c875ee3f/ChildrenInCare.
15 R. Hughes (1987) 'Child abuse in Cleveland', 25 June, file BN68/163.
16 Hughes, 'Child abuse in Cleveland'.
17 Hughes, 'Child abuse in Cleveland'.
18 S. Court, letter to Liam Donaldson, July 1987.
19 Cabinet minutes, 2 July 1987.
20 Cabinet minutes, 2 July 1987.
21 SSI (1987) *Child Abuse in Cleveland – Situation Report from SSD via SSI on 25 June 1987*.
22 NRHA (1987) *Report on Child Sexual Abuse in Cleveland*, 5 July.

23 A. Gamble (1989) 'The politics of Thatcherism', *Parliamentary Affairs*, 42(3), 1 July; J. Newman and J. Clarke (2009) *Publics, Politics and Power*, London: Sage.

24 The Cleveland files contain amended drafts of paragraph 13 of the Conclusions: paragraph 13, page 11 of the *Short Version* is altered, and notes attached to this file acknowledge that it is different from the Cleveland Report's paragraph 13 on page 224. The *Short Version* paragraph 13 ends thus: 'We understand that out of the 121 children, 98 are now at home.' The Cleveland Report's paragraph 13 does not. The *Short Version* therefore gives press and politicians a line on the children, which is usually interpreted as most of the children were not abused.

25 Moira Wallace, writing for the Chancellor of the Exchequer, 4 July 1988.

26 John Major, correspondence to ministers, 1 July 1988, National Archives.

27 Major, correspondence to ministers.

28 Letter from the prime minister's private secretary, 4 July 1988.

29 R.B. Saunders (1988) 'Confidential memorandum, Butler-Sloss Report', to the Chancellor of the Exchequer Nigel Lawson, Chief Secretary to the Treasury John Major, and officials, 5 July.

30 Saunders, 'Confidential memorandum'.

31 The chancellor was advised to endorse the prime minister's focus on the allocation of funds for training: £7 million. This was less than a quarter of the amount estimated by Shadow Health Secretary Robin Cook in the parliamentary debate to be necessary to bring two-year social training in the UK up to European three-year training levels.

32 John Major, Chief Secretary, to Tony Newton, 5 July 1988. In the parliamentary debate, Shadow Health Secretary Robin Cook lamented the meagre £7 million for training, especially because two months earlier Newton had 'failed to find £40 million to extend social work training from two to three years'.

33 The memorandum proposed that ministers avoid any positive commitment to the Butler-Sloss recommendation of an Office of Child Protection or the creation of a Family Court.

34 The family court was relaunched with the Children and Families Act 2014.

35 Interview with the author for this book, 2020.

36 A. Spackman (1988) 'Marietta Higgs', *Marxism Today*, January, available at: https://banmarchive.org.uk/marxism-today/january-1988/marietta-higgs/.

37 House of Commons debate, 6 July 1988, Hansard, vol 136, cc1061–77, available at: https://api.parliament.uk/historic-hansard/commons/1988/jul/06/child-abuse-cleveland.

38 Interview with the author, 2016.

Chapter 2

1 Hansard, 7 July 1987, vol 119.

2 D. Keay (1987) 'Interview', *Woman's Own*, September, available at: https://www.margaretthatcher.org/document/106689.

[3] C. Moore (2015) 'Margaret Thatcher biography, part 7: dealing with rumours without evidence', *The Telegraph*, 3 October, available at: https://www.telegraph.co.uk/news/politics/margaret-thatcher/margaret-thatcher-biography/11908220/margaret-thatcher-biography-sex-abuse-claims.html.

[4] IICSA (2020) 'Allegations of Child Sexual Abuse Linked to Westminster; E.3 the Conservative Party and Sir Peter Morrison, June', available at: https://www.iicsa.org.uk/reports-recommendations/publications/investigation/westminster/part-e-political-parties/e3-conservative-party-and-sir-peter-morrison.

[5] W v the UK, European Court of Human Rights, 8 July 1987, case number 4/1986/102/150, available at: http://hudoc.echr.coe.int/eng?i=001-57600. This case was lodged in 1982. It referred to a century-old legal instrument, modified in the Children and Young Persons Act 1969, to allow children to be removed from their parents for 28 days without appeal; it was still recommended in *Working Together*, but social workers were increasingly critical of Place of Safety Orders as a 'traumatic entry into the care system': see N. Parton (1991) *Governing the Family: Child Care, Child Protection and the State*, London: Macmillan, pp 34–6. The legal challenge was lodged by parents who were represented by Louis Blom-Cooper, QC. In his Beckford Report published in 1986, Blom-Cooper had recommended a 72-hour time limit and parents' rights to make immediate challenges – a proposal that the DHSS had rejected.

[6] Tony Newton announced the Cleveland Inquiry in the House of Commons, 9 July.

[7] Labour MP Michael Meacher's response to the proposed inquiry, available at: https://api.parliament.uk/historic-hansard/commons/1987/jul/09/child-abuse-cleveland.

[8] Interview with the author.

[9] R. Hughes (1987) 'Child abuse in Cleveland', 25 June, file BN68/163.

[10] See N. Parton (1991) *Governing the Family, Child Care, Child Protection and the State*, London: Macmillan.

[11] I. Butler and M. Drakeford (2005) *Scandal, Social Policy and Social Welfare*, Bristol: Policy Press, pp 3–4.

[12] A. Hegarty (2002) 'The government of memory: public inquiries and the limits of justice in Northern Ireland', *Fordham International Law Journal*, 26(4): 1148–92, available at: https://ir.lawnet.fordham.edu/cgi/viewcontent.cgi?httpsredir=1&article=1895&context=ilj.

[13] R. Susskind (1989) 'A conversation with Lady Justice Elizabeth Butler-Sloss', available at: https://www.gresham.ac.uk/lectures-and-events/a-conversation-with-lady-justice-elizabeth-butler-sloss.

[14] Susskind, 'A conversation'.

[15] Mathew Thorpe opening speech, on day 1 of the Cleveland Inquiry, 11 August 1987.

[16] Mathew Thorpe, closing speech, Cleveland Inquiry, 28 January 1988.

[17] Thorpe, closing speech.

[18] See B. Campbell (1997) *Unofficial Secrets*, London: Virago; John Urch of the Community Health Council, after the Chief Constable issued instructions to divisional commanders that 'unsubstantiated evidence from Dr Marietta Higgs will not be a matter for investigation'. In mid-June he rang Dr Higgs. 'I suppose I was rude … but she never lost her temper, she did not raise her voice. … I called her everything I could lay my tongue to really, in all sorts of ways, but the response was cool and calm.'

[19] Campbell, *Unofficial Secrets*.

[20] Jane Wynne and Chris Hobbs in 1986: 'Buggery in childhood: a common syndrome of child abuse', *The Lancet*, October, 4/2(8510): 792–6. They wrote that 'We have not seen this in normal children.'

[21] Mathew Thorpe, day 73 of the Cleveland Inquiry, 28 January 1988.

[22] Jane Wynne, day 25 of the Cleveland Inquiry, 25 November 1987.

[23] Days 73 and 74 of the Cleveland Inquiry, 29 and 30 January 1988.

[24] Eleanor Platt QC, day 72 of the Cleveland Inquiry, 27 January 1988.

[25] Robert Nelson QC, closing speech, day 73 of the Cleveland Inquiry, 29 January 1988.

[26] Dr Roberts had given evidence to the Inquiry on days 56 and 58, 23–4 November 1987.

[27] Robert Nelson QC, day 73 of the Cleveland Inquiry, 28 January 1987.

[28] Nelson, day 73.

[29] Israel Kolvin, day 39 of the Cleveland Inquiry.

[30] Dr Harry Zeitlin, day 48 of the Cleveland Inquiry, 4 November 1987.

[31] Ralph Underwager, day 70 of the Cleveland Inquiry, 14 December 1987.

[32] Underwager, day 70.

[33] Underwager, day 70.

[34] J.R. Conte, S. Wolf and T. Smith (1989) 'What sexual offenders tell us about prevention strategies', *Child Abuse and Neglect*, 13: 295–301, available at: http://ngolearning.com.au/files/face2face-courses/CP-dynamics/Whatsexualoffenderstellusaboutpreventionstrategies.pdf

[35] Interview with the author; see also Campbell, *Stolen Voices*, p 21.

[36] T.D. Lyon (1999) 'New wave in children's suggestibility research', *Cornell Law Review*, 1004, available at: http://scholarship.law.cornell.edu/clr/vol84/iss4/3.

[37] Lyon, 'New wave in children's suggestibility research'.

[38] R.C. Summit (1983) 'The child sexual abuse accommodation syndrome', *Child Abuse and Neglect*, 7(2): 177–93.

[39] J.L. Herman (1981) *Father–Daughter Incest*, Cambridge, MA: Harvard University Press.

[40] E. Butler-Sloss (1988) *Report of the Inquiry into Child Abuse in Cleveland 1987*, Cm 412, London: HMSO; see also B. Deer (1988) 'Why we must now start listening to children', *Sunday Times*, 10 July.

[41] Deborah Glassbrook's report was provided in her written evidence to the inquiry.

[42] Deborah Glassbrook, day 48 of the Cleveland Inquiry, 4 November 1987.

[43] Interview with the author for this book, 2016.

44 In the context of this rapid escalation in referrals since 1986, Dr Bob Nelson, Queen Elizabeth Hospital, Gateshead, distributed a questionnaire to all the region's paediatricians, 'The increasing involvement of paediatricians in child abuse', 27 May 1987. Nelson estimated further surveys would be needed because they were moving into the summer holiday period.

45 Liam Donaldson, statement to the Appeal Court, 20 February 1989. During Dr Higgs's legal proceedings, he said that in 1986 he 'began to give some thought to the problem of child sexual abuse. ... I had become aware that the problem of child sexual abuse was a growing one.' He said that he 'gave serious consideration to whether this was an issue which ought to be examined in policy terms at Regional level'. But there were 'factors which militated against such an approach'. First, it was a district – not regional – responsibility. Secondly, there were already many issues that were 'national priorities', and 'informal' conversations led him to believe that there was a national consultation on guidelines and 'definitive guidance was awaited'. In this statement he did not mention Dr Nelson's workload warning.

46 Nelson, 'The increasing involvement'.

47 Donaldson, statement to the Appeal Court; Sue Richardson, interview with the author for this book, 2016.

48 Eleanor Platt QC, day 73 of the Cleveland Inquiry, 29 January 1988.

49 Sue Richardson, interview with the author.

50 Platt, day 73, Cleveland Inquiry.

Chapter 3

1   T. Newton (1988) Undated draft of Parliamentary speech, National Archives, BN/68.

2   Tony Newton speech, House of Commons, 6 July 1988, available at: https://hansard.parliament.uk/commons/1988-07-06/debates/85bf6545-34e5-433b-a18f-edfbb702d74a/ChildAbuse(Cleveland).

3   E. Butler-Sloss (1988) Report of the Inquiry into Child Abuse in Cleveland 1987, Cm 412, London: HMSO.

4   https://hansard.parliament.uk/commons/1988-07-06/debates/85bf6545-34e5-433b-a18f-edfbb702d74a/ChildAbuse(Cleveland).

5   N. Parton (1991) Governing the Family: Child Care, Child Protection and the State, London: Macmillan, p 114.

6   https://hansard.parliament.uk/commons/1988-07-06/debates/85bf6545-34e5-433b-a18f-edfbb702d74a/ChildAbuse(Cleveland).

7   Later a minister and chief whip in the Labour government elected in 1987, before going to the House of Lords.

8   https://hansard.parliament.uk/commons/1988-07-06/debates/85bf6545-34e5-433b-a18f-edfbb702d74a/ChildAbuse(Cleveland).

9   https://hansard.parliament.uk/commons/1988-07-06/debates/85bf6545-34e5-433b-a18f-edfbb702d74a/ChildAbuse(Cleveland).

10 Butler-Sloss, Report of the Inquiry into Child Abuse.

11 Butler-Sloss, interview with the author.

[12] Butler-Sloss, *Report of the Inquiry into Child Abuse*.

[13] Butler-Sloss, *Report of the Inquiry into Child Abuse*.

[14] R.F. Badgley (1984) 'Sexual Offences Against Children, Report of the Committee on Sexual Offences Against Children and Youths, Canada, Department of Justice', Chapter 2, pp 29–36, available at: https://publications. gc.ca/site/eng/9.840126/publication.html.

[15] Parton, *Governing the Family*, p 113.

[16] Sue Richardson, interview with the author for this book, 2016.

[17] Prior guidance stated: 'doctors may disclose confidential information to police investigating a grave or very serious crime, provided always that they are prepared to justify their actions if called upon to do so'. The GMC publicised this toughening up, from *may* to *must*, in its 1987 Annual Report. Too late for Higgs or Wyatt – and their successors.

[18] Parton, *Governing the Family*, pp 113–14.

[19] E. Butler-Sloss (1988) *Report of the Inquiry into Child Abuse* (and the *Short Version*), 'Inter-Agency Co-operation', Section 8, para vi. They could also 'hold a watching brief or make informal inquiries'.

[20] Butler-Sloss (1988) *Report of the Inquiry into Child Abuse*, p 207.

[21] E. Butler-Sloss, day 73 of the Cleveland Inquiry, 28 January 1988.

Chapter 4

[1] The following cameos are taken from the confidential schedules given to the Inquiry summarising the legal, medical, social/health/welfare services' and police responses, the context and content of children's disclosures (if any), police action, court proceedings and final outcomes. S. Richardson and H. Bacon (2018) (eds) *Child Sexual Abuse: Whose Problem? – Reflections from Cleveland* (revised edition), Bristol: Policy Press.

[2] This account is based on the confidential analysis shared with the inquiry and my interviews with the children's mother: B. Campbell (1997) *Unofficial Secrets*, London: Virago; and interviews in 2018.

[3] E. Butler-Sloss (1988) Cleveland Report Short Version. This was noted by a local councillor with oversight responsibilities, who urged Brady to find a home outside the school.

[4] E. Butler-Sloss (1989) 'The Cleveland Enquiry', *Medico-Legal Journal*, 1 September, available at: https://journals.sagepub.com/doi/abs/10.1177/002581728905700304?journalCode=mljc.

[5] M. Raftery and E. O'Sullivan (2002) *Suffer the Little Children: The Inside Story of Ireland's Industrial Schools*, London: Continuum.

[6] B. Arnold (2009) *Irish Gulag, How the State Betrayed Its Innocent Children*, Dublin: Gill & Macmillan. After his conviction and imprisonment, a torrent of lawsuits hit the Catholic Church. Revelations about the 'Irish gulag' became uncontainable.

[7] *Northern Echo* (2004) 'Payout setback for abuse victim', 22 December, available at: https://www.thenorthernecho.co.uk/news/6967347.payout-setback-abuse-victim/.

[8] *Teesside Live* (2008) 'Kirklevington abuse man awarded £100,000 damages', 18 April, available at: https://www.gazettelive.co.uk/news/local-news/kirklevington-abuse-man-awarded-100000-3733451.

[9] W. Utting (1997) *People Like Us*, London: Stationery Office.

[10] Interview with the author, 2016.

[11] Interview with the author, 2015.

[12] Interview with the author, 2016.

[13] David Behan, communication with the author, 21 December 2015.

[14] L. Terr (1992) *Too Scared to Cry*, New York: Basic Books.

[15] A. Kleinman, V. Das and M.M. Lock (1997) *Social Suffering*, Oakland: University of California Press.

[16] Interview with the author, 2018.

[17] Interview with the author, 2017.

[18] 'National Circular HM (61)112 Disciplinary Proceedings in Cases Related to Hospital Medical and Dental Staff'.

[19] Eleanor Platt QC, day 72 of the Cleveland Inquiry, 27 January 1988.

[20] NRHA confidential minutes, December 1987, confirm that the plans had not yet been discussed with the paediatricians.

[21] The NRHA authority kept two sets of minutes of its meetings, only one of them public. Correspondence on 7 October between senior civil servants and the NRHA (in the National Archive) shows that the NRHA did not appreciate pressure 'to do as it's told' – that is, hold back from making a formal statement until the appeal had been heard.

[22] Senior officials involved in the Cleveland saga; W. Williams wrote to R. Merifield on 10 October that Dr Higgs would not be allowed back to Middlesbrough. The minister had asked all the agencies for their response to the Cleveland Report, and furthermore he was due to visit Middlesbrough in December, when the SSI inspection of Cleveland would be published, and wished to show that action had been taken. Dr Higgs's lawyers launched legal action against 'constructive dismissal'. The DHSS was hugely sensitive to this charge and ordered the NRHA to 'hold the line', and it wanted no evidence of its involvement: if its interventions were 'too overt the doctors might argue that their Appeals had been prejudiced'.

[23] Memorandum by Strachan Hepple, 1 November 1988: Cleveland: Report from NRHA, suggesting the line to take: 'cannot give any commitment to publishing the report at this stage'. In response to the health authority's request for reassurance that the minister's request for this report did not indicate lack of confidence in the authority, Strachan suggested that it be described as 'simply a natural follow-up'.

[24] Letter from E. Hay to M. Higgs, 18 February 1989.

[25] *The Guardian*, 18 February 1989.

[26] Interview with the authors, 2017.

[27] W. Williams memorandum, Cleveland *Guardian* letter, 21 February 1989. A briefing by senior civil servant Jim Furniss on 20 February 1989, 'The line to take', consolidated the narrative: 'Stuart Bell had tabled a Parliamentary Question in June ... in July the Minister announced the Inquiry ... the

Inquiry does not address the question as to how many of the cases examined were actually abused...'; Public statement by Cleveland paediatricians on 21 February 1989.

[28] J. Furniss (1989) to Parliamentary liaison P. Curd, Cleveland *Guardian* letter, 20 February.

[29] G. Bindman (1993) 'Obituary: Brian Raymond', *The Independent*, 31 May. The Cleveland Report had 'deliberately avoided reaching such certain conclusions in relation to individual cases, though it does say "we have in general no reason to question the accuracy of her (Dr Higgs's) clinical observations"'.

[30] On 19 October 1989 the conviction of the Guildford Four, three young Irish men and an English woman, for two IRA bombings, was quashed. Donaldson, the presiding judge, had notoriously lamented the abolition of the death penalty. K. Toolis (1990) 'When British justice failed', *New York Times*, 25 February.

[31] Brian Raymond personal letter to Dr Higgs, October 1989, outlining his impressions of the hearing.

[32] Dr Simon Court, interview with the author, 2018.

[33] Interview with the author, 2017.

[34] Interview with the author, 2018.

[35] NRHA correspondence to Dr Wyatt, 18 October 1988.

[36] NRHA public statement, December 1988.

[37] BBC Radio 4 (2007) *Cleveland: Twenty Years On*, presenter Jenny Cuffe, producer Smita Patel, 19 February.

[38] South Tees NHS Trust notification of Dr Wyatt's dismissal. He was dismissed on 5 July 2010.

[39] Interview with the author, 2016.

[40] Butler-Sloss, 'The Cleveland Inquiry'.

Chapter 5

[1] C. Smart (1999) 'A history of ambivalence and conflict in the discursive construction of the "child victim"', *Social and Legal Studies*, 8(3): 391–409, 406; J.L. Herman (1992) *Trauma and Recovery: From Domestic Abuse to Political Terrorism*, New York: Basic Books, p 7.

[2] The first text of forensic science was Song Ci's *The Washing Away of Wrongs*, written in China in 1247, to aid coroners and courts to bring justice to the living and the dead.

[3] T.A. Sebok (2001) *Signs: An Introduction to Semiotics*, 2nd edn, Toronto: University of Toronto Press.

[4] J. Labbé (2005) 'Ambroise Tardieu: the man and his work on child maltreatment a century before Kempe', *Child Abuse and Neglect*, 29(4): 311–24; A.A.Tardieu (1867) *Etude medico-legale sur les attentats aux mœurs*, Paris: J.B. Bailliere.

[5] A.A. Tardieu (1860) 'Etude medico-legale sur les services et mauvais traitements exerces sur des enfants', *Annales d'hygiène publique et de médecine légale*, 13, 361–98, available at: https://archive.org/details/

BIUSante_90141x1913x20. Labbé, *Ambroise Tardieu*, p 311: 'He tried to open the eyes of physicians to this horrendous reality.'

6   Tardieu, *Etude medico-legale sur les attentats aux mœurs*. From funnelling to changes in anal folds, skin colour, venereal diseases, and finally anal dilatation as an indicator of frequent buggery. Tardieu was careful to consider other possible causes: anal dilatation, he noted, also occurred after death (p 254). During the decade following the first edition, he reported that of 11,576 cases of rape or attempted rape in the courts, the majority of the victims, 9,125, were children, mostly girls.

7   L.A. Jackson (2000) *Child Sexual Abuse in Victorian England*, London: Routledge, p 173.

8   N. McKenna (2013) *Fanny and Stella: The Young Men Who Shocked Victorian England*, London: Faber & Faber. The progressive *Reynolds's News* described the clinical debates in the trial; the public was avid: crowds 'completely blockaded the thoroughfares' outside the court.

9   A.S. Taylor (1970) *Autograph Medical Report on Boulton and Park*, Cambridge: Cambridge University Press, available at: www.jnorman.com/pages/books/44785/alfred-swaine-taylor/autograph-medical-report-on-boulton-and-park (with thanks to Jeremy Norman). The medical report referred to the sign that was, 'according to Tardieu and others suspicious'; A. Clark (ed) (2011) *The History of Sexuality in Europe*, London: Routledge.

10   Labbé, 'Ambroise Tardieu'.

11   See J. Weeks (1977) *Coming Out*, London: Quartet; S. Brady (2005) *Masculinity and Male Homosexuality in Britain, 1861–1913*, Basingstoke: Palgrave; J.R. Walkowitz (1980) *Prostitution and Victorian Society*, Cambridge: Cambridge University Press.

12   K. Wellings, K. Mitchell and K. Collumbien (2012) *Sexual Health: A Public Health Perspective*, London: McGraw-Hill International, p 91. Studies in the UK and US confirm anal penetration experienced by between a quarter and a third of *both* gay and straight people; see B. Dodge, D. Herbenick, T-C. Fu, V. Schick, M. Reece, S. Sanders and D. Fortenberry (2016) 'Sexual behaviours of U.S. men by self-identified sexual orientation: results from the 2012 National Survey of Sexual Health and Behaviour', *Journal of Sexual Medicine*, 13, April: 637–49. In 2022 doctors Tabitha Gana and Lesley Hunt reported that around a third of young women experienced anal penetration – causing pain and ano-rectal disorders: T. Gana and L. Hunt (2022) 'Young women and anal sex', *BMJ*, 11 August, 378, available at: https://www.bmj.com/content/378/bmj.o1975. D. Campbell (2022) 'Rise in popularity of anal sex has led to health problems for women', *The Guardian*, 11 August, available at: https://www.theguardian.com/society/2022/aug/11/rise-in-popularity-of-anal-sex-has-led-to-health-problems-for-women

13   J.L. Herman (1986) *Father–Daughter Incest*, Cambridge, MA: Harvard University Press, p 9.

14   In 1896 Freud published *The Aetiology of Hysteria* and *Studies on Hysteria*. He wrote that the origin of every one of the 18 cases cited was of a childhood sexual trauma. This was his 'seduction theory'. Sigmund Freud, in a letter to

Wilhelm Fleiss, dated 21 September 1897, writes that he no longer believes his own seduction theory, partly because of disappointment that he could not bring his work with his patients to a conclusion, and 'Then the surprise that in all cases the father, not excluding my own, had to be accused ... surely such widespread perversions against children are not very probable.' See J. Masson (1985) *The Complete Letters of Sigmund Freud to Wilhelm Fleiss, 1887–1904*, Cambridge, MA: Harvard University Press, available at: http://ww3.haverford.edu/psychology/ddavis/ffliess.html.

[15] L. Gordon (1989) *Heroes of Their Own Lives: The Politics and History of Family Violence*, London: Virago, p 4.

[16] Smart, 'A history of ambivalence'.

[17] J. Crane (2015) '"The bones tell a story in children too young or too frightened to tell": the battered child syndrome in post-war Britain and America', *Social History of Medicine*, 28(4), 1 November: 767–88. In 1946 Pittsburgh physician John Caffey published evidence of children's injuries that he discovered using X-rays. Caffey became a founder of paediatric radiology, a field that was 'radical, innovative and unafraid to draw what were, for this period, bold conclusions about child maltreatment'. This was fearless, not least because the doctors wrestled with the discrepancies between the injuries and the carers' narratives. J. Caffey (1946) 'Multiple fractures in the long bones of infants suffering from chronic subdural hematoma', *Radiology*, 194: 163–74, available at: https://www.ncbi.nlm.nih.gov/pmc/articles/PMC3032844/.

[18] F. Silverman (1972) 'Unrecognized trauma in infants: the battered child syndrome, and the syndrome of Ambroise Tardieu', *Radiology*, 104(2): 337–53; P. Kleinman (2006) 'Multiple fractures in the long bones of children suffering from chronic subdural hematoma – a commentary', *American Journal of Roentgenology*, 187(6): 1403–4. Jennifer Crane gives a thorough narrative of the medical journey towards 'the battered-child syndrome' in Crane '"The bones tell a story"'. C.H. Kempe, F.N. Silverman, B.F. Steele, W. Droegmeuller and H.K. Silver (1985) 'The battered-child syndrome', *Child Abuse and Neglect*, 9: 143–54, available at: http://kempe.org/wp-content/uploads/2015/01/The_Battered_Child_Syndrome.pdf.

[19] Bentovim and his colleagues' 'family dysfunction' model was also being challenged as 'other-blaming' by feminist experts; see E. Saraga and M. MacLeod (1989) *Towards a Feminist Professional Practice, Report of a Conference Held by the Child Abuse Studies Unit*, April, London: CASU (Child Abuse Studies Unit).

[20] A. Bentovim (2013) 'Commentary on Kempe C.H. 1978 *Sexual Abuse, Another Hidden Paediatric Problem*', in R.D. Krugman and J.E. Korbin (eds) *C. Henry Kempe: A 50-Year Legacy to the Field of Child Sexual Abuse and Neglect*, Child Maltreatment 1, Dordrecht: Springer, pp 205–14.

[21] D. Finkelhor, G. Hotaling, I.A. Lewis and C. Smith (1990) 'Sexual abuse in a national survey of adult men and women: prevalence, characteristics and risk', *Child Abuse and Neglect*, 14: 19–28. Finkelhor's follow-up survey of

childhood experiences within and beyond the family found that 27 per cent of women and 16 per cent of men had suffered sexual abuse.

22 M. Koss and C. Oros (1980) 'The "unacknowledged" rape victim', paper presented to the Annual Convention of the American Psychological Association, Quebec, available at: https://files.eric.ed.gov/fulltext/ED199590.pdf.

23 M. Koss, C. Gidycz and N. Wisnieswski (1987) 'The scope, incidence and prevalence of sexual aggression and victimization in a national sample of higher education students', *Journal of Consulting and Clinical Psychology*, 55(2): 162–70.

24 D.E.H. Russell (1986) *The Secret Trauma: Incest in the Lives of Girls and Women*, New York: Basic Books.

25 G.E. Wyatt (1985) 'The sexual abuse of Afro-American and White-American women in childhood', *Child Abuse and Neglect*, 9: 507–19. Comparisons of major studies reveals significant differences: the Finkelhor findings on familial sexual abuse could have been low because he had included exhibitionism and Wyatt's could have been higher because the demographic was different. Older women were more likely to have reviewed their interpretation of events than students who were closer to their childhood interpretation of events.

26 A. Baker and S. Duncan (1985) 'Child sexual abuse: a study of prevalence in Britain', *Child Abuse and Neglect*, 9(4): 457–67.

27 B.S. Fisher (2009) 'The effects of survey question wording on rape estimates: evidence from quasi-experimental design', *Violence Against Women*, 15(2), February: 133–47; B.S. Fisher and F.T. Cullen (2000) 'Measuring the sexual victimization of women: evolution, current controversies and future research', *Criminal Justice*, 4: 317–90, available at: https://www.researchgate.net/publication/292731439_Measuring_the_sexual_victimization_of_women_Evolution_current_controversies_and_future_research.

28 N.J. Wild and J.M. Wynne (1986) 'Child sex rings', *British Medical Journal*, 293, August: 183–5, available at: https://www.jstor.org/stable/29523909; see also B. Campbell (1998) *Unofficial Secrets – Child Sexual Abuse: The Cleveland Case*, London: Virago. Tyneside's Women Police Doctors Group, a police–Rape Crisis Centre initiative, supported the findings. These doctors, too, were familiar with 'normal' and 'abnormal' and reported that reflex anal dilatation was observed in 8.5 per cent of the 224 children referred to them for suspected sexual abuse.

29 C.J. Hobbs and J.M. Wynne (1986) 'Buggery in childhood – a common syndrome of child abuse', *The Lancet*, October, 4/2(8510): 792–6. During a period of eight months signs of anal abuse were found in 35 cases of buggery in boys and girls aged between 14 months and eight years.

30 Campbell, *Unofficial Secrets*, p 60. Protective action would be relevant to 'differential diagnosis' because dilatation disappears in the process of the body healing.

31 R. Summit (1983) 'The child sexual abuse accommodation syndrome', *Child Abuse and Neglect*, 7: 177–93. The use of Summit's essay in the US courts became controversial, and Summit himself later cautioned that it should be

understood as a summary of clinical experience of victims' secondary trauma when faced with adults' disbelief and rejection: R. Summit (1993) 'Abuse of the child sexual abuse accommodation syndrome', *Journal of Child Sexual Abuse*, 1(4): 153–64.

[32] R. Badgley (1985) 'Report of the Committee on Sexual Offences Against Children and Youths', Canada, Department of Justice, available at: https://publications.gc.ca/site/eng/9.840126/publication.html; Truth and Reconciliation Commission of Canada (2015) *Honouring the Truth: Summary of the Final Report of the Truth and Reconciliation Commission of Canada*.

[33] Summit, 'The child sexual abuse accommodation syndrome'.

[34] R. Krugman, quoted in D.L. Kerns, D.L. Terman and C.S. Larson (1994) 'The role of physicians in reporting and evaluating child sexual abuse', *Future Child*, 4(2): 119–34.

[35] Krugman, 'The role of physicians'.

[36] J. Clarke and J. Newman (1997) *The Managerial State: Power, Politics and Ideology in the Remaking of Social Welfare*, London: Sage; B. Metriken-Gold (2005) 'Personal reflections about the work of the US Advisory Board on Child Abuse and Neglect', *Child Abuse and Neglect*, 41: 3–18.

[37] D. Keay (1987) 'Interview', *Woman's Own*, 31 October, available at: www.margaretthatcher.org/document/106689; E. Olafson (2002) 'When paradigms collide: Roland Summit and the rediscovery of child sexual abuse', in J. Conte (ed) *Critical Issues in Child Sexual Abuse: Historical, Legal and Psychological Perspectives*, London: Sage, pp 71–106.

[38] For a useful overview and discussion of this process, theories of 'public' and the state, see Newman and Clarke, *Publics, Politics and Power*; Clarke and Newman, *The Managerial State*, p 10.

[39] M. Dean (2015) 'Rupert Hughes obituary', *The Guardian*, 25 August.

Chapter 6

[1] Interview with the author, 2015.

[2] The Broxtowe narrative is based on interviews with senior officers, social workers, carers and members of the family, 1990.

[3] B. Campbell (1990) 'Listen to the children', *Diverse Reports*, Channel 4.

[4] Prison interview with perpetrator convicted in 1991.

[5] Campbell, 'Listen to the children'.

[6] D. White (1990) 'Report of the Director of Social Services, Child Abuse', 7 November, Nottinghamshire County Council.

[7] White, 'Report of the Director of Social Services', para 39.

[8] Appeal Court judgment (1988) EWCA Civ J0718-3, available at: https://cathyfox.substack.com/p/broxtowe-child-sexual-abuse-re-f-a-minor-and-others-supreme-court-18th-july-1988.

[9] White, 'Report of the Director of Social Services'.

[10] White, 'Report of the Director of Social Services', paras 36–9.

[11] (1995) EWCA Crim J0706-6, 6 July, L.J. Staughton, J. Scott Aker, J. Butterfield. Regina v VY and WX, available at: https://cathyfox.substack.com/p/broxtowe-child-sexual-abuse-court-of-appeal-6th-july-1995.

[12] Campbell, 'Listen to the children'.

[13] The JET Report (1990) *The Broxtowe Files*, available at: http://www.users. globalnet.co.uk/~dlheb/jetrepor.htm.

[14] R. Waterhouse (2014) 'Satanic abuse, false memories, weird beliefs and moral panics anatomy of a 24-hour investigation', PhD, London: City University.

[15] R. Waterhouse 'Satanic abuse'.

[16] White, 'Report of the Director of Social Services, Child Abuse': the JET Report's conclusions were leaked in March 1990 and 'soon gained wide currency as they were leaked to the media … in these leaks the excellent work which had been completed to rescue and care for children, and which led to the convictions, was ignored'.

[17] D. Aaronovitch (2015) 'Ritual sexual abuse: the anatomy of a panic', BBC Radio 4, parts 1 and 2, 25 May and 31 May, available at: https:// www.bbc.co.uk/programmes/b05vx63j.

[18] Psychologist, interview with the author, 1993.

[19] White, 'Report of the Director of Social Services'.

[20] David White's evidence to IICSA 8 October 2018 was remarkably candid about his role in the Broxtowe controversy, the unsteady state of social services and the 'appalling abuse of young people in the County Council's care', available at: https://www.iicsa.org.uk/key-documents/7181/view/ public-hearing-transcript-8-october-2018.pdf.

[21] Judith Jones, interview with the author, 1998.

[22] P. Gummer (n.d.) 'The Prescott case: key dates and events: Leeds, Grenville, Lanark, Health Unit', available at: https://web.archive.org/ web/20170203191702/http://www.healthunit.org/carekids/jericho/ STORY.htm.

[23] The investigation was named The Jericho Project in his memory.

[24] Gummer, 'The Prescott Case'.

[25] Rocci Pagnello, interview with the author, 2017.

[26] Gummer, 'The Prescott Case'.

[27] Sandra Lawn, interview with the author, 2017.

[28] Lawn, interview with the author, 2017.

Chapter 7

[1] J. Kitzinger (2004) *Framing Abuse: Media Influence and Public Understanding of Sexual Violence Against Children*, London: Pluto Press.

[2] Kitzinger, *Framing Abuse*, p 75.

[3] Kitzinger, *Framing Abuse*, p 75.

[4] Since the 1980s, statistics in the US and the UK have consistently indicated around 20 per cent of girls and 5 to 10 per cent of boys experience child sexual abuse of some kind: see US Center for Victims of Crime: https:// victimsofcrime.org/child-sexual-abuse-statistics/; UK NSPCC (2021) 'Child sexual abuse: statistics briefing', available at: https://learning.nspcc.org.uk/ research-resources/statistics-briefings/child-sexual-abuse.

5   C. Atmore (1999) 'Towards rethinking moral panic: child abuse conflicts and social constructionist responses', in C. Bagley and K. Mallick (eds) *Child Sexual Abuse and Adult Offenders*, London: Routledge, pp 11–26.

6   J.L. Herman (1995) 'Crime and memory', *Bulletin of the American Academy of Psychiatry and the Law*, 23(1): 57–76. The backlash against child sexual abuse synchronised with the resistance to feminist rape narratives; see Atmore (1999) 'Towards rethinking moral panic'.

7   Herman 'Crime and memory'.

8   D. Finkelhor (1994) 'The "backlash" and future of child protection advocacy: insights from the study of social issues', in J.E.B. Myers (ed) *Backlash: The Child Protection System Under Fire*, Los Angeles, CA: Sage, pp 1–14.

9   Myers, *Backlash*.

10   For an insightful overview and discussion of this process, see J. Newman and J. Clarke (2009) *Publics, Politics and Power*, London: Sage.

11   J.E.B. Myers (ed) (1994) *The Backlash: Child Protection Under Fire*, London: Sage, p 89.

12   J. Berry (2014) 'How the witch-hunt myth undermined American justice', *Daily Beast*, 7 December.

13   K. Beckett (1996) 'Culture and the politics of signification: the case of child sexual abuse', *Social Problems*, 43(1): 57–76. The false memory movement was a 'new and creative synthesis of (late) Freudian ideas regarding the impact of fantasy and suggestion on memory.'

14   In 2019 the US False Memory Syndrome Foundation disbanded.

15   J. Hollingsworth (1986) *Unspeakable Acts*, New York: Congdon & Weed, p 343. He appeared as an expert witness in the Jordan, Minnesota, trial in 1984 of more than 20 adults, including parents, accused of abusing children in a sex ring.

16   A. Salter (1992) *Accuracy of Expert Testimony in Child Sexual Abuse Cases: A Case Study of Ralph Underwager and Hollida Wakefield*, Alexandria, VA: American Prosecutors Research Institute; A. Salter (1998) 'Confessions of a whistle-blower: lessons learned', *Ethics and Behaviour*, 8(2): 115–24.

17   H.J. Wakefield and R. Underwager (1991) 'Interview: Hollida Wakefield and Ralph Underwager', *Paidika, The Journal of Paedophilia*, available at: https://theawarenesscenter.blogspot.com/1991/06/paidika-interview-hollida-wakefield-and.html.

18   Katherine Beckett notes that by then the false memory movement had been particularly successful in 're-signifying the issue of child abuse' in ways that the pro-paedophilia and male prerogatives advocates could not: Beckett, 'Culture and the politics of signification', 72. Underwager helped found the public campaigning organisation False Memory Syndrome Foundation in 1992 with Pamela and Peter Freyd – after their daughter, the academic Jennifer Freyd, had *privately* accused her father of childhood abuse.

19   B. Campbell (1995) 'Mind games', *Guardian Weekend*, 11 February.

20   This is a very condensed summary of an enduring, complex and technical conflict over memory, repression, recovered memories, trauma and children's memories.

[21] S.J. Dallam (1998) 'Dr. Richard Gardner: a review of his theories and opinions on atypical sexuality, pedophilia, and treatment issues', *Treating Abuse Today*, 8(1): 15–23; Leadership Council (2005) 'Overview of Richard Gardner's opinions on paedophilia and child sexual abuse', available at: http://www.leadershipcouncil.org/1/pas/RAG.html.

[22] World Health Organization (2020) 'WHO removes parental alienation from its classification index', 20 September, available at: https://reseauiml. wordpress.com/2020/02/23/world-health-organization-removes-parental-alienation-from-its-classification-index/.

[23] European Parliament (2021) 'Resolution on the impact of intimate partner violence and custody rights on women and children', 6 October, available at: https://www.europarl.europa.eu/doceo/document/TA-9-2021-10-06_EN.html.

[24] J.S. Meier (2020) 'Child custody outcomes involving parental alienation and abuse allegations: what do the data show?' *Journal of Social Welfare and Family Law*, January, 42(1): 92–105; available at: https://www.researchgate.net/publication/338437886_US_child_custody_outcomes_in_cases_involving_parental_alienation_and_abuse_allegations_what_do_the_data_show; A. Barnett (2020) 'A genealogy of hostility: parental alienation in England and Wales', *Journal of Social Welfare and Family Law*, 42(1): 18–29, available at: https://www.researchgate.net/publication/338453608_A_genealogy_of_hostility_parental_alienation_in_England_and_Wales; A. Barnett and A. Riley (2021) 'Experiences of parental alienation interventions', in J. Mercer & M. Drew (2021) *Challenging Parental Alienation*, Abingdon: Routledge; H. Summers and B. Campbell (2022) 'Parental alienation and the unregulated experts shattering children's lives', 12 June, *The Observer*; available at: https://www.theguardian.com/global-development/2022/jun/12/parental-alienation-and-the-unregulated-experts-shattering-childrens-lives.

[25] Meier, 'Child custody outcomes'.

[26] J. Birchall and S. Choudhry (2021) '"I was punished for telling the truth": how allegations of parental alienation are used to silence, sideline and disempower survivors of domestic abuse in family law proceedings', *Journal of Gender-Based Violence*, 6(1): 115–31; Summers and Campbell (2022) 'Parental alienation'; H. Summers (2022) 'Court-appointed expert can be named in "parental alienation" case', 31 July, *The Observer*, available at: https://www.theguardian.com/global-development/2022/jul/31/observer-victory-in-transparency-battle-in-family-courts-in-england-and-wales?amp.

[27] J. Doughty, N. Maxwell and T. Slater (2018) 'Review of research and case law on parental alienation', Cardiff: Welsh Government, available at: http://orca.cf.ac.uk/id/eprint/112511; J. Doughty, N. Maxwell and T. Slater (2019) *Professional Responses to Parental Alienation: Research Informed Practice*, RCA: Cardiff University; J. Doughty and M. Drew (2022) 'History of the parental alienation belief system', in J. Mercer and M. Drew (eds) (2022) *Challenging Parental Alienation*, Abingdon: Routledge, pp 21–39.

[28] Doughty, Maxwell and Slater, 'Review of research and case law'; Doughty, Maxwell and Slater, *Professional Responses to Parental Alienation*.

[29] See recent judgments: J. Keehan (2021) A and B (Parental Alienation: No. 1, No. 2, No. 3 and No. 4), 28 September, Courts and Tribunals Judiciary, available at: https://www.judiciary.uk/judgments/a-and-b-parental-alienation-no-1-no-2-no-3-and-no-4/; case before J. Lieven: Warwickshire County Council v the Mother & Ors [2022] EWHC 2146 (Fam), available at: https://www.bailii.org/ew/cases/EWHC/Fam/2022/2146.html, and Lieven's final judgment in this case: Warwickshire County Council v A Mother and A Father and X and Z [2023] EWHC 399 (Fam) [2023] EWHC 399 (Fam).

[30] E. Sheehy and S. Boyd (2020) 'Penalising women's fear: intimate partner violence and parental alienation in Canadian child custody', *Journal of Social Welfare and Family Law*, 42(1): 80–91; L. Neilson (2018) 'Parental alienation empirical analysis or child's best interests?', FREDA Centre for Research on Violence Against Women and Children, available at: https://fredacentre.com/wp-content/uploads/Parental-Alienation-Linda-Neilson.pdf.

[31] Neilson, 'Parental alienation'.

[32] E. Sheehy and S. Lapierre (2020) Introduction to the special issue on parental alienation, *Journal of Social Welfare and Family Law*, 42(1): 1–4, available at: https://www.tandfonline.com/doi/full/10.1080/09649069.2020.1702409.

[33] Barnett, quoted in S. McNichols-Thomas (2020) 'Playing the "Parental Alienation card": abusive parents use the system to gain access to children', Brunel University, 20 January; available at: https://www.brunel.ac.uk/news-and-events/news/articles/Playing-the-Parental-Alienation-card-Abusive-parents-use-the-system-to-gain-access-to-children.

[34] Royal Courts of Justice (2002) 'The judgment of Mr Justice Eady, in the Lillie and Reed v Newcastle City Council', available at: https://www.5rb.com/wp-content/uploads/2013/10/Lillie-v-Newcastle-CC-QBD-30-July-2002.pdf.

[35] E.F. Loftus and J.E.C. Pickrell (1995) 'Formation of false memories', *Psychiatric Annals*, 12 December, 25(12): 720–5, available at: https://www.myptsd.com/gallery/-pdf/1-96.pdf. The US psychologist Elizabeth Loftus became an academic doyenne of 'false memory' and appeared in hundreds of sexual abuse court cases. She had followed up a student's experimental study on implanted memories of being lost in a shopping mall with her own similar experiment involving 24 individuals and relatives: 75 per cent resisted the suggestion that they'd been lost in a mall; the others did not. She was a controversial figure, the subject of several complaints (she resigned from the American Psychological Association before two complaints could be heard by the ethics committee) and became embroiled in legal action after she outed 'Jane Doe'. This is her account: E. Loftus and M.J. Guyer (2002) 'Who abused Jane Doe? The hazards of the single case history Part 1', *Skeptical Inquirer*, 26(3), May–June: 24–32, available at: https://staff.washington.edu/eloftus/Articles/JaneDoe.htm. The psychologist Frank Putnam reviewed this startling case, 'a flashpoint in a long running, acrimonious debate about

the veracity of the delayed recall of traumatic memories', in F.W. Putnam (2014) 'Jane Doe: a cautionary tale for case reports', *Journal of Interpersonal Violence*, 29(18): 3277–89, available at: https://docksci.com/jane-doe-a-cautionary-tale-for-case-reports_5ad89613d64ab25daa0446e3.html. For archives of the memory debates see Accuracy About Abuse, founded by Marjorie Orr, journalist and former psychotherapist; and the Recovered Memory Project at Brown University, available at: https://blogs.brown.edu/recoveredmemory/.

[36] Nor did these experiments take account of the role of investigation in establishing the credibility, or otherwise, of allegations. T.D. Lyon (1999) 'The new wave of suggestibility research: a critique', *Cornell Law Review*, January: 1004–87, available at: https://works.bepress.com/thomaslyon/1/; see also T.D. Lyon, K. McWilliams and S. Williams (2019) 'Child witnesses', in N. Brewer and A.B. Douglass (eds) *Psychological Science and the Law*, London: Guilford Press. For a critique of Lyon, see D.A. Martindale (2001) 'On the importance of suggestibility testimony in assessing the credibility of children's testimony', *Court Review*, available at: https://www.researchgate.net/publication/228740582_Court_Review_Volume_38_Issue_3_On_the_Importance_of_Suggestibility_Research_in_Assessing_the_Credibility_of_Children%27s_Testimony; Lyon also challenged the salience of expert testimony in court cases where the child's testimony had been spontaneous and triggered investigation: T. Lyon (2002) *Expert Testimony on the Suggestibility of Children: Does It Fit?* New York: Cambridge University Press.

[37] S. Blackwell, F. Seymour and S. Mandeno (2020) 'Expert evidence about memory in New Zealand sexual violence trials and appellate courts', New Zealand Law Foundation, June, available at: https://apo.org.au/sites/default/files/resource-files/2020-07/apo-nid306776.pdf.

[38] C. Brewin and B. Andrews (2019) 'Memory accused: research on memory error and its relevance for the courtroom', *Criminal Law Review*, 9: 748–63; B. Andrews and C. Brewin (2016) 'False memories and free speech: is scientific debate being suppressed?', *Applied Cognitive Psychology*, 31(14), October: 45–9.

[39] Blackwell, Seymour and Mandeno, 'Expert evidence about memory'.

[40] Brewin and Andrews, 'Memory accused'; Andrews and Brewin, 'False memories and free speech'.

[41] Blackwell, Seymour and Mandeno, 'Expert evidence about memory'.

[42] A. Thomas (2020) 'Sexual abuse in care proceedings: a must read case', 27 November, available at: https://www.18sjs.com/sexual-abuse-care-proceedings-must-read-case/.

[43] He also reprised the comments of Judge Eady in a libel case in which he relied on the Ceci and Bruck studies: 'what the research has thrown into sharp relief is quite simply that very young children do not appear to have the same clear boundaries between fact and fantasy as that which adults have learned to draw': Lillie and others v Newcastle CC. See J. MacDonald (2019) 'Re P (Sexual Abuse – Finding of Fact Hearing)', EWFC 27.

44 R. Cheit (2014) *The Witch-Hunt Narrative: Politics, Psychology and the Sexual Abuse of Children*, Oxford: Oxford University Press.

45 M. Salter (2012) *Organised Sexual Abuse*, Abingdon: Routledge. For recitals of the moral panic/contamination thesis, see R. Waterhouse (2014) 'Satanic abuse, false memories, weird beliefs and moral panics', PhD thesis, London: City University; J. La Fontaine (1999) *Speak of the Devil: Tales of Satanic Abuse in Contemporary England*, Cambridge: Cambridge University Press.

46 D. Nathan and M.R. Snedeker (1995) *Satan's Silence: Ritual Abuse and the Making of a Modern American Witch Hunt*, New York: Basic Books.

47 Cheit, *The Witch-Hunt Narrative*; R. Summit (1994) 'The dark tunnels of McMartin', *Journal of Psychohistory*, 21(4), Spring: 397–416, available at: http://www.geocities.com/kidhistory/mcmartin.htm.

48 Cheit, *The Witch-Hunt Narrative*.

49 B. Gallagher, B. Hughes and H. Parker (1996) 'The nature and extent of known cases of organised child sexual abuse in England and Wales', in P. Bibby (ed) *Organised Abuse: The Current Debate*, Aldershot: Ashgate, pp 215–29.

50 Gallagher, Hughes and Parker, 'The nature and extent of known cases'; B. Gallagher (1998) *Grappling with Smoke, Investigating and Managing Organised Child Sexual Abuse: A Good Practice Guide*, London: NSPCC.

51 La Fontaine, *Speak of the Devil*.

52 La Fontaine, *Speak of the Devil*, p 169.

53 B. Gallagher (2001) 'Assessment and intervention in cases of suspected ritual child sexual abuse', *Child Abuse Review*, 10: 227–42.

54 Gallagher, 'Assessment and intervention'.

55 S. Nelson (2016) *Tackling Child Sexual Abuse: Radical Approaches to Prevention Protection and Support*, Bristol: Policy Press.

56 J. Clyde (1992) 'Report of the inquiry into the removal of children from Orkney in February 1991', Edinburgh: HMSO, 27 October, available at: https://assets.publishing.service.gov.uk/government/uploads/system/uploads/attachment_data/file/235702/0195.pdf.

57 Webster misunderstood/misrepresented Norman Cohn's book, *The Pursuit of the Millennium*: Cohn argued that unlike the great peasant revolts that were popular, organised, coherent and focused, the millenarians were isolated, alienated and marginal; B. Campbell (2020) 'The secret of Richard Webster', available at: http://www.beatrixcampbell.co.uk/the-secret-of-richard-webster/. See also R. Webster (2009) *The Secret of Bryn Estyn: The Making of a Modern Witch Hunt*, Halesworth: Orwell Press, p 574.

58 Webster, *The Secret of Bryn Estyn*, pp 574–5.

59 Home Affairs Select Committee (2001) 'Fourth report, conduct of investigations into past cases of abuse in children's homes', available at: https://publications.parliament.uk/pa/cm200102/cmselect/cmhaff/836/83605.htm.

60 Home Affairs Select Committee, 'Fourth report'.

61 L. Hood (2001) *A City Possessed*, Dunedin: Longacre Press.

[62] B. Tonkin (2014) 'The "moral entrepreneurs" who cash in on child abuse', *The Independent*, 11 July.

[63] A. O'Hagan (2012) 'Light entertainment', *London Review of Books*, 8 November.

[64] S. Cohen (1972) *Folk Devils and Moral Panics*, London: MacGibbon and Kee.

[65] H. Becker (1963) *Outsiders: Studies in the Sociology of Deviance*, New York: The Free Press.

[66] Stuart Hall and Chas Critcher and their cultural studies colleagues developed the theory to analyse the invention of 'the mugger' – the demonisation of young black men in the promotion of Thatcherism's law and order agenda – in their 1978 book, *Policing the Crisis: Mugging, the State and Law and Order*, Basingstoke: Palgrave. See also C. Critcher (2003) *Moral Panics and the Media*, Buckingham: Open University Press, pp 88, 98.

[67] Mass protests on Valentine's Day against violence against women: see www.onebillionrising.org/about/campaign/one-billion-rising/.

[68] K. Plummer (2016) 'Narrative power, sexual stories and the politics of story-telling', in I. Goodson (ed) *The Routledge International Handbook on Narrative and Life History*, London: Routledge, pp 290–302. A.M. Cole (2007) *The Cult of True Victimhood: From the War on Welfare to the War on Terror*, Stanford, CA: Stanford University Press.

[69] I. Hacking (1991) 'The making and molding of child abuse', *Critical Inquiry*, 17(2), Winter: 253–88.

[70] For a bracing critique of liberal, psychoanalytic and postmodern theorists, and the retreat from narratives of oppression, see Hacking, 'The making and molding of child abuse'.

[71] P. Jenkins (2010) 'The myth of Catholic crisis', *American Conservative*, 1 June, available at: https://www.theamericanconservative.com/myth-of-a-catholic-crisis/. In his 2013 book (*Moral Crusades in an Age of Mistrust*, Basingstoke: Palgrave) for example, he claimed that 'in 96 of the 121 cases the courts dismissed the allegations'. They didn't. See also P. Jenkins (2004) *Moral Panic: Changing Concepts of the Child Molester*, London: Yale University Press.

[72] F. Furedi (2018) *How Fear Works: Culture of Fear in the Twenty-First Century*, London: Bloomsbury; F. Furedi (2013) *Moral Crusades in an Age of Mistrust: The Jimmy Savile Scandal*, London: Palgrave Macmillan. Jenny Turner traces his political transition from the far left in the 1970s to the sceptical, libertarian right: J. Turner (2010) 'Who are they?: Jenny Turner reports from the battle of ideas', *London Review of Books*, 8 July.

[73] 'Open letter to the Criminal Code Revision Commission for the revision of certain texts governing relations between adults and minors, 1977', available at: http://www.dolto.fr/fd-code-penal-crp.html.

[74] H. Guesmi (2021) 'Reckoning with Foucault's alleged sexual abuse of boys in Tunisia', *Al Jazeera*, 16 April, available at: https://www.aljazeera.com/opinions/2021/4/16/reckoning-with-foucaults-sexual-abuse-of-boys-in-tunisia.

[75] C. Smart (1999) 'The history of ambivalence and conflict in the discursive construction of the "child victim" of sexual abuse', *Social and*

Legal Studies, 8(3): 391–409, available at: https://www.researchgate.net/
publication/249692271_A_History_of_Ambivalence_and_Conflict_in_the_
Discursive_Construction_of_the_%27Child_Victim%27_of_Sexual_Abuse.
76 Smart, 'The history of ambivalence'.
77 D. Pilgrim (2018) 'The perils of strong social constructionism: the case of child sexual abuse', *Journal of Critical Realism*, 16(3): 268–83.
78 K. Plummer (1991) 'Understanding childhood sexualities', *Journal of Homosexuality*, 20(1–2): 231–49. See also K. Plummer (2014) 'Child abuse and paedophilia: an open letter', available at: https://kenplummer.com/2014/07/27/child-abuse-and-paedophilia-an-open-letter/71.
79 Plummer, 'Child abuse and paedophilia'.
80 P. Jenkins (1998) *Moral Panic: Changing Concepts of the Child Molester in Modern America*, New Haven, CT: Yale University Press.
81 Pilgrim, 'The perils of strong social constructionism'.
82 Salter, *Organised Sexual Abuse*.
83 Kitzinger, *Framing Abuse*.

Chapter 8

1 Interview with the author for this book, 2020.
2 Streetwise lasted until it closed in 2005 – it gained large numbers of clients, but lost funding. See Richie McMullen's books about his childhood and boys involved prostitution: R. McMullen (1989) *Enchanted Boy*, London: Gay Men's Press; (1999) *Enchanted Youth*, London: Gay Men's Press.
3 Interview with the author, 2020.
4 Human Rights Watch (2016) 'Dignity debased: forced anal examinations in homosexuality prosecutions', 12 July, available at: https://www.hrw.org/report/2016/07/12/dignity-debased/forced-anal-examinations-homosexuality-prosecutions; A. Collins, G. Kendall and M. Michael (1998) 'Resisting a diagnostic technique: the case of reflex anal dilatation', *Sociology of Health and Illness*, 20, available at: https://eprints.lancs.ac.uk/id/eprint/18921/; S. Ashenden (2016) *Governing Child Sexual Abuse: Negotiating the Boundaries of Public and Private*, Abingdon: Routledge, pp 144–59.
5 Interview with the author.
6 In autumn 1987, Nottinghamshire's proactive child protection officers had correlated cases that combined similar forensic evidence and children's narratives.
7 R. Cheit (2014) *The Witch-Hunt Narrative*, Oxford: Oxford University Press; R. Cheit (2017) 'Special issue on the witch-hunt narrative', *Journal of Interpersonal Violence*, 32(6): available at: https://blogs.brown.edu/rcheit/2017/06/12/special-issue-on-the-witch-hunt-narrative/; D. Nathan and M. Snedeker (1996) *Satan's Silence: Ritual Abuse and the Making of a Modern American Witch Hunt*, New York: Basic Books; R.C. Summit (1994) 'The dark tunnels of McMartin', *The Journal of Psychohistory*, 21(4): 397–416.
8 D. Finkelhor, L.M. Williams and N. Burnes (1988) *Nursery Crimes: Sexual Abuse in Day Care*, London: Sage.

9   J. McCann, J. Voris, M. Simon and R. Wells (1989) 'Perianal findings in pre-pubertal children selected for non-abuse. A descriptive study', *Child Abuse and Neglect*, 13(2): 179–93.

10 McCann et al, 'Perianal findings in pre-pubertal children'.

11 Interview with the author, 2016.

12 McCann et al, 'Perianal findings in pre-pubertal children'.

13 Interview with the author for this book, 2021.

14 Interview with the author for this book, 2016.

15 Interview with the author for this book, 2016.

16 Interview with the author for this book, 2016.

17 S.J. Herriot Means and A. Heger (eds) (1992) *Evaluation of the Sexually Abused Child*, Oxford: Oxford University Press.

18 A. Heger, L. Ticson, O. Velasquez and R. Bernier (2002) 'Children referred for possible sexual abuse: medical findings in 2384 children', *Child Abuse and Neglect*, 6–7, 26 June: 645–59. This finding appeared closer to Wynne and Hobbs than to McCann et al – except that Dr Heger did not accept the association between RAD and anal abuse.

19 Leeds City Council v Mrs YX (2008) EWHC 802 (Fam), available at: https://www.casemine.com/judgement/uk/5a8ff7dd60d03e7f57eb28ad.

20 Newport City Council v W & Ors (2006) EWHC 3671 (Fam), available at: https://www.casemine.com/judgement/uk/5a8ff8ce60d03e7f57ecda4b. Masterman went on to say that Dr Heger endorsed the use of J. Adams (2005) 'Approach to the interpretation of medical and laboratory findings in suspected child sexual abuse: a 2005 revision', *The APSAC Advisor*, summer, available at: https://www.researchgate.net/publication/280950265_Approach_to_the_interpretation_of_medical_and_laboratory_findings_in_suspected_child_sexual_abuse_A_2005_revision.

21 Newport City Council v W & Ors (2006) EWHC 3671 (Fam), available at: https://www.familylawweek.co.uk/site.aspx?i=ed612.

22 Adams, 'Approach to the interpretation of medical and laboratory findings'.

23 Adams 'Approach to the interpretation of medical and laboratory findings'.

24 Interview with the author for this book, 2016.

25 Interview with the author for this book, 2016.

26 J. Adams, K. Harper, S. Knudson and J. Revilla (1994) 'Examination findings in legally confirmed sexual abuse: it's normal to be normal', *Pediatrics*, 94: 310–17, available at: https://publications.aap.org/pediatrics/article-abstract/94/3/310/59013/Examination-Findings-in-Legally-Confirmed-Child?redirectedFrom=fulltext.

27 McCann et al, 'Perianal findings in pre-pubertal children'.

28 It was followed in 1992 by the Child Welfare Act.

29 Interview with the author for this book, 2015.

30 C. Cameron, P. Moss and C. Owen (1999) *Men in the Nursery*, London: Paul Chapman Publishing, p 155.

31 Interview with the author for this book, 2015.

32 A.K. Myhre, K. Berntzen and D. Bratlid (2001) 'Perianal anatomy in non-abused pre-school children', *Acta Paediatrica*, 90: 1321–8.

[33] Interview with the author for this book, 2016.

[34] Interview with the author for this book, 2016.

[35] C. Hobbs and C. Wright (2014) 'Anal signs of child sexual abuse: a case-control study', *BMC Pediatrics*, 14: 128, available at: https://bmcpediatr.biomedcentral.com/track/pdf/10.1186/1471-2431-14-128.pdf. In addition to anal dilatation, they found venous congestion (another possible indicator of abuse) in 36 per cent of cases and only one control. Multiple signs were recorded among 43 per cent of cases, but in only 1 per cent of the control group.

[36] Dr Francesca Sfriso and her colleagues in Padua, Italy, published a study of non-abused children that challenged McCann and confirmed Hobbs and Wynne. It reported anal dilatation in only 1 per cent of the control children: F. Sfriso, S. Masiero, V. Mardegan, S. Bressan and A. Aprile (2014) 'Reflex anal dilatation: an observational study of non-abused children', *Forensic Science Journal*, 238, May: 22–5.

[37] Royal College of Paediatrics and Child Health (2015) *The Physical Signs of Child Sexual Abuse: Evidence-Based Review*, London: RCPCH.

[38] Interview with the author for this book, 2016.

[39] Interview with the author for this book, 2016.

[40] Royal College of Paediatrics and Child Health, *The Physical Signs of Child Sexual Abuse*, p 116: 'Sexual abuse should always be considered in the context of the history, medical assessment and other anogenital signs, and the absence of neurological condition'.

[41] 'Dynamic' is the preferred term used in the *Purple Book*.

[42] Interview with the author for this book, 2021.

[43] P. Kirk (1953) *Crime Investigation: Physical Evidence and the Police Laboratory*, New York: Interscience Publishers.

[44] See John Berger's path-breaking BBC television series (with Michael Dibb) in 1972, *Ways of Seeing*, and the book of the same name, London: Penguin.

[45] C. Hyde (2016) 'Serious case review: Child N', Cumbria Local Safeguarding Children Board, 13 June, available at: https://www.cumbria.gov.uk/eLibrary/Content/Internet//537/6683/7080/4253494137.pdf.

[46] Following submissions by media organisations.

[47] Hyde, 'Serious case review'.

[48] This narrative is derived from the published judgements of Mr Justice Peter Jackson, the 2017 report by the Cumbria coroner, David Roberts, and the serious case review by Clare Hyde: D. Roberts (2018) 'Poppi Iris Worthington Deceased', available at: https://www.cumbria.gov.uk/elibrary/Content/Internet/17318/43115155356.pdf; Hyde, 'Serious Case Review'.

[49] Independent Police Complaints Commission (2014) 'Operation Lavender: independent investigation, final report', Ref 2014/ 029756, available at: https://policeconduct.gov.uk/sites/default/files/Documents/investigation_reports/Op%20Lavender%20Report%20for%20Publication%20Online.pdf.

[50] See the Transparency Project, available at: https://www.transparencyproject.org.uk.

51 The judge had ruled that 'as much information as possible' be placed in the public domain: H. Pidd (2015) 'Judge criticizes "minimal" investigation into death of 13-month-old girl', *The Guardian*, 25 November, available at: https://www.theguardian.com/uk-news/2015/nov/25/judge-criticises-minimal-investigation-into-death-of-13-month-old-girl.

52 N. Hines (2009) 'Profile: Nat Cary Britain's top pathologist', *The Times*, 17 April, available at: https://www.thetimes.co.uk/article/profile-nat-cary-britains-top-pathologist-qm7nhblmgw7.

53 Dr Aziz insisted that the injuries were not severe enough to have been caused by penetration – a conclusion she reiterated at a second inquest in 2017: C. Barber (2017) 'Poppi inquest: experts continue to disagree over whether tot suffered abuse', *Times and Star*, 13 December, available at: https://www.timesandstar.co.uk/news/17017408.poppi-inquest-experts-continue-to-disagree-over-whether-tot-suffered-abuse/.

54 B. Campbell (2016) 'Poppi Worthington case takes us back to the Cleveland abuse scandal', *The Independent*, 23 January, available at: https://www.independent.co.uk/voices/comment/poppi-worthington-case-takes-us-back-to-the-cleveland-abuse-scandal-a6830011.html.

55 Cumbria County Council v M and F (2014) EWHC 2596 (Fam), 28 July 2014, available at: https://www.bailii.org/ew/cases/EWHC/Fam/2014/2596.html.

56 (2014) EWHC 2596 (Fam), available at: https://www.bailii.org/ew/cases/EWHC/Fam/2014/2596.html.

57 S. Ashenden (2016) *Governing Child Sexual Abuse; Negotiating the Boundaries of Public and Private*, Abingdon: Routledge, pp 144–58.

58 H. Quirk (2016) 'Poppi Worthington and the risk of "ghost" miscarriages of Justice', *The Justice Gap*, 26 January, available at: https://www.thejusticegap.com/poppi-worthington-and-the-risk-of-ghost-miscarriages-of-justice/.

59 L. Reed (2016) 'Debating the standard of proof for really serious stuff', *Pink Tape*, 30 January, available at: http://www.pinktape.co.uk/legal-news/debating-the-appropriate-standard-of-proof-for-really-serious-stuff/.

60 HMIC (2015) 'In harm's way: the role of the police in keeping children safe', HMIC, July, available at: https://www.justiceinspectorates.gov.uk/hmicfrs/wp-content/uploads/in-harms-way.pdf.

61 Hyde, 'Serious case review'.

62 D. Leatherdale (2018) 'Poppi Worthington: father declined to answer questions', BBC News, 15 January, available at: https://www.bbc.com/news/uk-england-cumbria-42371133.

63 According to the coroner, there was a significant amount of blood that accumulated in the rectum and was released post mortem when the anus dilated: D. Roberts, D. (2018) 'In the matter of Poppi Iris Worthington: deceased, review of evidence, findings and conclusion', HM Coroner's Court for the County of Cumbria.

64 Hyde, 'Serious case review'.

65 Hyde, 'Serious case review'.

Chapter 9

1   M. MacLeod and E. Saraga (1988) *Child Sexual Abuse: Towards a Feminist Professional Practice: report of the conference held by the Child Abuse Studies Unit, 6, 7 and 8 April 1987, at the Polytechnic of North London,* London: PNL Press.

2   MacLeod and Saraga, *Child Sexual Abuse*; Arnon Bentovim's and his colleagues' 'family dysfunction' model was also being challenged as 'mother-blaming' by feminist experts.

3   Interview with the author for this book, 2017.

4   Interview with the author for this book, 2017.

5   The origins of the false memory movement can be found in J. Freyd (1998) *Betrayal Trauma,* Cambridge, MA: Harvard University Press; K. McMaugh and W. Middleton (2022) 'The rise and fall of the false memory movement', *International Society for the Study of Trauma and Discussion,* available at: https://news.isst-d.org/the-rise-and-fall-of-the-false-memory-syndrome-foundation/.

6   S. Sedley (1987) 'Whose child? The report of the panel appointed to inquire into the death of Tyra Henry', Lambeth Social Services; L. Blom Cooper (1986) 'A child in trust: the report of the panel of inquiry into the circumstances surrounding the death of Jasmine Beckford', Brent Social Services; L. Blom Cooper (1987) 'Report into the death of Kimberley Carlile', London Borough of Greenwich, Greenwich Health Authority. See also R. Dingwall (1986) 'Reports of committees: the Jasmine Beckford affair', available at: https://onlinelibrary.wiley.com/doi/pdf/10.1111/j.1468-2230.1986.tb01700.x.

7   The Children Act 1989. The legal framework for investigation was Section 47; the local authority social worker would take the lead, with other agencies – health, education and the police – required to cooperate. The act was a welcome improvement and brought together all matters involving children and young people in public and private law, in criminal justice, in alternative care. It emphasised the paramount principle of children's best interests as the focus of the court, and identified their holistic needs and the basis on which a threshold of significant harm would be crossed if those needs were not met. In particular, parents' responsibility was stressed, and the emphasis was on children's best interests being within their families (in the widest sense) and that local authorities should work in partnership with parents. https://www.legislation.gov.uk/ukpga/1989/41/section/47.

8   N. Parton (1991) *Governing the Family: Child Care, Child Protection and the State,* London: Macmillan, pp 160–92 and 206.

9   Parliamentary debate on the Second Reading of the Children Bill, 27 April 1989, available at: https://api.parliament.uk/historic-hansard/commons/1989/apr/27/children-bill-lords.

10 Parton, *Governing the Family,* pp 162–3. With unrepentant grandiosity, Bell declared, 'I came to the House rather in the manner of Mark Antony, because I came to bury not Caesar but Cleveland as an issue of child abuse. In the past two years the county has suffered enormously due to a great deal of irresponsible comment. A great stigma lay across the county. That stigma

has now been erased. All the major participants in the Cleveland child abuse crisis are no longer in their jobs.'

[11] Parliamentary debate on the Second Reading of the Children Bill, 27 April 1989, available at: https://api.parliament.uk/historic-hansard/commons/1989/apr/27/children-bill-lords.

[12] B. Campbell and J. Jones (1999) *Stolen Voices*, London: The Women's Press, pp 74–84.

[13] Interview with the author for this book, 1990.

[14] Interview with the author for this book, 1990.

[15] Campbell and Jones, *Stolen Voices*, pp 74–84.

[16] Department of Health (1995) 'Child protection and child abuse: messages from research: studies in child protection', 1 June, HMSO Child Protection, available at: https://www.semanticscholar.org/paper/Child-Protection%3A-Messages-From-ResearchDepartment-Middleton/f7f7de8f00c6c5b7f9e9cf10f84c1db257faf6d0.

[17] Department of Health (1995) 'Child protection and child abuse'.

[18] Parton, *Governing the Family*.

[19] H. Cleaver and P. Freeman (1995) *Parental Perspectives in the Cases of Suspected Child Abuse*, London: HMSO.

[20] Parton, *Governing the Family*, p 113.

[21] M. Calder (2000) *The Complete Guide to Sexual Abuse Assessments*, London: Russell House Publishing; interview with the author for this book, 2021.

[22] H. Westcott and G. Davies (1999) 'Interviewing child witnesses under the Memorandum of Good Practice: a research review', Home Office.

[23] Interview with the author, 1995.

[24] Interview with the author, 1995.

[25] National Commission of Inquiry into the Prevention of Child Abuse (1996) *Childhood Matters*, London: HMSO.

[26] P. Gregg, S. Harkness and S. Machin (1999) 'Poor kids: trends in child poverty in Britain, 1968–96', *Fiscal Studies*, 20(2): 163–98.

[27] P. Freeman (2015) 'Child neglect and behavioural parent education', *Journal of Social Work*, 5(4): 453–5.

[28] B. Hearn (1997) 'Putting child and family support and the protection of children into practice', in N. Parton (ed) *Child Protection and Family Support*, London: Routledge, pp 243–61.

[29] Calder, *The Complete Guide to Sexual Abuse Assessments*.

[30] HMSO (2000) *Assessing Children in Need and their Families: Practice Guidance*, London: HMSO, available at: https://dera.ioe.ac.uk/15599/1/assessing_children_in_need_and_their_families_practice_guidance_2000.pdf.

[31] E. Munro (2011) 'Munro review of child protection: a child-centred system', Department of Education, available at: https://www.gov.uk/government/publications/munro-review-of-child-protection-final-report-a-child-centred-system.

[32] Interviews with the author for this book, 2021.

[33] Interview with the author for this book, 2021.

[34] J. Thoburn (2019) 'The Children Act 1989: 30 years on', *Children and Young People Now*, available at: https://www.cypnow.co.uk/features/article/the-children-act-1989-30-years-on.

[35] Institute for Government (2020) 'Local government funding in England', available at: https://www.instituteforgovernment.org.uk/explainers/local-government-funding-england; P. Butler (2019) 'Children's services are in financial crisis, say charities', *The Guardian*, 26 February.

[36] K. Karsna and L. Kelly (2021) 'Measuring the scale and nature of child sexual abuse', London Centre of Expertise on Child Sexual Abuse, June, pp 42–3, available at: https://www.csacentre.org.uk/our-research/the-scale-and-nature-of-csa/measuring-the-scale-and-nature-of-csa/.

[37] H. Laming (2003) *The Victoria Climbié Inquiry*, CM5730, available at: https://www.gov.uk/government/publications/the-victoria-climbie-inquiry-report-of-an-inquiry-by-lord-laming.

[38] R. Jones (2014) *The Story of Baby P: Setting the Record Straight*, Bristol: Policy Press.

[39] Court of Appeal (2010) EWCA Crim 4 Case No: 2009/02867/C5, 21 January, available at: http://www.bailii.org/ew/cases/EWCA/Crim/2010/4.html.

[40] P. Cooper and D. Wurtzel (2010) 'Through the eyes of a child', *Counsel*, 28 February, available at: https://www.counselmagazine.co.uk/articles/through-the-eyes-of-child.

Chapter 10

[1] David Mellor correspondence with John Patten, 7 December 1988.

[2] John Patten reply to David Mellor, 7 December 1988.

[3] Patten reply to Mellor.

[4] Bill Utting letter to David Mellor, 30 November 1988.

[5] Utting letter to Mellor. SSI (1988) *Report of Cleveland Social Services Department's Arrangements for Handling Child Sexual Abuse*, London: Department of Health.

[6] Utting letter to Mellor.

[7] C. Yates (1990) 'The Pigot Committee report: children, evidence and videotape', *The Journal of Child Law*, 2(3): 96.

[8] T. Pigot (1989) *Report of the Advisory Group on Video-Recorded Evidence*, London: HMSO. Pigot proposed that children's evidence should be recorded contemporaneously, before the trial, and shown behind a screen, via video link, to save the child from facing the defendant. Only part of the report was adopted, and crucially, cross-examination was excluded. This meant that the child's first conversation with the court was the shattering moment when they would be cross-examined. Unsurprisingly, outcomes were no better for children. See the 2012 statement by Joyce Plotnikoff and Kathy Rowe to the Parliamentary Education Committee on provision for children and young people giving evidence to the courts, available at: https://publications.parliament.uk/pa/cm201213/cmselect/cmeduc/137/137vw71.htm; A. Bramner and P. Cooper (2011) *Still Waiting for a Meeting of Minds:*

Child Witnesses in the Criminal and Family Justice Systems, London: Sweet and Maxwell; P. Cooper and D. Wurtzel (2010) 'Through the eyes of a child', *Counsel*, 28 February, available at: https://www.counselmagazine.co.uk/articles/through-the-eyes-of-child.

9   S. Drew and L. Gibbs (2017) 'A united approach', *Counsel*, 21 February, available at: https://www.counselmagazine.co.uk/articles/united-approach.

10 Israel Kolvin evidence, day 39 of the Cleveland Inquiry.

11 E. Butler-Sloss (1989) 'The Cleveland Enquiry', *Medico-Legal Journal*, 57(3): 149–63, available at: https://journals.sagepub.com/doi/abs/10.1177/002581728905700304.

12 Interview with the author, 1995.

13 G. Davis, L. Hoyano, C. Keenan, L. Maitland and L. Morgan (1999) *The Admissibility and Sufficiency of Evidence in Child Abuse Prosecutions*, available at: https://www.bbc.co.uk/radio4/today/print/politics/bain_20031111.shtml.

14 See Islington Survivors Network for an archive of Eileen Fairweather's prolific investigations into child abuse in Islington, available at: https://islingtonsurvivors.co.uk/eileen-fairweather-freelance-investigative-journalist/.

15 S. Hall (2003) 'The Guardian profile: Margaret Hodge', *The Guardian*, 21 November, available at: https://www.theguardian.com/society/2003/nov/21/childrensservices.schools.

16 A. Stickler (2003) 'Paedophile investigation', *Today*, BBC Radio 4, available at: http://www.bbc.co.uk/radio4/today/reports/politics/bain_20031111.shtml.

17 P. Waugh (2003) 'Hodge apology fails to satisfy abuse victim', *The Independent*, 15 November, available at: https://www.independent.co.uk/news/uk/politics/hodge-apology-fails-to-satisfy-abuse-victim-78498.html. Demetrious Panton was by then not only a tenacious survivor, he was a civil servant and government adviser.

18 *EC1 Echo* (2021) 'Payments for survivors of abuse in Islington', available at: https://www.ec1echo.co.uk/payments-for-survivors-of-child-abuse-in-islington/; see also: https://islingtonsurvivors.co.uk/author/islingtonsn/page/3/.

19 C. Wolmar (2000) *Forgotten Children: The Secret Abuse Scandal in Children's Homes*, London: Vision Paperbacks.

20 Wolmar, *Forgotten Children*.

21 A. Winning (2014) '"Too many of them": warnings on paedophiles operating in Westminster were "ignored"', *Reuters*, 12 July, available at: https://www.bishop-accountability.org/news2014/07_08/2014_07_12_RT_lsquo_Too.htm.

22 B. Hughes, H. Parker and B. Gallagher (1996) 'Policing child sexual abuse: the view from police practitioners', University of Huddersfield, available at: https://www.semanticscholar.org/paper/Policing-child-sexual-abuse%3A-the-view-from-police-Hughes-Parker/9a8bbfdaee4a5b936e1d9606d84153daf38fb011.

23 B. Robinson (2008) 'ABE interviews: is the child's "best evidence" being achieved in alleged sexual abuse cases?', parts 1 and 2, *Family Law Week*, available at: http://www.familylawweek.co.uk/site.aspx?i=ed24715;

https://www.familylawweek.co.uk/site.aspx?i=ed24931. Robinson concluded that far from being planned, 'Rather, an "it'll be alright on the night" approach appeared to constitute the most common planning "strategy".'

24 Sexual Offences Act 2003, available at: https://www.legislation.gov.uk/ukpga/2003/42/contents.

25 L. Kelly, J. Lovett and L. Regan (2005) 'A gap or a chasm?', Home Office research study 293.

26 J. Temkin and B. Krahe (2008) *Sexual Assault and the Justice Gap: A Question of Attitude*, Oxford: Hart Publishing.

27 E. Stanko (2007) *The Attrition of Rape Allegations in London: A Review*, London: Metropolitan Police Service.

28 Interview with the author, 2005.

29 K. Hohl and E. Stanko (2015) 'Complaints of rape and the criminal justice system: fresh evidence on the attrition problem in England and Wales', *European Journal of Criminology*, 12(3): 324–41, available at: https://openaccess.city.ac.uk/id/eprint/5923/.

30 K. Karsna and L. Kelly (2021) 'The scale and nature of child sexual abuse: a review of evidence', Centre of Expertise on Child Sexual Abuse, June, available at: https://www.csacentre.org.uk/documents/scale-nature-review-evidence-0621/.

31 ONS (Office for National Statistics) (2018) 'Sexual offending: victimisation and the path through the criminal justice system', 13 December.

32 J. Plotnikoff and R. Woolfson (2005) 'In their own words: the experiences of 50 young witnesses in criminal proceedings', NSPCC and Victim Support, available at: https://www.researchgate.net/publication/344177101_In_their_own_words_The_experiences_of_50_young_witnesses_in_criminal_proceedings_The_NSPCC_in_partnership_with_Victim_Support.

33 Cooper and Wurtzel, 'Through the eyes of a child'.

34 J. Plotnikoff and R. Woolfson (2019) 'Falling short? A snapshot of young witnesses policy and practice', NSPCC, February, available at: www.researchgate.net/publication/338506075_Falling_short_A_snapshot_of_young_witness_policy_and_practice_A_report_for_the_NSPCC_revisiting_%27Measuring_up_Evaluating_implementation_of_Government_commitments_to_young_witnesses_in_criminal_proceed.

35 Justice Inspectorates (2012) 'Forging the links: rape investigation and prosecution', a joint review by HMIC and HMCPSI, February.

36 HMIC (2015) 'In harm's way: the role of the police in making children safe', 2 July, available at: https://www.justiceinspectorates.gov.uk/hmicfrs/wp-content/uploads/in-harms-way.pdf.

Chapter 11

1 R. Bichard (2004) *The Bichard Inquiry Report*, House of Commons, HC653, London: HMSO; C. Kelly (2004) 'Serious case review: Ian Huntley, North-East Lincolnshire, 1995–2001', North East Lincolnshire Area Child Protection Committee.

2   Bichard, *The Bichard Inquiry Report*.

3   Kelly, 'Serious case review'.

4   L. Gordon (1989) *Heroes of Their Own Lives*, London: Virago, p 292.

5   Youth worker Sara Rowbotham, evidence to Home Affairs Select Committee, 6 November 2012, available at: https://publications.parliament. uk/pa/cm201213/cmselect/cmhaff/uc182-v/uc182-v.pdf, Q281, Q291. She said that 'it was absolute disrespect that vulnerable young people did not have a voice. They were overlooked. They were discriminated against. They were treated appallingly by protective services.' She believed ethnicity was a factor – with White girls abused by older, more powerful Asian men whose language they did not speak – but 'I seriously believe that protective services didn't not respond because it was an issue of ethnicity. That seriously was not the case.' Rather it was contempt for the girls and pessimism about their competence as witnesses: 'I think we need an absolute shift in what constitutes a reliable witness.' The Rochdale story was dramatised in a BBC One television series, *Three Girls*, during May 2016.

6   M. Newsam and G. Ridgway (2020) 'Independent assurance review of the effectiveness of multi-agency responses to child sexual exploitation in Greater Manchester, part one', available at: www.greatermanchester-ca.gov. uk/media/2569/operation_augusta_january_2020_digital_final.pdf.

7   A. Jay (2014) 'The independent inquiry into sexual exploitation of children in Rotherham 1997–2013', Rotherham Metropolitan Council, available at: https://www.rotherham.gov.uk/downloads/download/31/independent-inquiry-into-child-sexual-exploitation-in-rotherham-1997---2013. See also, for vivid chronicles of the services for girls and political sabotage, J. Senior (2016) *Broken and Betrayed*, London: Pan Macmillan; A. Gladman and A. Heal (2017) *Child Sexual Exploitation after Rotherham*, London: Jessica Kingsley.

8   Gladman and Heal, *Child Sexual Exploitation after Rotherham*; House of Commons, Home Affairs Committee (2015) 'Child sexual exploitation and the response to localised grooming: follow-up', available at: https:// publications.parliament.uk/pa/cm201415/cmselect/cmhaff/203/203.pdf.

9   Adele Gladman told me that her academic mentor, Jalna Hamner, had warned her: copy everything and keep it safe. So, she did. And all was not lost.

10   Gladman and Heal, *Child Sexual Exploitation after Rotherham*.

11   Jay, 'The independent inquiry into sexual exploitation of children in Rotherham'.

12   J. Drew (2016) 'An independent review into South Yorkshire Police's handling of child sexual exploitation, 1999–2016', available at: www. drewreview.uk/wp-content/uploads/2016/03/SYP030-Final-report.pdf.

13   A. Bedford (2015) 'Serious case review into child sexual exploitation in Oxfordshire: from the experiences of Children A, B, C, D, E and F', 14 March, Oxfordshire Safeguarding Children Board.

14   T. Symonds (2010) 'Derby rape gang targeted children', BBC News, 24 November, available at: https://www.bbc.com/news/uk-11819732.

[15] Derbyshire Safeguarding Children Board (2019) 'Derby and Derbyshire child at risk of exploitation (CRE) risk assessment toolkit', available at: https://www.proceduresonline.com/derbyshire/scbs/user_controlled_lcms_area/uploaded_files/City-and-County-CRE-Risk-Assessment-Toolkit%20-%20FINAL%20May%202019.pdf; Symonds, 'Derby rape gang targeted children'.

[16] Symonds, 'Derby rape gang targeted children'.

[17] D. Spicer (2018) 'Joint serious case review concerning sexual exploitation of children and adults with needs for care and support in Newcastle-upon-Tyne', Newcastle Safeguarding Children Board and Newcastle Safeguarding Adults Board, February, available at: https://www.newcastle.gov.uk/sites/default/files/Final%20JSCR%20Report%20160218%20PW.pdf.

[18] Spicer, 'Joint serious case review'.

[19] Spicer, 'Joint serious case review'.

[20] After the convictions, Detective Superintendent Steve Barron, one of the investigators, commented that the perpetrators had 'hugely underestimated' the strength of their very vulnerable victims: 'they thought nobody would believe them. We believed them, as did the jury': J. Halliday (2017) 'Woman who helped Newcastle grooming gang jailed for six years', *The Guardian*, 8 September.

[21] Gladman and Heal, *Child Sexual Exploitation after Rotherham*.

[22] J. Bindel (2007) 'The mothers of prevention', *Sunday Times*, 30 September. Julie Bindel had been researching prostitution for years, but it took until 2007 before she could get any newspaper to publish her voluminous research on this issue.

[23] Rochdale Borough Safeguarding Children Board (2013) 'The overview report of the serious case reviews in respect of young people 1, 2, 3, 4, 5 and 6', 20 December, available at: https://www.rochdaleonline.co.uk/uploads/f1/news/document/20131220_93449.pdf

[24] C. Alexander (2000) *The Asian Gang: Ethnicity, Identity, Masculinity*, London: Bloomsbury.

[25] K. Elliott (2019) 'Child sexual exploitation: a comparative frame analysis of media coverage over time', *Feminist Legal Studies*, 11 February, available at: https://www.tandfonline.com/doi/abs/10.1080/14680777.2019.1690021?journalCode=rfms20; see A. Norfolk (2012) 'Exploitation of white girls "is an Asian problem"', *The Times*, 8 June, available at: https://www.thetimes.co.uk/article/exploitation-of-white-girls-is-an-asian-problem-r8c826l63nh; A. Norfolk (2012) '"Media prejudice" claim as child-sex report turns blind eye to Asian gangs', *The Times*, 21 November, available at: https://www.thetimes.co.uk/article/media-prejudice-claim-as-child-sex-report-turns-a-blind-eye-to-asian-gangs-f6qk3tfdsf9.

[26] E. Cockbain (2013) 'Grooming and the "Asian sex gang predator": the construction of a racial crime threat', *Race and Class*, 28 March, 54(4): 22–32, available at: https://journals.sagepub.com/doi/full/10.1177/0306396813475983.

[27] D. Aaronovitch (2012) 'Let's be honest, there's a clear link with Islam', *The Times*, 10 May, available at: https://www.thetimes.co.uk/article/lets-be-

honest-theres-a-clear-link-with-islam-twm9hvfgqf3; D. Batty (2011) 'White girls seen as "easy meat" by Pakistani rapists, says Jack Straw', *The Guardian*, 8 January, available at: https://www.theguardian.com/world/2011/jan/08/jack-straw-white-girls-easy-meat.

28 A. Gentleman (2014) 'Nazir Afzal: "There is no religious basis for the abuse in Rotherham"', *The Guardian*, 3 September, available at: https://www.theguardian.com/society/2014/sep/03/nazir-afzal-there-is-no-religious-basis-for-the-abuse-in-rotherham.

29 Sara Rowbotham, evidence to Home Affairs Select Committee, 6 November 2012, available at: https://publications.parliament.uk/pa/cm201213/cmselect/cmhaff/uc182-v/uc182-v.pdf.

30 D. Cameron (2013) 'It happens everywhere', *Trouble & Strife*, 28 June, available at: http://www.troubleandstrife.org/new-articles/it-happens-everywhere/.

31 P. Vallely (2012) 'Child sex grooming: the Asian question', *The Independent*, 10 May, available at: https://www.independent.co.uk/news/uk/crime/child-sex-grooming-the-asian-question-7729068.html.

32 A. Gill and K. Harrison (2015) 'Child grooming and sexual exploitation: are South Asian men the UK media's new folk devils?', *International Journal of Crime, Justice and Social Democracy*, 4(2): 34–49, available at: https://hydra.hull.ac.uk/assets/hull:10899/content.

33 Muslim Women's Network UK (2013) *Unheard Voices: The Sexual Exploitation of Asian Girls and Young Women*, September, p 7.

34 Interview with the author for this book, 2020.

35 Elliott, 'Child sexual exploitation'.

36 There was disproportionality between Black/Asian and White people stopped and searched by the police in England and Wales at that time, consistent with the preceding and succeeding years, and in the Greater Manchester and Yorkshire areas there was a high disproportionality ratio: Equality and Human Rights Commission (2010) 'Stop and think: a critical review of the use of stop and search powers in England and Wales', London, EHRC, available at: https://www.equalityhumanrights.com/en/publication-download/stop-and-think-critical-review-use-stop-and-search-powers-england-and-wales; Gov.uk (2019) 'Ethnicity facts and figures, stop and search', available at: https://www.ethnicity-facts-figures.service.gov.uk/crime-justice-and-the-law/policing/stop-and-search/latest.

37 M. Hussain (2018) 'The 12 Pakistani men from Rotherham you probably haven't heard about', *The Independent*, 14 February; F. Perraudin (2016) 'Call for inquiry as Asian men who fought far right extremists are cleared', *The Guardian*, 16 November.

38 E. Cockbain and H. Brayley (2012) 'The truth about Asian gangs', *The Guardian*, 8 May, available at: https://www.theguardian.com/commentisfree/2012/may/08/asian-sex-gangs-on-street-grooming; Cockbain, 'Grooming and the "Asian gang predator"'; B. Cathcart and P. French (2019) 'Unmasked: Andrew Norfolk, *The Times* newspaper and

anti-Muslim reporting – a case to answer', available at: www.mediareform. org.uk/wp-content/uploads/2019/06/Norfolk_Report-FINAL.pdf.

39 A. Topping (2012) 'Children's Commissioner defends child sex abuse report', *The Guardian*, 21 November; Norfolk, '"Media prejudiced" claim'.

40 S. Berelowitz, J. Clifton, C. Firimin, S. Gulyurtlu and G. Edwards (2013) '"If only someone had listened": Office of the Children's Commissioner's inquiry into child sexual exploitation in gangs and groups, final report', November, Children's Commissioner; Office of the Children's Commissioner (2012) '"I thought I was the only one in the world": inquiry into child sexual exploitation in gangs and groups, interim report', November, available at: www.childrenscommissioner.gov.uk/wp-content/uploads/2017/07/I-thought-I-was-the-only-one-in-the-world.pdf.

41 Jay, 'The independent inquiry into sexual exploitation of children in Rotherham'.

42 Ofsted, Care Quality Commission, HM Inspectorate of Constabulary and Fire and Rescue Services, HM Inspectorate of Probation (2020) 'Multi-agency response to child sexual abuse in the family environment: joint targeted inspections', 4 February, available at: https://www.gov.uk/government/publications/the-multi-agency-response-to-child-sexual-abuse-in-the-family-environment. This had grave consequences for their mental well-being, because children were prohibited from receiving therapeutic support before their cases came to court.

43 NSPCC (2022) 'Child sexual abuse prosecutions and convictions roughly halve in 4 years', 19 January, available at: https://www.nspcc.org.uk/about-us/news-opinion/2022/child-sexual-abuse-prosecutions-convictions-halve/.

44 M. Newman (2014) 'Exclusive: rape of vulnerable women "has been effectively decriminalised"', 28 February, available at: https://www.independent.co.uk/news/uk/crime/exclusive-rape-of-vulnerable-women-has-been-effectively-decriminalised-9161336.html.

45 A report into North Wales by a team led by John Jillings had been suppressed – under pressure from municipal insurers – but it had been covertly shared with a few reporters, who felt free to write up their old files when a redacted version was finally published in 2013 following Freedom of Information requests. A North Wales police superintendent, Gordon Anglesea, who successfully sued *The Independent on Sunday* and other media over a 1991 cutting-edge investigation into North Wales, finally met his comeuppance: in 2016 he was jailed for sex offences against boys.

46 D. Ponsford (2015) 'Meirion Jones: "Everyone on the right side of the Savile argument has been forced out of the BBC"', *Press Gazette*, 29 July. See also N. Pollard (2012) *The Pollard Review*, available at: http://downloads.bbc.co.uk/bbctrust/assets/files/pdf/our_work/pollard_review/pollard_review.pdf; J. Smith (2016) *The Jimmy Savile Investigation Report*, BBC, 25 February, available at: http://downloads.bbci.co.uk/bbctrust/assets/files/pdf/our_work/dame_janet_smith_review/savile/jimmy_savile_investigation.pdf.

47 D. Davies (2014) *In Plain Sight: The Life and Lies of Jimmy Savile*, London: Quercus. It had taken Davies years to secure a publisher.

48 B. Kirkup and B. Marshall (2014) 'Jimmy Savile investigation: Broadmoor Hospital', Department of Health, 2 June. The report said he wielded power over staff; he was 'grandiose, narcissistic, arrogant and lacking any empathy. He was also very manipulative, and many staff were convinced that he had close connections in high places and had the power to have them dismissed.'

49 HMIC (2013) 'Mistakes were made: HMIC's review into allegations and intelligence material concerning Jimmy Savile, between 1964 and 2012', HMIC, March, available at: https://www.justiceinspectorates.gov.uk/hmicfrs/media/review-into-allegations-and-intelligence-material-concerning-jimmy-savile.pdf.

50 J. Smith (2014) *The Jimmy Savile Investigation Report*, 25 February, available at: http://downloads.bbci.co.uk/bbctrust/assets/files/pdf/our_work/dame_janet_smith_review/savile/jimmy_savile_investigation.pdf; L. Mangan (2022) '*Jimmy Savile: A British Horror Story*: a welter of devastating detail', *The Guardian*, 6 April, available at: https://www.theguardian.com/tv-and-radio/2022/apr/06/jimmy-savile-a-british-horror-story-review-a-welter-of-devastating-detail.

51 Tom Watson cited an unnamed source in the House of Commons on 24 October 2012, when he claimed that a paedophile network was linked to Parliament and Number 10. UK Parliament (2012) 24 October, available at: https://publications.parliament.uk/pa/cm201213/cmhansrd/cm121024/debtext/121024-0001.htm

52 Simon Danczuk followed up with a book, co-written with Matthew Baker (2014) *Smile for the Camera: The Double Life of Cyril Smith*, Hull: Biteback Publishing.

53 G. Sammon (2014) 'The article that first exposed Cyril Smith', *Rochdale Observer*, 2 May, available at: https://www.manchestereveningnews.co.uk/news/local-news/rochdale-observer-re-prints-article-exposed-7064068.

54 ITV (2014) 'Westminster child abuse claims: what we know', 7 July, available at: https://www.itv.com/news/2014-07-07/westminster-child-sex-abuse-claims-what-we-know.

55 Gov.uk (2014) 'Independent investigation into the payment of Home Office funding to the Paedophile Information Exchange: final report', available at: https://assets.publishing.service.gov.uk/government/uploads/system/uploads/attachment_data/file/327927/InvestigationFundingPIE.pdf; see also P. O'Brien (2014) 'Leon Brittan: I was handed "paedophile" dossier', Channel 4, 2 July, available at: https://www.channel4.com/news/lord-leon-brittan-home-office-paedophile-dossier; Dossier PREM 19/588, National Archives.

56 Margaret Thatcher, written answer, House of Commons, 15 November 1982: 'nothing has been discovered to suggest that he was' a PIE member.

57 K. Mudie (2012) 'Abuse scandals probe widens: the man who may hold key to biggest paedophile network ever', *The Mirror*, 11 November, available at: https://www.mirror.co.uk/news/uk-news/paedophile-scandal-charles-napier-could-1430365.

[58] He was finally arrested in the context of post-Savile vigilance, see BBC News (2014) 'Charles Napier jailed for 13 years for child sex abuse', 23 December, available at: https://www.bbc.com/news/uk-30591158.

[59] BBC News, 'Charles Napier jailed for 13 years'.

[60] BBC News (2014) 'Abuse claims: senior whip "would help colleagues"', 8 July, available at: www.bbc.co.uk/news/av/28207066/abuse-claims-senior-whip-would-help-colleagues.

[61] BBC News (2014) 'Child abuse "may well have been" covered up – Norman Tebbit', 6 July, available at: https://www.bbc.co.uk/news/uk-politics-28182373.

[62] HMIC, HMCPSI (2012) 'Forging the links: rape investigation and prosecution', HMIC, HMCPSI, London, available at: https://www.justice inspectorates.gov.uk///hmicfrs/media/forging-the-links-rape-investigation-and-prosecution-20120228.pdf.

[63] V. Dodd (2020) 'Police uncovering "epidemic" of child abuse in 1970s and 80s', *The Guardian*, 5 February, available at: https://www.theguardian.com/uk-news/2020/feb/05/police-uncovering-epidemic-of-child-abuse-in-1970s-and-80s.

[64] D. Aaronovitch (2012) 'Beware a modern Salem of child abuse', *The Times*, 12 November, available at: https://www.thetimes.co.uk/article/beware-a-modern-salem-over-child-abuse-mhdw9lmjmzc.

[65] A. O'Hagan (2012) 'Light entertainment', *London Review of Books*, 8 November, available at: https://pugpig.lrb.co.uk/the-paper/v34/n21/andrew-o-hagan/light-entertainment.

[66] B. Tonkin (2014) 'The "moral entrepreneurs" who cash in on child abuse', *The Independent*, 11 July, available at: https://www.independent.co.uk/voices/comment/the-moral-entrepreneurs-who-cash-in-on-child-abuse-9600692.html.

[67] D. Lawson (2015) 'In this rush to believe abuse claims we destroy both justice and lives', *Sunday Times*, 11 September. The investigative journalist Tim Tate complained to the *Sunday Times* about Lawson's errors. The online version was amended. Orkney and Cleveland were removed.

[68] J. La Fontaine (2015) 'Jean La Fontaine on satanic ritual abuse panic', British False Memory Society, 19 November, available at: https://bfms.org.uk/jean-la-fontaine-on-satanic-ritual-abuse-panic/.

[69] J. Kitzinger (2015) *Framing Abuse: Media Influence and Public Understanding of Sexual Violence*, London: Pluto.

Chapter 12

[1] V.K. Vojdik (2022) *Beyond Repatriation: Combating Peacekeeper Sexual Abuse and Exploitation*, 2 May, available at: https://gjia.georgetown.edu/2022/05/02/beyond-repatriation-combating-peacekeeper-sexual-abuse-and-exploitation/

[2] M. Salter (2020) 'The transitional space of public inquiries: the case of the Royal Commission into Institutional Forms of Child Sexual Abuse', *Australian & New Zealand Journal of Criminology*, 53(2): 213–30.

3   A.W. Richard (1994) 'Priest sex abuse case stirs political storm in Northern Ireland', National Catholic Reporter, 2 December, available at: https://www.bishop-accountability.org/news3/1994_12_02_Richard_PriestSex_Brendan_Smyth_1.htm.

4   F. O'Toole (1997) *The Ex-Isle of Erin: Images of a Global Ireland*, Dublin: New Island Books, p 198.

5   The *Irish Times* (1996) 'Revelations of abuse by priests and religious has had "immense impact on Catholic Church"', 31 January.

6   M. Raftery and E. O'Sullivan (2002) *Suffer the Little Children*, London: Continuum.

7   B. Arnold (2009) *The Irish Gulag: How the State Betrayed Its Innocent Children*, Dublin: Gill & Macmillan.

8   Judge Sean Ryan took over as chair from Judge Mary Laffoy after she quit over her concerns about resources and independence. P. Anderson (2003) 'Former counsel to Ferns Inquiry to succeed Laffoy', *Irish Times*, 26 September, available at: https://researchbriefings.files.parliament.uk/documents/CDP-2016-0244/CDP-2016-0244.pdf.

9   Interview with the author, 2018.

10   Y. Murphy (2010) 'Report into the Catholic diocese of Cloyne', available at www.justice.ie/en/JELR/Cloyne_Rpt.pdf/Files/Cloyne_Rpt.pdf.

11   C. Holohan (2011) 'In plain sight: responding to the Ferns, Ryan, Murphy and Cloyne reports', Amnesty International Ireland, available at: https://www.amnesty.ie/wp-content/uploads/2016/10/In-Plain-Sight-Responding-to-the-Ferns-Ryan-Murphy-and-Cloyne-Reports.pdf.

12   J. McCarthy (2016) 'The point in the film Spotlight that had me in tears', *Sydney Morning Herald*, 26 February, available at: https://www.smh.com.au/national/the-point-in-the-film-spotlight-that-had-me-in-tears-20160226-gn47hv.html.

13   J. Reynolds (2016) 'Pell's late night of tough questions', BBC News, 29 February, available at: https://www.bbc.com/news/world-australia-35683790.

14   B. Mathews and M.N. Bernard Thomas (2020) 'How George Pell won in the High Court on a legal technicality', *The Conversation*, 7 April, available at: https://theconversation.com/how-george-pell-won-in-the-high-court-on-a-legal-technicality-133156.

15   Interview with the author for this book, 2017.

16   Salter, 'The transitional space of public inquiries'.

17   Salter, 'The transitional space of public inquiries'.

18   Royal Commission into the Institutional Response to Child Sexual Abuse (2017) *Final Report*, available at: https://www.childabuseroyalcommission.gov.au/sites/default/files/final_report_-_preface_and_executive_summary.pdf.

19   Royal Commission into the Institutional Response to Child Sexual Abuse (2017) *Criminal Justice Report*, Executive Summary and Parts I–II, Commonwealth of Australia, available at: https://www.bishopaccountability.org/reports/2017_08_14_Royal_Commission_Criminal_Justice_Final_Report/RC_Criminal_Justice_Final_Parts_I_to_II.pdf.

[20] Royal Commission into the Institutional Response to Child Sexual Abuse (2017) *Message to Australia*, available at: https://www.childabuseroyal commission.gov.au/message-australia.

[21] A. Hegarty (2002) 'The government of memory: public inquiries and the limits of justice in Northern Ireland', *Fordham International Law Journal*, 24(4): 1148–92.

[22] Murunbuch (2014) 'Sir Michael Havers, brother of Baroness Butler-Sloss', Spotlight, available at: https://spotlightonabuse.wordpress.com/2014/07/08/sir-michael-havers-brother-of-baroness-butler-sloss/.

[23] Phil Johnson had campaigned for this independent inquiry and became one of its core participants, see www.youtube.com/watch?v=e4sZu-DdCfM.

[24] C. Moore (2014) 'Our Establishment is running scared about historic abuse', *The Telegraph*, 24 October, available at: https://www.telegraph.co.uk/news/uknews/crime/11185442/Our-Establishment-is-running-scared-about-historic-sex-abuse.html. See also C. Moore (2020) 'The real establishment ring is the one that gave credence to vile sex abuse lies', 28 February, available at: https://www.telegraph.co.uk/news/2020/02/28/real-establishment-ring-one-gave-credence-vile-sex-abuse-lies/.

[25] Moore, 'Our Establishment is running scared'.

[26] R. Mendick (2016) 'Dame Lowell Goddard accuses former colleagues of forcing her to quit', *The Telegraph*, 2 November, available at: https://www.telegraph.co.uk/news/2016/11/02/dame-lowell-goddard-accuses-former-colleagues-of-forcing-her-to/.

[27] Moore, 'Our Establishment is running scared'.

[28] Alexis Jay had been Scotland's Chief Social Work Inspector until 2013. She had produced a landmark report, the 'Inspection into the care and protection of children in Eilean Siar' (2005), unnoticed in England, but acclaimed in Scotland, and her indictment of an English scandal, the 'Independent inquiry into child sexual exploitation in Rotherham', stunned public opinion.

[29] Its leading counsel, Ben Emmerson, an eminent human rights lawyer, was accused of sexually harassing a Matrix Chambers colleague who also worked with the inquiry. He denied it. The IICSA's passive response did not square with an inquiry into sexual abuse. Emmerson was suspended. The managers of his own chambers ordered an inquiry that exonerated him. Outraged Matrix barristers complained, and Matrix called in Dame Laura Cox, who had investigated sexual harassment in Parliament. Her report criticised Matrix for failing to protect the woman involved and failing to apply Equality Act protections. Neither Matrix nor IICSA emerged with any honour. See J. Morris (2017) 'Investigation into child abuse inquiry QC criticised', 16 October, BBC Newsnight, available at: https://www.bbc.com/news/uk-41644277.

[30] IICSA Rochdale Hearing, 12 October 2017, available at: https://www.iicsa.org.uk/key-documents/2858/view/public-hearing-transcript-12-october-2017.pdf.

[31] IICSA Rochdale Hearing, 12 October 2017.

[32] IICSA Rochdale Hearing, 12 October 2017.

[33] BBC News (2017) 'Rochdale inquiry: MI5 "told of Cyril Smith abuse case lie"', 9 October, available at: https://www.bbc.com/news/uk-41547471.

[34] IICSA (2018) 'Cambridge House, Knowl View and Rochdale investigation report', 12 April, available at: https://www.iicsa.org.uk/document/cambridge-house-knowl-view-and-rochdale-investigation-report-april.

[35] See lawyer Richard Scorer's forensic summing up on 29 March 2019, available at: https://www.iicsa.org.uk/key-documents/10541/view/public-hearing-transcript-29-march-2019.pdf; IICSA (2020) 'Allegations of child sexual abuse linked to Westminster investigation report', 25 February, available at: https://www.iicsa.org.uk/document/allegations-child-sexual-abuse-linked-westminster-investigation-report.

[36] IICSA, 'Allegations of child sexual abuse linked to Westminster'.

[37] IICSA, 'Cambridge House, Knowl View and Rochdale investigation report'.

[38] IICSA, 'Cambridge House, Knowl View and Rochdale investigation report'.

[39] IICSA Rochdale Hearing, 27 October 2017, available at https://www.iicsa.org.uk/key-documents/3289/view/public-hearing-transcript-27-october-2017.Pdf.

[40] IICSA Rochdale Hearing, 11 October 2017, available at : https://www.iicsa.org.uk/key-documents/2785/view/public-hearing-transcript-11-october-2017.pdf.

[41] IICSA Rochdale Hearing, 11 October 2017.

[42] IICSA Rochdale Hearing, 27 October 2017.

[43] Dr Mellor also advanced the notion that horror videos might have contributed to children's narratives of abuse: B. Campbell (1995) 'Moral panic', *Index on Censorship*, 24(2): 57–61, available at: https://journals.sagepub.com/doi/abs/10.1080/03064229508535901. See also IICSA Rochdale Hearing, 27 October 2017.

[44] IICSA Rochdale Hearing, 27 October 2017.

[45] D. O'Donaghue (2020) 'Former Liberal leader David Steel quits House of Lords after damning child abuse inquiry', 25 February, *Press and Journal*, available at: https://www.pressandjournal.co.uk/fp/politics/uk-politics/2037719/former-liberal-leader-david-steel-quits-house-of-lords-after-damning-child-abuse-inquiry/. Steel claimed that after investigations into other Establishment figures failed to secure a parliamentary scalp, 'I fear that I have been made a proxy for Cyril Smith.'

[46] IICSA, 'Allegations of child sexual abuse linked to Westminster'.

[47] See lawyer Richard Scorer's quietly fierce summing up on 29 March 2019, available at: https://www.iicsa.org.uk/key-documents/10541/view/public-hearing-transcript-29-march-2019.pdf; IICSA, 'Allegations of child sexual abuse linked to Westminster'.

[48] IICSA, 'Cambridge House, Knowl View and Rochdale investigation report'.

[49] B. Campbell (1993) 'A dangerous place to be young: why have 18 vulnerable children died in Nottinghamshire in 18 months?', *The Independent*, 22 December, available at: https://www.independent.co.uk/voices/a-dangerous-place-to-be-young-why-have-18-vulnerable-children-died-in-nottinghamshire-in-18-months-beatrix-campbell-reports-1468975.html.

50 David White oral evidence: IICSA (2018) 'Hearing into children in the care of Nottinghamshire councils', 8 October, available at: https://www.iicsa.org.uk/key-documents/7181/view/public-hearing-transcript-8-october-2018.pdf.

51 IICSA, 'Hearing into children in the care of Nottinghamshire councils'.

52 Her Majesty's Inspectorate of Constabulary and Fire & Rescue Services (2016) 'PEEL: police effectiveness 2016: a vulnerability revisit inspection of Nottinghamshire Police', available at: www.justiceinspectorates.gov.uk/hmicfrs/wp-content/uploads/nottinghamshire-peel-vulnerability-revisit-2016.pdf.

53 IICSA, 'Hearing into children in the care of Nottinghamshire councils'.

54 IICSA (2019) 'Children in the care of the Nottinghamshire councils', available at www.iicsa.org.uk/publications/investigation/nottinghamshire-councils.

55 Interview with the author for this book, 2019.

56 Interview with the author for this book, 2019.

57 IICSA (2019) 'Anglican Church case studies: Chichester/Peter Ball investigation report', 2 May, available at: www.iicsa.org.uk/document/anglican-church-case-studies-chichesterpeter-ball-investigation-report; Archbishop Justin Welby's evidence.

58 IICSA (2018) 'Anglican Church hearing', available at: https://www.iicsa.org.uk/document/21-march-2018-anglican-public-hearing-transcript.

59 BBC News (2015) 'Retired Bishop Peter Ball jailed for sex assault', 7 October, BBC News, available at: https://www.bbc.com/news/uk-england-34466842.

60 IICSA, 'Anglican Church case studies'.

61 IICSA, 'Chichester case study report'; IICSA, 'Chichester/Peter Ball investigation report', p 197.

62 IICSA, 'Chichester/Peter Ball investigation report'.

63 IICSA public hearing, 24 July 2018, transcript, available at: https://www.iicsa.org.uk/document/public-hearing-transcript-24-july-2018.

64 M. Gibb (2017) 'The independent Peter Ball review: an abuse of faith, Church of England', June, available at, https://www.churchofengland.org/sites/default/files/2017-11/report-of-the-peter-ball-review-210617.pdf. Witnesses familiar with Ball's personal life provided the inquiry with other insights. His chaplain, the Reverend Stephen Eldridge, recalled that when the closure of mental hospitals abandoned many vulnerable people to hostels or the streets, clergy houses in Gloucester were seen 'as places where they could find help and a kind word', but 'Ball would have nothing to do with anyone who was homeless, sick or needy who came to his door'. He did, however, have an eye for attractive boys or young men, and enjoyed an extravagant lifestyle.

65 IICSA (2019) 'The Anglican Church case studies, the response to the allegations against Peter Ball', available at: https://www.iicsa.org.uk/reports-recommendations/publications/investigation/anglican-chichester-peter-ball.html.

66 For a full account of Carroll's role, see IICSA (2018) 'Ampleforth and Downside (English Benedictine Congregation case study) investigation report', August, available at: https://www.iicsa.org.uk/key-documents/6583/ view/ampleforth-downside-investigation-report-august-2018.pdf.

67 IICSA (2018) 'Ampleforth and Downside'.

68 Interview with the author for this book, 2019; see also R. Scorer (2014) *Betrayed: the English Catholic Church and the Sexual Abuse Crisis*, London: Biteback.

69 L. Jenkins (2016) 'London priest arrested in Kosovo', *The Guardian*, 14 May, available at: https://www.theguardian.com/world/2016/may/14/fugitive-london-priest-arrested-kosovo.

70 Father Gerard Doyle evidence: IICSA (2019) 'The Roman Catholic Church (Archdiocese of Birmingham case study) investigation report, part B.3: Samuel Penney', available at: https://www.iicsa.org.uk/reports-recommendations/publications/investigation/birmingham-archdiocese/ part-b-archdiocese-birmingham/b3-samuel-penney. Leonard then changed his mind, but Penney was allowed to escape. In 1993 he was later arrested and imprisoned.

71 IICSA (2019) 'The Roman Catholic Church (Archdiocese of Birmingham case study) investigation report, part C.3: Father John Tolkien, an example of safeguarding response pre and post-Nolan', available at: https://www.iicsa. org.uk/reports-recommendations/publications/investigation/birmingham-archdiocese/part-c-post-nolan-safeguarding-archdiocese/c3-father-john-tolkien.

72 IICSA (2019) 'The Roman Catholic Church investigation report, part D: the Nolan and Cumberlege reviews', available at: https://www.iicsa.org. uk/reports-recommendations/publications/investigation/roman-catholic-church/part-d-nolan-and-cumberlege-reviews/d1-nolan-report-2001.

73 IICSA, 'The Roman Catholic Church investigation report'.

74 Interview with the author for this book, 2019.

75 IICSA (2020) 'Allegations of child sexual abuse linked to Westminster: Investigation Report, Part K, conclusions and recommendations', available at: https://www.iicsa.org.uk/reports-recommendations/publications/ investigation/westminster/part-k-conclusions-and-recommendations/ k1-conclusions.

76 The inquiry did not investigate allegations of abuse in Dolphin Square, a block of more than 1,000 flats near the River Thames, home to many MPs and members of the House of Lords. The Exaro news agency promoted allegations by Carl Beech that were investigated by the police in Operation Midland. Beech was jailed in 2019 for perverting the course of justice. IICSA, 'Allegations of child sexual abuse linked to Westminster'.

77 S. Phelps (2015) 'Leon Brittan and Geoffrey Dickens' notes from 1983', BBC News, 4 June. At a meeting (also attended by David Mellor, later health minister) Brittan took the view that advocacy of sex with children did not necessarily imply actual sexual acts with children; it was 'the mischief that should be banned, not the organisation'.

[78] IICSA (2020) 'Allegations of child sexual abuse linked to Westminster: Investigation Report, Part K, conclusions and recommendations', available at: https://www.iicsa.org.uk/reports-recommendations/publications/investigation/westminster/part-k-conclusions-and-recommendations/k1-conclusions.

[79] IICSA, 'Allegations of child sexual abuse linked to Westminster, Part K'.

[80] For a useful accounts of the discourses, see J. Lovett, M. Coy and L. Kelly (2018) 'Deflection, denial and disbelief: Social and political discourses about child sexual abuse and their influence on institutional responses', IICSA, available at www.iicsa.org.uk/publications/research/social-political-discourses; L. Kelly (2016) 'The conducive context of violence against women and girls', *Discover Society*, 1 March, available at: https://archive.discoversociety.org/2016/03/01/theorising-violence-against-women-and-girls/; https://archive.discoversociety.org/2016/03/01/theorising-violence-against-women-and-girls/; A. Glinski (2021) 'We mustn't rely on a child to tell us verbally in order to take action', 26 November, London: Centre of Expertise on Child Sexual Abuse.

Chapter 13

[1] R.C. Summit (1994) 'The dark tunnels of McMartin', *The Journal of Psychohistory*, 21(4): 397–416, available at: https://ritualabuse.us/ritualabuse/articles/the-dark-tunnels-of-mcmartin-dr-roland-c-summit-journal-of-psychohistory/.

[2] D. Pilgrim (2018) 'The perils of strong social constructionism: the case of child sexual abuse', *Journal of Critical Realism*, 16(3): 268–83, available at: https://www.researchgate.net/publication/315978716_The_Perils_of_Strong_Social_Constructionism_The_Case_of_Child_Sexual_Abuse.

[3] D. Garland (2008) 'On the concept of moral panic', *Crime Media Culture*, 4(1): 9–30, available at: https://vdocument.in/garland-moral-panic-concept.html?page=2.

[4] See Alyson Cole's critique in A.M. Cole (2007) *The Cult of True Victimhood: From the War on Welfare to the War on Terror*, Redwood, CA: Stanford University Press.

[5] S. Cavell (2006) 'Foreword', in V. Das (ed) *Life and Words: Violence and the Descent into the Ordinary*, Oakland: University of California Press, p xi.

[6] S. Felman and D. Laub (1992) *Testimony: Crises of Witnessing in Literature, Psychoanalysis and History*, London: Routledge.

[7] J.L. Herman (2015) *Trauma and Recovery*, New York: Basic Books, p i.

[8] Cavell, 'Foreword', p xiii.

[9] R. Susskind (2003) 'A conversation with Lady Justice Elizabeth Butler-Sloss, Gresham House', available at: https://www.gresham.ac.uk/watch-now/conversation-lady-justice-elizabeth-butler-sloss.

[10] B. Campbell (2004) *End of Equality*, London: Seagull; see also M. Kaldor (2012) *New and Old Wars: Organized Violence in a Global Era*, Cambridge: Polity Press.

[11] B. Kidron (2021) 'Evidence to US Senate hearings on protecting kids online: internet privacy and manipulative marketing', available at: https://www.commerce.senate.gov/services/files/2CE3A83F-D678-4F0C-A623-B3790C4EE29B; Internet Watch Foundation (2023) 'Sexual abuse imagery of primary school children 1000 per cent worse since lockdown', 23 January, available at: https://www.iwf.org.uk/news-media/news/sexual-abuse-imagery-of-primary-school-children-1-000-per-cent-worse-since-lockdown/.

[12] Interview with the author for this book, 2020.

[13] R.B. Saunders, correspondence with Chief Secretary John Major, 5 July 1988.

[14] J. Barr (2006) 'Reframing the Idea of an educated public', *Discourse: Studies in the Cultural Politics of Education*, 27(2), 225–39, available at: https://www.tandfonline.com/doi/abs/10.1080/01596300600676185?journalCode=cdis20

[15] Ofsted, Care Quality Commission, HM Inspectorate of Probation, HM Inspectorate of Constabulary, Fire and Rescue Services (2020) 'The multi-agency response to child sexual abuse in the family environment', available at: https://www.gov.uk/government/news/unseen-evil-sex-abuse-in-families-going-under-the-radar-say-inspectorates.

[16] https://api.parliament.uk/historic-hansard/commons/1988/jul/06/child-abuse-cleveland.

[17] H. Cashman (1989) 'Speaking no evil', *Marxism Today*, May, available at: https://banmarchive.org.uk/marxism-today/may-1989/speaking-no-evil/.

[18] Cashman, 'Speaking no evil'.

[19] R. Moss (2011) 'Middlesbrough MP Sir Stuart Bell fights laziest MP tag', BBC, 9 September, available at: https://www.bbc.co.uk/news/uk-england-14847291.

[20] H. Arendt (1971) 'Lying in politics: reflections on the Pentagon Papers', *New York Review of Books*, 18 November; R. Norton-Taylor (1995) *Truth Is a Difficult Concept: Inside the Scott Inquiry*, London: 4th Estate, pp 88–99; P. Hennessy (1996) *The Hidden Wiring: Unearthing the British Constitution*, London: Gollancz.

[21] H. Arendt (1972) *Lying in Politics, in Crises of the Republic*, New York, Harvest HBJ, p 6.

[22] See Norton-Taylor, *Truth Is a Difficult Concept*, p 16.

[23] Hennessy, *The Hidden Wiring*; O. Gay (1996) 'Questions of procedure for ministers', House of Commons Research Paper, 96/53, 1 April, available at: https://researchbriefings.parliament.uk/ResearchBriefing/Summary/RP96-53.

[24] Gay, 'Questions of procedure for ministers'.

[25] For a fastidious account of the development of PQM and its 'constitutional importance', see Gay, 'Questions of procedure for ministers'. For insight into its limits, see P. Hennessy (2022) 'Peter Hennessy on Johnson's breach of the ministerial code', 17 April, available at: https://soundcloud.com/user-773097207-787181974/peter-hennessy-on-johnsons-breach-of-the-ministerial-code-1; M. Gordon (2022) 'The prime minister, the parties

and the ministerial code', Political Studies Association Specialist Group on Parliaments, 29 April, available at: https://psaparliaments.org/2022/04/29/the-prime-minister-the-parties-and-the-ministerial-code/.

26 Norton-Taylor, *Truth Is a Difficult Concept*, pp 88–99.
27 Norton-Taylor, *Truth Is a Difficult Concept*, pp 88–99.
28 On this occasion, MPs had access to the exhaustive inquiry by the Committee of Privileges (2023) Matter referred on 21 April 2022 (conduct of the Rt Hon Boris Johnson) Final Report, Fifth Report of Session 2022–2033, House of Commons, 15 June, available at: https://hansard.parliament.uk/commons/2023-06-19/debates/E15A1DF8-31A1-4FEF-B007-3CBF444BAA11/PrivilegeConductOfRightHonBorisJohnson
29 https://www.iicsa.org.uk/victims-and-survivors/truth-project.
30 https://www.iicsa.org.uk/document/public-hearing-transcript-5-october-2018.
31 L. Kelly and K. Karsna (2017–18) 'Measuring the scale and changing nature of child sexual abuse and sexual exploitation', Centre of Expertise on Child Sexual Abuse and London Metropolitan University, August, pp 19–20, available at: https://www.csacentre.org.uk/cprodv2/assets/File/CSA%20Scale%20and%20Nature%20full%20report%202018.pdf; S. Parke and K. Karsna (2019) 'Measuring the scale and changing nature of child sexual abuse', Centre of Expertise on Child Sexual Abuse, 1 April, p 6, available at: https://www.csacentre.org.uk/documents/scale-and-nature-update-2019/.
32 Welsh Government (2019) 'National action plan: preventing and responding to child sexual abuse', available at: https://www.gov.wales/sites/default/files/publications/2019-07/national-action-plan-preventing-and-responding-to-child-sexual-abuse.pdf'; Home Office (2021) *Tackling Child Sexual Abuse Strategy*, available at: https://assets.publishing.service.gov.uk/government/uploads/system/uploads/attachment_data/file/973236/Tackling_Child_Sexual_Abuse_Strategy_2021.pdf.
33 Home Office, *Tackling Child Sexual Abuse Strategy*.
34 Welsh Government, 'National action plan'.
35 Home Office, (2021) *Tackling Child Sexual Abuse Strategy*, London: HM Government, pp 21–2.
36 B. Kidron (2021) 'Amendment 23', Trade Bill, available at: https://www.theyworkforyou.com/lords/?id=2021-01-06b.193.1.
37 By the end of the year, however, age verification for internet pornography sites had not been implemented: H. Grant and D. Milmo (2021) 'Campaigners threaten UK legal action over porn sites' lack of age verification', *The Guardian*, 5 December, available at: https://www.theguardian.com/global-development/2021/dec/05/campaigners-threaten-uk-legal-action-over-porn-sites-lack-of-age-verification; John Carr chronicles the sorry history in his blog: 'A very poor show', available at: https://johncarr.blog/2022/08/03/a-very-poor-show/.
38 Home Office, *Tackling Child Sexual Abuse Strategy*, pp 21–2.

39 See Ella Cockbain's bracing critique: E. Cockbain (2021) 'Continuing to racialise child sexual abuse by focusing on "grooming gangs" won't lead to systemic change', *Byline Times*, 2 February, available at: https://bylinetimes.com/2021/02/02/continuing-to-racialise-child-sexual-abuse/. See also Home Office (2021) 'Group-based child sexual exploitation characteristics of offending', London: HM Government, October, available at: https://www.gov.uk/government/publications/group-based-child-sexual-exploitation-characteristics-of-offending/group-based-child-sexual-exploitation-characteristics-of-offending-accessible-version.

40 J. Proulx, F. Cortoni, L.A. Craig and E. Letourneau (2020) *The Wiley Handbook of What Works with Sex Offenders: Contemporary Perspectives in Theory, Assessment, Treatment, and Prevention*, Hoboken, NJ: Wiley Blackwell; Centre of Expertise on Child Sexual Abuse (2020) 'A new typology of child sexual abuse offending', CECSA and Centre for Abuse and Trauma Studies, Middlesex University, available at: https://www.csacentre.org.uk/documents/new-typology-of-child-sexual-abuse-offending/.

41 S. Osborne (2018) 'Number of people seeking help from looking at child sexual abuse images increases by 40%', *The Independent*, 5 April, available at: https://www.independent.co.uk/news/uk/crime/stop-child-sex-images-paedophile-help-charity-stop-it-now-lucy-faithfull-foundation-online-internet-latest-a8286501.html.

42 On 23 September 2022, Victims' Commissioner Dame Vera Baird resigned in protest against the government's approach and 'lack of engagement at the top' of the Ministry of Justice; 'it is no exaggeration', she said, 'that the criminal justice system is in chaos': J. Kelly (2022) 'Dame Vera Baird: Victims' champion resigns, claiming her role was sidelined', BBC News, 23 September, available at: https://www.bbc.co.uk/news/uk-63009853.

43 S. Braverman (2023) 'Government response to the final report of the Independent Inquiry into Child Sexual Abuse', May, Gov.UK, available at: https://www.gov.uk/government/publications/response-to-the-final-report-of-the-independent-inquiry-into-child-sexual-abuse/government-response-to-the-final-report-of-the-independent-inquiry-into-child-sexual-abuse. The exception was the creation of a cabinet-level minister.

44 S. Veale (2023) 'Child sexual abuse compensation scheme to be set up in England', available at: https://www.theguardian.com/uk-news/2023/may/22/child-sexual-abuse-inquiry-compensation-scheme-england.

45 S. Bailey (2017) The scale of child sexual abuse means we cannot solely prosecute our way out', National Police Chiefs Council and NSPCC, 28 February, available at: https://news.npcc.police.uk/releases/the-scale-of-child-sexual-abuse-means-we-cannot-solely-prosecute-our-way-out; see also Elizabeth Letourneau's work with juvenile sex offenders: E.J. Letourneau and M.H. Miner (2005) 'Juvenile sex offenders: a case against the legal and clinical status quo', *Sexual Abuse, Journal of Research and Treatment*, 17(3): 293–312; E.J. Letourneau and K. Armstrong (2008) 'Recidivism rates for registered and non-registered juvenile sex offenders', *Sex Abuse*, 20(4): 393–408.

46   In 2022 Ireland's Justice Minister Helen McEntee launched a pioneering zero tolerance strategic timetable, with 144 detailed actions, ranging from teaching children about consent and coercive control, gender and violence, to safe spaces for victims, doubling of resources for women's shelters, regular research and the establishment of a statutory agency for gendered violence and abuse: 'Zero tolerance, third national strategy on domestic, sexual and gender-based violence, 2022–2026', Government of Ireland, available at: https://www.gov.ie/en/policy-information/9e169-dsgbv-strategies/#third-national-strategy-on-domestic-sexual-and-gender-based-violence. In 2021 Australia launched a National Strategy to Prevent and Respond to Child Sexual Abuse 2021–2030, involving three phased action plans to build community and organisational awareness and to promote cultural change and prevention, available at: https://www.childsafety.gov.au/system/files/2022-09/national-strategy-2021-30-english.pdf.

47   D. Campbell (2023) 'Children in mental health crisis spend more than 900,000 hours in England', *The Guardian*, 9 February, available at: https://www.theguardian.com/society/2023/feb/09/children-mental-health-crisis-a-and-e-england.

48   L. Casey (2023) 'Final Report, independent review into the standards of behaviour and internal culture of the Metropolitian Police Service', p 140, available at: https://www.met.police.uk/SysSiteAssets/media/downloads/met/about-us/baroness-casey-review/update-march-2023/baroness-casey-review-march-2023a.pdf.

49   HMIC (2016) *State of Policing Report*, p 21, available at: https://www.justiceinspectorates.gov.uk/hmicfrs/wp-content/uploads/state-of-policing-2016-double-page.pdf.

50   Casey, 'Final report', p 140.

51   Home Office, *Tackling Child Sexual Abuse Strategy*, introduction by Priti Patel; see Cockbain, 'Continuing to racialise child sexual abuse'.

52   Y. Johansson (2022) 'Regulation is needed in the fight against child sexual abuse online', European Commission, available at: https://ec.europa.eu/commission/commissioners/2019-2024/johansson/blog/regulation-needed-fight-against-child-sexual-abuse-csa-online-companies-must-use-their-technical_en.

53   World Health Organization (2017) 'Responding to children and adolescents who have been sexually abused: WHO clinical guidelines', Geneva: WHO, available at: https://apps.who.int/iris/bitstream/handle/10665/259270/9789241550147-eng.pdf;sequence=1.

54   F. Singhateh (2021) 'One year on: how COVID-19 has impacted the sexual exploitation of children including the "drive-by sale of children"', ECPAT, available at: https://www.ecpat.org/news/one-year-on-how-has-covid-19-impacted-the-sexual-exploitation-of-children/.

55   NSPCC (2021) 'Calls to the NSPCC surge during the pandemic', 29 April, available at: https://www.nspcc.org.uk/about-us/news-opinion/2021/nspcc-child-abuse-helpline-pandemic/.

56 M. de Boer-Buquicchio (2020) 'Sale and sexual exploitation of children, United Nations Human Rights Council', 21 January, available at: https://undocs.org/en/A/HRC/43/40.

57 S. Zuboff (2019) *The Age of Surveillance Capitalism: The Fight for the Future of the Frontier of Power*, London: Profile Books.

58 V. Das and A. Kleinman (2001) 'Introduction', in V. Das, A. Kleinman, M. Lock, M. Ramphele and P. Reynolds (eds) *Remaking a World: Violence, Social Suffering, and Recovery*, Berkeley: University of California Press, pp 20–2.

59 https://www.iicsa.org.uk/document/public-hearing-transcript-5-october-2018.

Epilogue

1 S. Bell (1988) *When Salem Came to the Boro: The True Story of the Cleveland Child Abuse Case*, London: Pan Macmillan; B. Campbell (1988) *Unofficial Secrets*, London: Virago.

2 Interview with the author, 2018.

3 V. Das and A. Kleinman (2001) 'Introduction', in V. Das, A. Kleinman, M. Lock, M. Ramphele and P. Reynolds (eds) *Remaking a World: Violence, Social Suffering, and Recovery*, Berkeley: University of California Press, p 20.

Timeline

1 Kempe, Silverman and Steele, 'The battered child syndrome'.

2 D. Finkelhor (1979) *Sexually Victimised Children*, Riverside, NJ: Macmillan Publishing.

3 Government of Canada (1984) *Sexual Offences Against Children*, Ottawa: Canadian Government Publishing Services.

4 D. Finkelhor (1986) *A Sourcebook on Child Sexual Abuse*, London: Sage.

5 Barker, 'Sir Stuart Bell'.

6 E. Butler-Sloss (1988) *Report of the Inquiry into Child Abuse in Cleveland 1987*, Cm 412, London: HMSO.

7 Saunders, 'Confidential memorandum'.

8 Hansard, 7 July 1987, vol 119.

9 *The Guardian*, 18 February 1989.

10 McCann et al, 'Perianal findings in pre-pubertal children'.

11 Hobbs and Wynne, 'Buggery in childhood'.

12 Webster, *The Secret of Bryn Estyn*, pp 574–5.

13 Salter, *Accuracy of Expert Testimony in Child Sexual Abuse Cases*.

14 Islington Survivors Network, https://islingtonsurvivors.co.uk/eileen-fairweather-freelance-investigative-journalist/

15 Wakefield and Underwager, 'Interview', available at https://spotlightonabuse.wordpress.com/2013/05/30/ralph-underwager-the-paidika-interview/

16 Morris, S. (2016) 'Ex-police chief Gordon Anglesea jailed for child sexual abuse', *The Guardian*, available at: https://www.theguardian.com/uk-news/2016/nov/04/ex-police-chief-gordon-anglesea-jailed-child-sexual-abuse-north-wales.

[17] Campbell, 'Mind games'.
[18] BBC News, 'Abuse claims'. See also M. Cockerell (1995) 'Westminster's Secret Service', BBC 2, 20 May, available at, https://www2.bfi.org.uk/films-tv-people/4ce2b7e5833e6.
[19] Utting, *People Like Us*.
[20] Department of Health (2000) *Lost in Care*, London: The National Archives.
[21] Bichard, *The Bichard Inquiry Report*; Kelly, 'Serious case review'.
[22] Kelly et al, 'A gap or a chasm?'.
[23] Gladman and Heal, *Child Sexual Exploitation after Rotherham*.
[24] Stanko, *The Attrition of Rape Allegations in London*.
[25] B. Cathcart and P. French (2019) *Unmasked: Andrew Norfolk*, London: Unmasked Books, available at, https://hackinginquiry.org/wp-content/uploads/2019/06/Norfolk_Report_Unmasked.pdf
[26] Ponsford, 'Meirion Jones'.
[27] Children's Commissioner (2012) *Research into Gang-Associated Sexual Exploitation and Sexual Violence*, University of Bedfordshire.
[28] UK Parliament, 24 October.
[29] Home Office (2013) *Jillings Report*, London: HM Government.
[30] A. Jay (2014) *Alexis Jay's Independent Inquiry into Child Sexual Exploitation in Rotherham*, Rotherham: HM Government.
[31] Criminal Justice Joint Inspection (2014) *Achieving Best Evidence in Child Sexual Abuse Cases*, London: HMCPSI.
[32] K. Hohl and E. Stanko (2015) 'Complaints of rape and the criminal justice system: fresh evidence on the attrition problem in England and Wales', *European Journal of Criminology*, 12(3): 324–41.
[33] Welsh Government, 'National action plan'.
[34] Pidd, 'Judge criticizes "minimal" investigation'.
[35] Royal College of Paediatrics and Child Health, *The Physical Signs of Child Sexual Abuse*.
[36] Roberts, 'In the matter of Poppi Iris Worthington'.
[37] Roberts, 'In the matter of Poppi Iris Worthington'.
[38] *EC1 Echo*, 'Payments for survivors of abuse in Islington'.
[39] Ofsted et al, 'Multi-agency response to child sexual abuse'.
[40] R. Fewkes (2021) *Operation Hydrant Annual Report*, available at: https://www.vkpp.org.uk/assets/Files/Hydrant/Operation-Hydrant-Annual-Report-2021.pdf.
[41] Home Office (2021) *Tackling Child Sexual Abuse Strategy*, London: HM Government.

Index

References to endnotes show both the page
number and the note number (231n3).

Index

IICSA (2014 Independent Inquiry into
Child Sexual Abuse) (continued)
as rebuke to the Cleveland Inquiry
and Report 164–5
reports 173, 178, 180
Rochdale 167–73
sexual harassment within the inquiry
itself 166–7, 252n29
Smith, Sir Cyril 167–73
social media 165, 193
Truth Project 193, 194
victims/witnesses 165, 167, 170,
171–2, 176, 177, 178, 193–4,
197, 254n64
Westminster cases/Report 181–4
wish of witness D31 193–4, 199
Woolf, Fiona 166
see also Smith, Sir Cyril
incest 34, 71–2, 73–4, 225–6n14
see also child sexual abuse
Independent on Sunday (broadsheet) 82
Internet
Children's Code 195–6
online child pornography 187, 198,
258n37
IPCC (Independent Police Complaints
Commission) 121, 125
Ireland (Republic of Ireland)
Catholic Church and child sexual
abuse 160–2
government and child sexual abuse
160–2
'Irish gulag' 51, 161, 222n6
Ryan Commission 161, 163, 251n8
Third National Strategy on
Domestic, Sexual and Gender-
Based Violence (DSGBV) 197,
260n46
Irish Times 161
Irvine, Alistair (Dr) 11
challenging medical evidence of
child sexual abuse 1–2
criticism of 14, 29
media and 11, 14
RAD 1, 28
Islington: children's homes scandal 140–1
ITV: *Exposure* documentary 155–6

J

Jackson, Louise 70
Jackson, Peter, Mr Justice 120–1, 122,
123–4
James II, King of England and Ireland
176
Jay, Alexis 154, 252n28
IICSA chairperson 166, 167,
171–2, 197
Jenkins, Philip 104
Jillings, John 248n45
Johansson, Ylva (European Union
Home Affairs Commissioner)
198
Johnson, Boris 189, 192
Johnson, Phil 165, 166, 252n23
Jones, Judith (child abuse consultant)
80, 85
Jones, Meirion 156
Jones, Ray (Social Services Director)
135
justice system 199
children's participation in 139, 145
Cleveland children, failed by justice
system xiv, xvi, xviii, 4, 33, 47,
204
Criminal Justice Bill 139
crisis in 259n42
'justice gap' 143
Pigot Report 139, 242n8
rape cases 155
victims of sexual exploitation
151–2
young witnesses, failed by justice
system 144
see also Cleveland child abuse:
judicial proceedings

K

Karsna, Kairika: 'Measuring the scale
and nature of child sexual abuse'
135
Kelly, Sir Christopher 146–7
Kelly, Liz 143, 144
'Measuring the scale and nature of
child sexual abuse' 135

Index

Prime, Geoffrey 165
Private Eye 168–9, 170, 171
Project Jericho (Prescott, Canada) 79,
    86–9, 229n23
  child abuse: medical signs 86
  collegial co-operation and solidarity
    86, 87, 88–9
  media 87–8
  perpetrators' admissions 86
  police 89
  prosecution and conviction 87, 88
  sadism 86
  social work 86–7
  state: resources and positive interest
    86, 87, 89
prostitution 50, 51, 148, 175
  child prostitution 76, 79, 104–5,
    107, 152, 175
  West End, London 108, 169
  see also sexual exploitation of
    children
public opinion 5, 14, 35, 190, 252n28

Q
Quirk, Hannah 124

R
RAD (Reflex Anal Dilatation) 74–5,
    108–9, 215n4
  Adams, Joyce (Dr) 114–15,
    116–17
  Asian, Scandinavian and European
    research on 117
  backlash against the diagnosis
    108–10
  Butler-Sloss, Elizabeth 109
  Cleveland children 1–2, 17, 27,
    47–9, 50, 108
  Cleveland Inquiry and 27, 28, 30,
    109, 120
  Cleveland Report and 17, 109,
    117
  dismissed as evidence of child
    abuse 28, 30, 110, 112–15, 123,
    237n18

as evidence of child abuse 28, 30,
    74–5, 108, 113, 115, 116–17,
    123, 227n28, 238n37
forensic pathology and 75, 119–20
Heger, Astrid (Dr) 112–14,
    237n18
Hobbs and Wynne (Drs) 1–2, 28,
    74–5, 109, 111, 113, 117–18,
    215n4, 227n29, 238nn35–6
homosexuality and 28, 71, 75, 108,
    120
Irvine, Alistair (Dr) 1, 28
McCann and Voris (Drs) 110–12,
    113, 114–15, 116–17, 123,
    238n36
Myhre, Arne K. (Dr) 115–16
Norwegian research 115–16
Royal College: *Purple Book* 118,
    123
as signifier of buggery 108
Tardieu, Auguste Ambroise on anal
    dilatation 70, 75, 109, 225n6
timing and child's position during
    examination 111–12, 115, 116
UK/US research comparison
    111–12, 113–14, 115, 116, 118
Worthington case 123
see also child sexual abuse: medical
    signs
Raftery, Mary: *States of Fear* (TV
    series) 51, 161
rape 187, 230n6
  2003 Sexual Offences Act 143
  acknowledged/unacknowledged
    rape victims 73
  campaign of rape against children
    149–52
  'culture of scepticism' 143
  decriminalisation of 155
  low rape conviction rates 144
  mass protests in India against rape
    103
  no prosecution/criminal charge of
    rapists xviii, 47, 48, 49
  police focus on victims rather than
    perpetrators 143
  police records on 143, 144

Printed in the USA
CPSIA information can be obtained
at www.ICGtesting.com
JSHW021548111223
53613JS00005B/68